Reflections on America, 1984

REFLECTIONS ON AMERICA, 1984

AN ORWELL SYMPOSIUM

Edited by Robert Mulvihill

The University of Georgia Press
Athens and London

© 1986 by the University of Georgia Press
Athens, Georgia 30602
All rights reserved

Designed by Sandra Strother Hudson
Set in 10 on 12 Linotron 202 Times Roman with Gill Sans display

The paper in this book meets the guidelines for
permanence and durability of the Committee on
Production Guidelines for Book Longevity of the
Council on Library Resources.

Printed in the United States of America

90 89 88 87 86   5 4 3 2 1

Library of Congress Cataloging in Publication Data
Main entry under title:

Reflections on America, 1984.

Includes index.
Results of a symposium held at Rosemont College
in March, 1984.
    1. Orwell, George, 1903–1950. Nineteen eighty-four—
Congresses. I. Mulvihill, Robert.
PR6029.R8N664 1985   823'.912   85-2538
ISBN 0-8203-0778-5 (alk. paper)
ISBN 0-8203-0780-7 (pbk.)

Allie, Kate, Matt

1

CONTENTS

Contents

viii

ACKNOWLEDGMENTS

This book is one of the results of a three-day symposium held at Rosemont College in March 1984. I am grateful to all those who helped put both the symposium and the book together. My deepest thanks go, of course, to the contributors, each of whom produced an original paper for this volume. Their insight and analysis make this volume a distinctive contribution to American cultural criticism.

The symposium was made possible by the generous financial assistance of the Pennsylvania Endowment for the Humanities and the International Telephone and Telegraph Corporation. President Dorothy Brown of Rosemont College strongly supported the project; her encouragement is evidence of her genuine commitment to a liberal education. Many members of the Rosemont community gave their time and expertise, especially Bob Davis, Dev Thielens, Maureen Cullen, Sue Seltzer, and the entire Development Office. The high attendance at the conference was due largely to the efforts of Marguerite Goff and Nancy Sokoloff.

So many of my colleagues contributed to the planning for the book and the meeting that I am hard pressed to thank them selectively. They helped me to clarify the scope and focus of the project and to refine my ideas about its interdisciplinary nature. Eleanor Gubins listened to every idea and every complaint for two years, and yet she helped, always. Gary Bolger gave freely of ideas, time, and energy. Ron Duska offered suggestions that enlivened and enriched both meeting and book. To these and all the other members of the Rosemont faculty who helped go my sincerest thanks.

Some people, of course, helped in ways that are not easy to categorize. I am especially grateful to Sr. Eleanor Rice, Melvin Barg, Margie Malanoski, Frank West, Jo Gavin, Ann Redpath, Kathy and Ted Beal, Michael Willsie, Irene Moretti Shank, and Barbara Cox.

I am greatly indebted to Jennifer Tyndale of the British Council and to Janet Percival of the Orwell Archive at the Library, University College, London, for their unfailing help in arranging for permission to use the photographs contained in the exhibit prepared by Bernard Crick and the British Council.

Acknowledgments

At the University of Georgia Press, Malcolm Call was consistently supportive from beginning to end. Ellen Harris provided the kind of editorial expertise without which projects of this kind would certainly flounder.

Finally, four people deserve that gratitude that defies description: Penny Columbus, Dotty Curry, Margaret Loftus, and Allie.

Robert Mulvihill

INTRODUCTION

Because of its underlying moral commitments and its identification of problems central to the democratic political experience, *Nineteen Eighty-Four* is a story for all seasons. The novel continues to provoke us to consider the substance of political decency and the threats to its survival. The title should not tempt us to judge Orwell as a prophet (his whole life militated against such an interpretation), but rather it should elicit a thoughtful attempt to cast some light on important dimensions of American public life. It was for just this purpose that we brought together eleven distinguished scholars at Rosemont College in March 1984. The papers that they presented at this meeting, "Reflections on America, 1984: an Orwell Symposium," are published in revised form in this volume.

Hovering over and around these essays, despite their differences in substance and perspective, is the question of decency—liberty and justice. Nowhere more eloquently does Orwell allow us to glimpse his commitment to decency than in the famous passage from "A Hanging" where he describes his reaction to the condemned man's effort to avoid stepping into a puddle on his way to the gallows.

> When I saw the prisoner step aside to avoid the puddle I saw the mystery, the unspeakable wrongness of cutting a life short when it is in full tide. This man was not dying, he was alive just as we are alive. . . . He and we were a party of men walking together, seeing, learning, feeling, understanding the same world; and in two minutes, with a sudden snap, one of us would be gone—one mind less, one world less.

It is not surprising, then, that one so concerned with providing decency for individual human beings should at the same time be concerned with the accumulation and employment of power in all areas of society: thus the wide range of targets of his criticism as well as the conscious mixing of the personal and the systemic, especially in *Nineteen Eighty-Four*. Clearly, it is inevitable that discussions of Orwell will cut across many aspects of modern life. Although never abandoning what by contemporary hyperbolic standards must be viewed as modest ideals, Orwell understood that none of us touches more than a small slice of the truth. In this volume we receive different reflections of the truth, each reflection somewhat altered and enhanced in the context of the other contributions.

The most neglected aspect of *Nineteen Eighty-Four,* namely, the role of cold war in the generation and persistence of totalitarianism, is the subject of the opening essay, by Murray Rothbard. Rothbard warns us that, while trying to protect the liberal substance of society, we may actually be preparing its disintegration. The central place of cold war in Orwell's scheme certainly demands a reconsideration of the impact of the contemporary cold war on the origins and dynamics of repression.

The next three essays provide the context necessary for an understanding of *Nineteen Eighty-Four* and for the consideration of the essays that follow. Orwell's writing was, of course, a reflection of his own convictions. The reporter's detail, the intricate yet detached portrayal of the individual, the absorption in the final consequences of the exercise of power, all find their fruition in his writing. The essays by Bernard Crick, Hugh Kenner, and Robert Coles testify in various ways to this coherence of style and substance.

Bernard Crick focuses on the text itself, providing a necessary re-introduction to the story. Crick, who knows the Orwell story as well as anyone, has given us a thorough and faithful interpretation that alerts us to the complexity of Orwell's effort. Robert Coles draws a human and sensitive portrait of the writer himself, based largely on some of Orwell's documentary writing. In this way Coles helps us to understand the sensibility of the man and, consequently, the spirit of the book. The final essay in this section, by Hugh Kenner, reveals the subtle and provocative links between the style and substance of Orwell's work. We are left not only with a greater understanding of Orwell's use of language but with a finer appreciation of the book's capacity to evoke varied responses. Taken together, these essays enlarge our understanding of the book and its deepest commitments and thereby help to establish a foundation for the cultural criticisms that follow.

There is a widespread assumption that the best defense against totalitarianism is the kind of public philosophy, liberal individualism, found in contemporary America. Among the important consequences of such a view is one that exempts social and political concentrations of power from adequate scrutiny. The threats to decency from big business, medicine, computers, and television, to name the areas we will consider, are often examined out of context, without regard to the philosophical milieu in which they are developing. The essays by Sheldon Wolin and Robert Solomon help to overcome this void by drawing our attention to the critical relationship between philosophy and society.

Wolin, assuming that Orwell was warning the West rather than simply photocopying totalitarian society, examines those dimensions of liberal society which may themselves be involved in the generation of totalitarianism. His attention to the historical dimensions of *Nineteen Eighty-Four* vividly connects Orwell's thought and the present state of American society. Solomon's criticism, in the form of an allegorical take-off on *Animal Farm,* is directed mainly at 'Enlightenment' liberalism and is not nearly so apocalyptic as much criticism of liberalism appears to be. A faulty and inadequate conception of liberalism, especially among those who are its most ardent defendants, may be a more imminent problem for us than the path to totalitarian doom depicted by Orwell.

The means of social and technological control in the areas of economic organization, medicine, computers, and television are the subjects of the next four essays. They deal with substantive threats to privacy and freedom, issues at the very heart of liberal thought. Of even greater concern today than they were in Orwell's time, these threats expose the ambiguities and vulnerabilities of our society.

In Joseph Weizenbaum's paper, one of the pioneers of computer science vigorously speaks out, not so much against computer technology as against the social and philosophical thought which gives computer technology its increasingly important place in American life. Especially in the areas of education and military thought and technology, we see the computer put to use in ways that seem to make our hold on liberal values more and more tenuous.

Ivar Berg takes the apparently ironic course of examining the implications for social control of the now much-loved mechanism of economic deregulation. In a manner recalling Orwell's vituperations against intellectual arrogance, Berg argues that the ideological rigidity of many of the adherents of deregulation prevents them, and us, from seeing the potential for social control embedded in deregulation. This essay emphasizes the complex relationships between different levels of social control and different political philosophies.

Ruth Macklin examines behavior control, so often associated with *Nineteen Eighty-Four* yet strangely consigned to the alleyways of public attention. She argues that an understanding of the concept of autonomy is required before we can pass judgment on the practice and technology of behavior control. Macklin concludes that we have more to fear from the attempts of social and political authorities and agencies to secure conformity than we do from psychotechnology.

Mark Crispin Miller's essay begins by examining the ironic inner workings of the Enlightenment view of the world. Miller sees Orwell arguing against the morally vacuous rationalistic faith in progress, wherein the enlightened come to resemble most closely that which they most reject. In a chilling analysis, Miller applies his understanding of *Nineteen Eighty-Four* to an analysis of television and warns that today's television viewer may embody the substance of Winston Smith.

The final essay, by James Billington, is, like the first by Murray Rothbard, a broadly historical analysis. It uncovers the origins of modern totalitarianism in the demands for social intimacy, in the form of fraternity and equality. With this perspective, Billington parts company from those who see America as seriously threatened by the kind of degradation inflicted on Oceania. Billington's is an implied defense of Western liberalism and, at the same time, a plea for its reinvigoration.

His crankiness aside, Orwell's affection for humanity is revealed in his faith that a turn inward, devoid of self-indulgent abstractions, would uncover the sources of decency in each of us. With their implicit and wary concern for power and its many manifestations, these essays tug at the great political and social obstacles to that very decency which so preoccupied Orwell. The varied perspectives of the authors testify to the richness, complexity, and importance of the subject matter. They will have succeeded if they lead us, in our turn, to renewed reflection on America.

Murray N. Rothbard

GEORGE ORWELL
AND THE COLD WAR:
A RECONSIDERATION

n a recent and well-known article, Norman Podhoretz has attempted to conscript George Orwell into the ranks of neoconservative enthusiasts for the newly revitalized cold war with the Soviet Union.[1] If Orwell were alive today, this truly "Orwellian" distortion would afford him considerable wry amusement. It is my contention that the cold war, as pursued by the three superpowers of *Nineteen Eighty-Four,* was the key to their successful imposition of a totalitarian regime upon their subjects. We all know that *Nineteen Eighty-Four* was a brilliant and mordant attack on totalitarian trends in modern society, and it is also clear that Orwell was strongly opposed to communism and to the regime of the Soviet Union. But the crucial role of a perpetual cold war in the entrenchment of totalitarianism in Orwell's "nightmare vision" of the world has been relatively neglected by writers and scholars.

In *Nineteen Eighty-Four* there are three giant superstates or blocs of nations: Oceania (run by the United States, and including the British Empire and Latin America), Eurasia (the Eurasian continent), and Eastasia (China, southeast Asia, much of the Pacific). The superpowers are always at war, in shifting coalitions and alignments against each other. The war is kept, by agreement between the superpowers, safely on the periphery of the blocs, since war in their heartlands might actually blow up the world and their own rule along with it. The perpetual but basically phony war is kept alive by unremitting campaigns of hatred and fear against the shadowy foreign Enemy. The perpetual war system is then used by the ruling elite in each country to fasten totalitarian collectivist rule upon their subjects. As Harry Elmer Barnes wrote, this system "could only work if the masses are always kept at a fever heat of fear and excitement and are effectively prevented from learning that the wars are actually phony. To bring about this indispensable deception of the people requires a tremendous development of propaganda, thought-policing, regimentation, and mental terrorism." And finally, "when it becomes impossible to keep the people any longer at a white heat in their hatred of one enemy group of nations, the war is shifted against another bloc and new, violent hate campaigns are planned and set in motion."[2]

From Orwell's time to the present day, the United States has fulfilled his analysis or prophecy by engaging in campaigns of unremitting hatred and fear of the Soviets, including such widely trumpeted themes (later quietly admitted to be incorrect) as "missile gap" and "windows of vulnerability." What Garet Garrett perceptively called "a complex of vaunting and fear" has been the hallmark of the American as well as of previous empires:[3] the curious combination of vaunting and braggadocio that insists that a nation-state's military might is second to none in any area, combined with repeated panic about the intentions and imminent actions of the "empire of evil" that is marked as the Enemy. It is the sort of fear and vaunting that makes Americans proud of their capacity to "overkill" the Russians many times and yet agree enthusiastically to virtually any and all increases in the military budget for mightier weapons of mass destruction. Senator Ralph Flanders (Republican, Vermont) pinpointed this process of rule through fear when he stated, during the Korean War: "Fear is felt and spread by the Department of Defense in the Pentagon. In part, the spreading of it is purposeful. Faced with what seem to be enormous armed forces aimed against us, we can scarcely expect the Department of Defense to do other than keep the people in a state of fear so that they will be prepared without limit to furnish men and munitions."[4]

This applies not only to the Pentagon but to its civilian theoreticians, the men whom Marcus Raskin, once one of their number, has dubbed "the megadeath intellectuals." Thus Raskin pointed out that

> their most important function is to justify and extend the existence of their employers. . . . In order to justify the continued large-scale production of these [thermonuclear] bombs and missiles, military and industrial leaders needed some kind of theory to rationalize their use. . . . This became particularly urgent during the late 1950's, when economy-minded members of the Eisenhower Administration began to wonder why so much money, thought, and resources, were being spent on weapons if their use could not be justified. And so began a series of rationalizations by the "defense intellectuals" in and out of the Universities. . . . Military procurement will continue to flourish, and they will continue to demonstrate why it must. In this respect they are no different from the great majority of modern specialists who accept the assumptions of the organizations which employ them because of the rewards in money and power and prestige. . . . They know enough not to question their employers' right to exist.[5]

In addition to the manufacture of fear and hatred against the primary Enemy, there have been numerous Orwellian shifts between the Good Guys and the Bad Guys. Our deadly enemies in World War II, Germany and Japan, are now considered prime Good Guys, the only problem being their unfortunate reluctance to take up arms against the former Good Guys, the Soviet Union. China, having been a much lauded Good Guy under Chiang Kai-shek when fighting Bad Guy Japan, became the worst of the Bad Guys under communism, and indeed the United States fought the Korean and Vietnamese wars largely for the sake of containing the expansionism of Communist China, which was supposed to be an even worse guy than the Soviet Union. But now all that is changed, and Communist China is now the virtual ally of the United States against the principal Enemy in the Kremlin.

Along with other institutions of the permanent cold war, Orwellian Newspeak has developed richly. Every government, no matter how despotic, that is willing to join the anti-Soviet crusade is called a champion of the "free world." Torture committed by "totalitarian" regimes is evil; torture undertaken by regimes that are merely "authoritarian" is almost benign. While the Department of War has not yet been transformed into the Department of Peace, it was changed early in the cold war to the Department of Defense, and President Reagan has almost completed the transformation by the neat Orwellian touch of calling the MX missile "the Peacemaker."

As early as the 1950s, an English publicist observed that "Orwell's main contention that 'cold war' is now an essential feature of normal life is being verified more and more from day to day. No one really believes in a 'peace settlement' with the Soviets, and many people in positions of power regard such a prospect with positive horror." He added that "a war footing is the only basis of full employment."[6]

And Harry Barnes noted that "the advantages of the cold war in bolstering the economy, avoiding a depression, and maintaining political tenure after 1945 were quickly recognized by both politicians and economists."

The most recent analysis of Orwell's *Nineteen Eighty-Four* in terms of permanent cold war was in *U.S. News and World Report,* in its issue marking the beginning of the year 1984:

> No nuclear holocaust has occurred but Orwell's concept of perpetual local conflict is borne out. Wars have erupted every year since 1945, claiming more than 30 million lives. The Defense Department reports that there currently are 40 wars raging that involve one-fourth of all nations in the world—from El Salvador to Kampuchea to Lebanon and Afghanistan.
>
> Like the constant war of 1984, these post-war conflicts occurred not within superpower borders but in far-off places such as Korea and Vietnam. Unlike Orwell's fictitious superpowers, Washington and Moscow are not always able to control events and find themselves sucked into local wars such as the current

conflict in the Middle East heightening the risk of a superpower confrontation and use of nuclear armaments.[7]

But most Orwell scholars have ignored the critical permanent-cold-war under-pinning to the totalitarianism in the book. Thus, in a recently published collection of scholarly essays on Orwell, there is barely a mention of militarism or war.[8]

In contrast, one of the few scholars who have recognized the importance of war in Orwell's *Nineteen Eighty-Four* was the Marxist critic Raymond Williams. While deploring the obvious anti-Soviet nature of Orwell's thought, Williams noted that Orwell discovered the basic feature of the existing two- or three-superpower world, "oligarchical collectivism," as depicted by James Burnham in his *Managerial Revolution* (1940), a book that had a profound if ambivalent impact upon Orwell. As Williams put it:

> Orwell's vision of power politics is also close to convincing. The transformation of official "allies" to "enemies" has happened, almost openly, in the generation since he wrote. His idea of a world divided into three blocs— Oceania, Eurasia, and Eastasia, of which two are always at war with the other though the alliances change—is again too close for comfort. And there are times when one can believe that what "had been called England or Britain" has become simply Airstrip One.[9]

A generation earlier, John Atkins had written that Orwell had "discovered this conception of the political future in James Burnham's *The Managerial Revolution.*" Specifically, "there is a state of permanent war but it is a contest of limited aims between combatants who cannot destroy each other. The war cannot be decisive. . . . As none of the states comes near conquering the others, however, the war deteriorates into a series of skirmishes [although] . . . the protagonists store atomic bombs."[10]

To establish what we might call this "revisionist" interpretation of *Nineteen Eighty-Four,* we must first point out that the book was not, as in the popular interpretation, a prophecy of the future so much as a realistic portrayal of existing political trends. Thus, Jeffrey Meyers points out that *Nineteen Eighty-Four* was less a "nightmare vision" (Irving Howe's famous phrase) of the future than "a very concrete and naturalistic portrayal of the present and the past," a "realistic synthesis and rearrangement of familiar materials." And again, Orwell's "statements about *1984* reveal that the novel, though set in a future time, is realistic rather than fantastic, and deliberately intensifies the actuality of the present." Specifically, according to Meyers, *Nineteen Eighty-Four* was not "totalitarianism after its world triumph" as in the interpretation of Howe, but rather "the very real though unfamiliar political terrorism of Nazi Germany and Stalinist Russia transposed into the landscape of London in 1941–44."[11] And not only Burnham's work but the reality of the 1943 Teheran Conference gave Orwell the idea of a world ruled by three totalitarian superstates.

Bernard Crick, Orwell's major biographer, points out that the English reviewers of *Nineteen Eighty-Four* caught on immediately that the novel was supposed to be an intensification of present trends rather than a prophecy of the future. Crick notes that these reviewers realized that Orwell had "not written utopian or anti-utopian fantasy . . . but had simply extended certain discernible tendencies of 1948 forward into 1984."[12] Indeed, the very year 1984 was simply the transposition of the existing year, 1948. Orwell's friend Julian Symons wrote that 1984 society was meant to be the "near future," and that all the grim inventions of the rulers "were just extensions of 'ordinary' war and post-war things." We might also point out that the terrifying Room 101 in *Nineteen Eighty-Four* was the same numbered room in which Orwell had worked in London during World War II as a British war propagandist.

But let Orwell speak for himself. Orwell was distressed at many American reviews of the book, especially in *Time* and *Life,* which, in contrast to the British, saw *Nineteen Eighty-Four* as the author's renunciation of his long-held devotion to democratic socialism. Even his own publisher, Frederic Warburg, interpreted the book in the same way. This response moved Orwell, terminally ill in a hospital, to issue a repudiation. He outlined a statement to Warburg, who, from detailed notes, issued a press release in Orwell's name. First, Orwell noted that, contrary to many reviews, *Nineteen Eighty-Four* was not prophecy but an analysis of what *could* happen, based on present political trends. Orwell then added: "Specifically, the danger lies in the structure imposed on Socialist and on liberal capitalist communities by the necessity to prepare for total war with the USSR and the new weapons, of which of course the atomic bomb is the most powerful and the most publicized. But danger also lies in the acceptance of a totalitarian outlook by intellectuals of all colours." After outlining his forecast of several world superstates, specifically the Anglo-American world (Oceania) and a Soviet-dominated Eurasia, Orwell went on:

> If these two great blocs line up as mortal enemies it is obvious that the Anglo-Americans will not take the name of their opponents. . . . The name suggested in *1984* is of course Ingsoc, but in practice a wide range of choices is open. In the USA the phrase "American" or "hundred per cent American" is suitable and the qualifying adjective is as totalitarian as any could wish.[13]

9

We are about as far from the world of Norman Podhoretz as we can get. While Orwell is assuredly anti-Communist and anticollectivist, his envisioned totalitarianism can and does come in many guises and forms, and the foundation for his nightmare totalitarian world is a perpetual cold war that keeps brandishing the horror of modern atomic weaponry.

Shortly after the atom bomb was dropped on Japan, George Orwell prefigured his world of *Nineteen Eighty-Four* in an incisive and important analysis of the new phenomenon. In an essay entitled "You and the Atom Bomb," he noted that when weapons are expensive (as the A-bomb is) politics tends to become despotic, with power concentrated into the hands of a few rulers. In contrast, in the day when weapons were simple and cheap (as was the musket or rifle, for instance) power tends to be decentralized. After noting that Russia was thought to be capable of producing the A-bomb within five years (that is, by 1950), Orwell writes of the "prospect," at that time, "of two or three monstrous super-states, each possessed of a weapon by which millions of people can be wiped out in a few seconds, dividing the world between them." It is generally supposed, he noted, that the result will be another great war, a war which this time will put an end to civilization. But isn't it more likely, he added, "that surviving great nations make a tacit agreement never to use the bomb against one another? Suppose they only use it, or the threat of it, against people who are unable to retaliate?"

Returning to his favorite theme, in this period, of Burnham's view of the world in *The Managerial Revolution,* Orwell declares that

> Burnham's geographical picture of the new world has turned out to be correct. More and more obviously the surface of the earth is being parcelled off into three great empires, each self-contained and cut off from contact with the outer world, and each ruled, under one disguise or another by a self-elected oligarchy. The haggling as to where the frontiers are to be drawn is still going on, and will continue for some years.

Orwell then proceeds gloomily:

> The atomic bomb may complete the process by robbing the exploited classes and peoples of all power to revolt, and at the same time putting the possessors of the bomb on a basis of equality. Unable to conquer one another, they are likely to continue ruling the world between them, and it is difficult to see how the balance can be upset except by slow and unpredictable demographic changes.

In short, the atomic bomb is likely "to put an end to large-scale wars at the cost of prolonging 'a peace that is no peace.' " The drift of the world will not be toward anarchy, as envisioned by H. G. Wells, but toward "horribly stable . . . slave empires."[14]

Over a year later, Orwell returned to his pessimistic perpetual-cold-war analysis of the postwar world. Scoffing at optimistic press reports that the Americans "will agree to inspection of armaments," Orwell notes that "on another page of the same paper are reports of events in Greece which amount to a state of war between two groups of powers who are being so chummy in New York." There are two axioms, he added, governing international affairs. One is that "there can be no peace without a general surrender of sovereignty," and another is that "no country capable of defending its sovereignty ever surrenders it." The result will be no peace, a continuing arms race, but no all-out war.[15]

Orwell completes his repeated wrestling with the works of James Burnham in his review of *The Struggle for the World* (1947). Orwell notes that the advent of atomic weapons has led Burnham to abandon his three-identical-superpowers view of the world, and also to shuck off his tough pose of value-freedom. Instead, Burnham is "virtually demanding an immediate preventive war against Russia," which has become *the* collectivist enemy, a preemptive strike to be launched before Russia acquires the atomic bomb.

While Orwell is fleetingly tempted by Burnham's apocalyptic approach, and asserts that domination of Britain by the United States is to be preferred to domination by Russia, he emerges from the discussion highly critical. After all, Orwell writes, the

> Russian regime may become more liberal and less dangerous a generation hence. . . . Of course, this would not happen with the consent of the ruling clique, but it is thinkable that the mechanics of the situation may bring it about. The other possibility is that the great powers will be simply too frightened of the effects of atomic weapons ever to make use of them. But that would be much too dull for Burnham. Everything must happen suddenly and completely.[16]

George Orwell's last important essay on world affairs was published in *Partisan Review* in the summer of 1947. He there reaffirmed his attachment to socialism but conceded that the chances were against its coming to pass. He added that there were three possibilities ahead for the world. One (which, as he had noted a few months before, was the new Burnham solution) was that the United States would launch an atomic attack on Russia before Russia developed the bomb. Here Orwell was more firmly opposed to such a program than he had been before. For even if Russia were annihilated, a preemptive attack would only lead to the rise of new empires, rivalries, wars, and use of atomic weapons. At any rate, the first possibility was not likely. The second possibility, declared Orwell, was that the cold war would continue until Russia got the bomb, at which point world war and the destruction of civilization would take place. Again, Orwell did not consider this possibility very likely. The third, and most likely, possibility is the old vision of perpetual cold war between blocs of superpowers. In this world,

> the fear inspired by the atomic bomb and other weapons yet to come will be so great that everyone will refrain from using them. . . . It would mean the division of the world among two or three vast super-states, unable to conquer one another and unable to be overthrown by any internal rebellion. In all probability their structure would be hierarchic, with a semi-divine caste at the top and outright slavery at the bottom, and the crushing out of liberty would exceed anything the world has yet seen. Within each state the necessary psychological atmosphere would be kept up by complete severance from the outer world, and by a continuous phony war against rival states. Civilization of this type might remain static for thousands of years.[17]

Orwell (perhaps, like Burnham, now fond of sudden and complete solutions) considers this last possibility the worst.

It should be clear that George Orwell was horrified at what he considered to be the dominant trend of the postwar world: totalitarianism based on perpetual but peripheral cold war between shifting alliances of several blocs of super-states. His positive solutions to this problem were fitful and inconsistent; in *Partisan Review* he called wistfully for a Socialist United States of Western Europe as the only way out, but he clearly placed little hope in such a development. His major problem was one that affected all democratic socialists of that era: a tension between their anticommunism and their opposition to imperialist, or at least interstate, wars. And so at times Orwell was tempted by the apocalyptic preventive-atomic-war solution, as was even Bertrand Russell during the same period. In another, unpublished article, "In Defense of Comrade Zilliacus," written at some time near the end of 1947, Orwell, bitterly opposed to what he considered the increasingly procommunist attitude of his own Labour magazine, the *Tribune,* came the closest to enlisting in the cold war by denouncing neutralism and asserting that his hoped-for Socialist United States of Europe should ground itself on the backing of the United States of America. But despite these aberrations, the dominant thrust of Orwell's thinking during the postwar period, and certainly as reflected in *Nineteen Eighty-Four,* was horror at a trend toward perpetual cold war as the groundwork for a totalitarianism throughout the world. And his hope for eventual loosening of the Russian regime, if also fitful, still rested cheek by jowl with his more apocalyptic leanings.

NOTES

1. Norman Podhoretz, "If Orwell Were Alive Today," *Harper's,* January 1983, pp. 30–37.

2. Harry Elmer Barnes, "How 'Nineteen Eighty-Four' Trends Threaten American Peace, Freedom, and Prosperity," in *Revisionism: A Key to Peace and Other Essays* (San Francisco: Cato Institute, 1980), pp. 142–43. Also see Barnes, *An Intellectual and Cultural History of the Western World,* 3d rev. ed., 3 vols. (New York: Dover, 1965), 3:1324–1332; and Murray N. Rothbard, "Harry Elmer Barnes as Revisionist of the Cold War," in *Harry Elmer Barnes, Learned Crusader,* ed. A. Goddard (Colorado Springs: Ralph Myles, 1968), pp. 314–38. For a similar analysis, see F. J. P. Veals, *Advance to Barbarism* (Appleton, Wis.: C. C. Nelson, 1953), pp. 266–84.

3. Garet Garrett, *The People's Pottage* (Caldwell, Idaho: Caxton Printers, 1953), pp. 154–57.

4. Quoted in Garrett, *The People's Pottage,* p. 154.

5. Marcus Raskin, "The Megadeath Intellectuals," *New York Review of Books,* November 14, 1963, pp. 6–7. Also see Martin Nicolaus, "The Professor, the Policeman and the Peasant," *Viet-Report,* June–July 1966, pp. 15–19; and Fred Kaplan, *The Wizards of Armageddon* (New York: Simon and Schuster, 1983).

6. Barnes, " 'Nineteen Eighty-Four' Trends," p. 176.

7. *U.S. News and World Report,* December 26, 1983, pp. 86–87.

8. Irving Howe, ed., *1984 Revisited: Totalitarianism in Our Century* (New York: Harper and Row, Perennial Library, 1983). There is a passing reference in Robert Nisbet's essay and a few references in Luther Carpenter's article on the reception given to *Nineteen Eighty-Four* by his students at a community college on Staten Island (pp. 180, 82).

9. Raymond Williams, *George Orwell* (New York: Columbia University Press, 1971), p. 76.

10. John Atkins, *George Orwell* (London: Caldor and Boyars, 1954), pp. 237–38.

11. Jeffrey Meyers, *A Reader's Guide to George Orwell* (London: Thames and Hudson, 1975), pp. 144–45. Also, "Far from being a picture of the totalitarianism of the future, *1984* is, in countless details, a realistic picture of the totalitarianism of the present" (Richard J. Voorhees, *The Paradox of George Orwell,* Purdue University Studies, 1961, pp. 85–87).

12. Bernard Crick, *George Orwell: A Life* (London: Secker and Warburg, 1981), pp. 393. Also see p. 397.

13. George Orwell, *The Collected Essays, Journalism and Letters of George Orwell,* ed. Sonia Orwell and Ian Angus, 4 vols. (New York: Harcourt Brace Jovanovich, 1968), 4:504 (hereafter cited as *CEJL*). Also see Crick, *George Orwell,* pp. 393–95.

14. George Orwell, "You and the Atom Bomb," *Tribune,* October 19, 1945, reprinted in *CEJL,* 4:8–10.

15. George Orwell, "As I Please," *Tribune,* December 13, 1946, reprinted in *CEJL,* 4:255.

16. George Orwell, "Burnham's View of the Contemporary World Struggle," *New Leader* (New York), March 29, 1947, reprinted in *CEJL,* 4:325.

17. George Orwell, "Toward European Unity," *Partisan Review,* July–August 1947, reprinted in *CEJL,* 4:370–75.

Bernard Crick

READING *NINETEEN EIGHTY-FOUR* AS SATIRE

Nineteen *Eighty-Four* has been read with amazingly diverse interpretations. Serious people have seen it as a deterministic prophecy, as a conditional projection, as a humanistic satire of events, as nihilistic misanthrophy, as a libertarian socialist satire of power in general, as predominantly an attack on the Soviet Union. Anthony Burgess has seen it as a comic novel. For a man who cultivated the skills and reputation of plain living, plain thinking, and plain writing, this diversity of reception, this propensity to be body-snatched by nearly everyone (except the Communists), is at least curious.

Partly Orwell brought the trouble on himself. The book is indeed a satire, but it is also the most complex and ambitious work he ever undertook, probably too complex for its own good, both aesthetically considered (compared to *Animal Farm,* for instance) and in the crowded jostle of its substantive ideas. Orwell used *satire* and *parody* synonymously. In the now well-known press release he issued after reading the first reviews of *Nineteen Eighty-Four,* he denied that he was saying that "something like this will happen," but that "allowing for the book being after all a parody, something like *Nineteen Eighty-Four* could happen."[1] And in his letter to an official of the United Automobile Workers, also worried at some of the American reviews, he says: "I do not believe that the kind of society I describe necessarily will arrive, but I believe (allowing of course for the fact that the book is a satire) that something resembling it could arrive."[2] In the same letter he calls it a "show-up" of the "perversions to which a centralized economy is liable and which have already been partly realized in Communism and Fascism." And in the letter to his publishers about the "blurb," he had said that he was "parodying . . . the intellectual implications of totalitarianism," which he then links, as in the press release, to the division of the world by the Great Powers;[3] but in the press release he had added the specific dangers to freedom in having to rearm with the new atomic weapons. Strictly speaking, parody mocks a style or the

15

external characteristics of a person, whereas satire mocks ideas, institutions, or behavior purporting to be good. In the vernacular, *take-off* and *show up* express the difference. But the line is fine in some writing. *Nineteen Eighty-Four* as a whole is clearly satire, although with some elements of parody to be found in the Goldstein section and in the appendix.

The targets of the satire in the actual text are more than Orwell's two statements might imply. In my reading of the internal symbolic structure, seven main satiric themes emerge: the division of the world by the superstates; the mass media as an agent of prolerization; power hunger in general and totalitarianism in particular; the untrustworthiness of the intellectuals; the abuse and degradation of language; the control of history for political purposes; and the theses of James Burnham.

However, all that is interpretation. And what an author intends a book to be or says that it was is not always what we find in the text. So I simply want to demonstrate that the book is a satire of continuing events, not a prophecy of the future, by a slow reading of the text following the actual plot or story line. This is tedious (or scholarly) but it is seldom done: commentators tend to seize on one element or other in the book and then preach a sermon upon it.

First, there is the title. A title or a name creates preconceptions. Orwell first intended it to be called, as he had headed his outline of 1943, "The Last Man in Europe."[4] As late as October 1948, when he was beginning to revise and retype the final version of the manuscript (an effort that brought on his final collapse), he told his publisher, "I haven't definitely fixed on the title but I am hesitating between NINETEEN EIGHTY-FOUR and THE LAST MAN IN EUROPE.[5] Perhaps the publisher felt strongly that *The Last Man in Europe* would give too much of the game away, was too leading and gloomily didactic. *Nineteen Eighty-Four* would invoke more of a surprise, arousing expectations of some new *Brave New World* or Utopia. The dashing of those expectations would then add to the satiric effect.

Consider the title as if we are reading the book in 1949. If thirty-five or under, the reader will think to himself that he will probably be alive to see if it is so. He may quickly realize that any precise date is a joke, but he will relish the joke that though it sounds like a utopian, antiutopian or possibly science-fiction novel, the date is well adjusted to be within the lifetime of some of us and in their childrens' lifetime for others, sounding both closer and more precise than Huxley's year 2000. It is overwhelmingly probable that the date is simply 1948, when Orwell finished the book, turned inside out; the date had been used before by other writers, but it is most unlikely that they could have influenced Orwell's choice.

In other words, the novel inhabits what Julian Symons well calls "a near future": "In one of its aspects *Nineteen Eighty-Four* was about a world familiar to anybody who lived in Britain during the war that began in 1939. The reductions in rations, the odious food, the sometimes unobtainable and always dubiously authentic drink, these were with us still when the book appeared." And he concluded a perceptive "appreciation" of Orwell: "*Nineteen Eighty-Four* is about a possible future, but through the fantasy we see always the outline of our own real world"[6]—the same point but with a different emphasis. Surely it looks both at his present and, allowing for fantasy, at a near future. Anthony Burgess's *A Clockwork Orange* and Doris Lessing's *The Memoirs of a Survivor* are other examples of "near futures"; perhaps they worry us more than dystopias because they are less easy to distance. Nonetheless, commentators try to distance *Nineteen Eighty-Four* by putting it in the tradition of Wells, Zamyatin, and Huxley, rather than seeing it as a mutant of social novel and satiric polemic. This is made easier if the title is misrendered (as is the usual American custom) as a date, *1984*, rather than spelled out. A date suggests a prophecy, whereas a title or name suggests a fiction.

The opening pages are full of recognizable images of immediate postwar London, albeit with sardonic exaggeration. The experience described in the very first paragraph of not being able to close the door quickly enough "to prevent a swirl of gritty dust from entering along with him" was a familiar experience: the dust from the bombsites and from the rarely cleaned streets. "Victory Mansions" was familiar, and what a victory it seemed: food shortages and rationing had actually increased after the end of the war with the end of Lend-Lease and a world shipping shortage. "The clocks were striking thirteen": the armed forces, civil defense, and railways had gone over to the "Continental" twenty-four-hour system during the war, but the man in the street still dragged his unprogressive feet, and still does. And the next two paragraphs have the smell of "boiled cabbage" (something never in short supply), propaganda posters, elevators that don't work, the electric current cut off for certain hours as part of the economy drive (indeed the winter of 1947 saw widespread power failures; in London one was forever getting stuck in lifts); also Winston's tiredness, his blue overalls, coarse soap, and blunt razor blades. All these things were very familiar to the British reader in 1949. Winston drags himself up "seven flights" of stairs: few apartment buildings in London were then of that height, but Orwell was the kind of gloomy person who feared that in the future they all would be so, and the elevators still no better. Some of the posters are torn and flapping and "little eddies of wind were swirling dust and torn paper into spirals"—most familiar. How bold and bright the design of wartime exhortatory posters and of political campaigns; how dirty and torn they quickly became.

The only new inventions we meet immediately are the telescreen and the helicopter, and these only new in their adaption for surveillance. All this is consistent with a "near future," quite unlike science fiction or fantasies. The BBC had begun television broadcasting just before the war and had recently resumed, so all Orwell did was to imagine its extension, as now used for security in banks and supermarkets. Helicopters had been used by the American army during the invasion of Europe for artillery observation and guidance, so the fantasy of police using them for general surveillance was not a very great one and soon came true. And when in the fourth paragraph the telescreen is "still babbling away about pig-iron and the over-fulfillment of the Ninth Three-Year Plan," while the last phrase would take the politically literate reader's mind to the USSR, the general gabbling of triumphant and possibly imaginary production statistics was not unfamiliar to wartime listeners to the BBC. And while the BBC's morning exercises were not compulsory (as in Oceania), they were there and made absurd claims that millions of patriotic people did them to keep fit for the war effort.

As we read on into the first section, the inventions continue to be familiar, recognizable caricatures that look a little way ahead and a little way back, quite unlike the biological fantasies of Aldous Huxley or the engineering fantasies of Zamyatin. "Ink-pens" were simply the new and still-expensive Biros; "speakwrites" were simply dictaphones that typed, though we can't quite yet dispense with human secretaries; and the "pneumatic tubes" that transmitted Winston's work in the ministry had linked, since the 1920s, the sales staff to the cashiers in big department stores. The great ministries are named Minitrue, Minipax, Miniluv, and Miniplenty. Abbreviated names and acronyms became a fashion in the 1930s—it seemed very modern and futuristic to be CP, Nazi, FBI, or Coop, for example—and during the war the fashion became a contagion and spread rapidly.

"The Ministry of Truth . . . was startlingly different from any other object in sight. It was an enormous pyramidal structure of glittering white concrete, soaring up, terrace after terrace, three hundred meters into the air." Now the Senate House Tower of the University of London is a mere 64.5 meters high, but it was the tallest new building in London in the 1930s and 1940s and, more to the point, housed the wartime Ministry of Information, which everybody knew to be Newspeak for Ministry of Propaganda. Admittedly, working conditions within Minitrue closely resemble those of the wartime BBC, with which Orwell was very familiar; but the terraced structure and the location of the Ministry of Information make Senate House the primary target of Orwell's detestation. And the first of the three great slogans of the Party on the wall of the tower, "War Is Peace," is pleasantly reminiscent of the "Fight for Peace" beloved of Communist Front organizations in the Popular Front days and revived after the war to oppose British and American intervention in the Greek civil war and anything else that ran counter to Russian interests.

The more we see through Winston Smith's eyes of the townscape of London as the provincial capital of Airstrip One (the genial anti-Americanism of the name escapes most commentators, even though the United States Air Force bases of 1942 are now reopening, and some never closed), the more we are aware of a desolate and colorless world. (*Colorless* is used in the descriptions almost as often as *dust*.) A bleak contrast is painted between the glittering machines in the modern-style ministries and the drab grime and dirt of the streets and the crumbling homes of both the Outer Party and the proles. This awful gulf between theory and practice, the ideal and the actual, the best and the ordinary, is literally Swiftian: despite all the marvellous schemes of the projecteers of Balnibari, "the whole country lies miserably waste." Dust means a dead world—not literally dead, but with all liveliness and humanity gone out of it.

One of the later passages on this theme, however, while it brings totalitarian projects and pretensions down to London earth, is yet of such power that a prophetic note is undeniable.

> Life, if you looked about you, bore no resemblance not only to the lies that poured out of the telescreens, but even to the ideals that the Party was trying to achieve. Great areas of it, even for a Party member, were neutral and non-political, a matter of slogging through dreary jobs, fighting for a place on the Tube, darning a worn-out sock, cadging a saccarine tablet, saving a cigarette end. The ideal set up by the Party was something huge, terrible and glittering—a world of steel and concrete, of monstrous machines and terrible weapons—a nation of warriors and fanatics, marching forward in perfect unity, all thinking the same thoughts and shouting the same slogans, perpetually working, fighting, triumphing, persecuting—three hundred million people all with the same face. The reality was decaying, dingy cities where underfed people shuffled to and fro in leaky shoes, in patched up nineteenth century houses that smelt always of cabbage and bad lavatories. He seemed to see a vision of London, vast and ruinous, city of a million dustbins.

This vision must go far beyond (though it still includes) the actuality of London in 1948. Different readers will read very different things into it: the essence of our own time, the decaying "inner city," or various precise locations ranging from Eastern Europe to China through sundry pretentious, cruel, but inefficient military dictatorships.

Winston begins his diary. The keeping of the diary is the major theme of the plot until two minor themes, his interest in Julia and then O'Brien, introduced quietly and casually early in part 1, suddenly and dramatically become dominant in part 2, but not until part 2. The diary thus carries the story through the first third of the book, serving both to tell us a lot about Winston and to broach the two-edged theme of memory: private memory as essential to humanity, but also its terrible uncertainty. The diary itself "was a peculiarly beautiful book. Its smooth creamy paper, a little yellowed by age, was of a kind that had not been manufactured for at least forty years past." So it was manufactured about the time he was born, "since he was fairly sure that his age was thirty-nine, and he believed that he had been born in 1944 or 1945; but it was never possible nowadays to pin down any date within a year or two." His probable year of birth accounts for his first name, of course, but the important point is that the diary exists in itself physically, even before it becomes a diary by his writing in it, before his memory. The author writes in an empiricist tradition: he shows no doubt that there is an external world independent of the consciousness of the observer. And though finally Winston Smith is attacked and destroyed by O'Brien on this very point, the author does give us, very early on, this simple, external point of reference. We are never meant to doubt that two plus two equals four.

The first thing Winston sets down is a tense account of a night at "the flicks," a sadistic newsreel of the war during which the prole woman starts shouting "they didn't oughter of showed it not in front of the kids." And Winston "did not know what had made him pour out this stream of rubbish." "Pour out" suggests an instinctive attempt at cleansing himself, trying to use the diary as therapy; indeed the sadism of the scene he describes, the audience applauding the killing of the child, makes him think of the hateful-looking young woman from the novel-writing machines, who wore the "narrow scarlet sash, emblem of the Junior Anti-Sex League." Orwell thus deliberately links the sadistic with the erotic; the regime turns sexual frustration into violent hatred—the famous orgiastic Two Minutes Hate is a daily event, and it even affects Winston's perceptions. When later Winston recounts to his diary his visit to the horrible prostitute, the naturalistic vividness of the description suggests not just another embellishment of the consequences of an imaginary regime, but a fairly conventional progressive view that modern society creates sexual frustration of the kind of Winston's marriage.

Yet the same film also makes him think of a member of the Inner Party whom he had seen from time to time but never talked to, but to whom "he felt deeply drawn." As the relationship develops, even into the final torture chambers of Miniluv, he thinks he finds a father figure, almost a god; but in fact O'Brien becomes antifather, anti-Christ.

The next thing he writes in the diary is "Down With Big Brother," repeatedly, although the trust he is to give to O'Brien shows that he wants a real big brother, father, family even. For as we read on, more and more of Winston's diary entries, to which are soon added his dreams, are concerned with memories of his mother, his childhood, and not just his vanished wife's sexual coldness and Party warmth but the specific fact that he and his wife failed, however many times they went at "making a baby" or "our duty to the Party," to produce a child. Immediately after the first diary-writing scene, Orwell takes Winston in next door to help Mrs. Parsons clear a blocked pipe. I don't think that small piece of symbolism is very important; he had used it before and far more effectively in *The Road to Wigan Pier*, when he himself watches remotely from a train the helplessness of a young working-class woman trying to clear a blocked external drainpipe. The image is Sisyphean, of squalor and oppression, not sexual. But what is important is to meet the truly horrible children so early: "'You're a traitor!' yelled the boy. 'You're a thought-criminal! You're a Eurasian spy! I'll shoot you, I'll vaporize you, I'll send you to the salt mines! Want to see the hanging! Want to see the hanging!' chanted the little girl, still capering round." How ghastly that a regime can render the time of innocence so sadistic—and that these young members of "the Spies" do finally betray their proud father, the zealous Parsons. All this makes us think of both the Soviet Young Pioneers and the Nazi Youth groups (and I suspect that Orwell had dark suspicions that the Boys Brigade and the Boy Scouts were potential paramilitaries). But there is something about these neighbors, not shared by Winston, that is so obvious that we might miss it: they are a family, a satiric family, a black joke on the real thing, but nonetheless a family.

Winston tells his diary that he had bullied his mother and stolen his frail sister's chocolate ration just before they both disappeared. His memories of his family life were bad, but nonetheless he wants a child. So there is a strong suggestion in the text that the family should be the primary school of that "mutual trust" which is the precondition of a wider fraternity and general decency toward others. Some moralists, like Plato, or social philosophers, like Marx, have seen the family, or rather family ties and affections, as inherently a vested, selfish interest, corrupting to justice. The socialist Orwell did not like family privilege, still less rule or influence by privileged families; but he did quite sensibly suggest that any regime that destroys the primary institution in which we first learn mutual trust and mutual aid and how to behave toward others, destroys any possibility that morality rather than force will govern general social relations. Despite his strong belief in the influence and injustice of the class system, he had called England "a family with the wrong members in control"—a metaphor that still embarrasses some socialists.

The diary quickly returns to the theme of mutuality when Winston addresses the future—an important passage because it is his first clear statement of what he believes in, this last man in Europe:

> To the future or the past, a time when thought is free, when men are different
> from one another and do not live alone—to a time when truth exists and what
> is done cannot be undone: From the age of uniformity, from the age of solitude,
> from the age of Big Brother, from the age of doublethink—greetings!

Freedom and *truth* are the great and obvious affirmations. Not merely their
defense but examples of their use run through all Orwell's writings and the
way he led his life, and at the very least *Nineteen Eighty-Four* is a satire of all
attempts to justify the unfree and the untrue. Only in this passage are they
explicit; elsewhere and throughout they are found in the negation of their
negation (the technique of satire). The importance of freedom and truth both
in the text and to the author is common ground among critics, but not so the
theme of mutuality, mutual trust, sociability, even fraternity. Some critics see
Orwell as always an individualist, in a strict liberal or neoconservative sense,
or as returning right at the end, in crisis and under stress, to the individualism
that had preceded his socialist writings.[7] But notice that in this passage, far
from defending individualism as privacy and autonomy, he looks to a time
"when men are different" but also one in which "they do not live alone," and
he makes, paradoxically to some, "the age of uniformity" also "the age of
solitude." Orwell's individualism was not of a liberal kind but either of a
republican (sometimes called "civic humanism") or of a modern socialist
kind: a person cannot be truly human except in relationships with others. My
uniqueness consists not in my "personality" but in the "identity" by which
others recognize my actions: it is a mutual, social process, not solitude.[8]
Privacy is important to Orwell, but it depends on political action to preserve
it: the whole man must move backward and forward, constantly and easily,
between public and private: man must be both citizen and individual. Orwell
is closer to Rousseau than to Adam Smith or John Stuart Mill.

The ideals are clear, far clearer than the hope of ever regaining what we
could lose. Winston has a panic sense of doom, in which Julia shares, when
they embark on their illicit affair, "free love" indeed. He had begun actually
writing the illegal diary "in sheer panic, only imperfectly aware of what he
was setting down"; just before he was interrupted while writing his first entry,
he had been "seized by a kind of hysteria" and scribbled: "theyll shoot me i
dont care theyll shoot me in the back of the neck i dont care down with big
brother." Even when he writes more calmly, "to the future or to the past," he
has no confidence that anyone in the future will read his diary or know freedom, truth, and sociability ever again; and he enters the foreboding words:
"Thoughtcrime does not entail death: thoughtcrime IS *death."* Orwell is
clearly saying that once one gets into a totalitarian regime there is no way out,
no hope through conspiracy or rebellion. This view is far from irrationally pessi-

mistic: the Nazis were only defeated externally by war, and it is unlikely that Orwell would have believed that the death of Stalin meant the end of totalitarianism. "The moral to be drawn from this dangerous nightmare situation," he said in the postpublication press release, "is a simple one: *Don't let it happen. It depends on you.*" Our resistance to totalitarian tendencies will be greater if we fight without illusions, above all with no false belief in the inevitability of progress. The worst could happen. And here Orwell drops prudential calculation, as in effect did Winston Smith. Implicitly he is saying that a man, to remain human, *must* exercise his freedom; he must rebel, however hopelessly: *"theyll shoot me i dont care."* Winston, often dismissed, or labeled as an antihero, is actually a very brave man: he holds out for truth under torture astonishingly long, though it can do him no good at all— "pointless," says O'Brien.

This part of the satire is specifically antitotalitarian. The autocracies of the past had only demanded passive obedience; ceremonies of occasional conformity were all that was needed for law and order. But Orwell implies that totalitarianism demands *complete* loyalty, no reservations being allowed, and continuous enthusiasm, not just occasional conformity.[9] Hence even to think a heterodox thought is a crime, and life without the Party is impossible: *"Thoughtcrime is death."* But precisely because this is *not* typical of autocracies in general, some of the satire aimed at the power-hungry in general or the Party seen as a savage caricature of all bureaucracies, appears both implausible and diffuse. *Totalitarianism* is both too big and too precise to appear relevant to every jack-in-office. Most bureaucrats "let sleeping dogs lie" rather than prosecute vigorously for "Thoughtcrime." Neither bureaucratization nor totalitarianism are to be commended; but they are different phenomena, and threaten each other. Orwell attacks both, but using the same imagery can be confusing. The two birds are hard to kill with the same stone.

"Thoughtcrime" is not commonly found in autocracies, unless Orwell shifts and blurs the focus of the argument from totalitarian regimes to totalitarian *tendencies* (of which there may be some in quite unlikely places). Matthew 5:28—"Whosoever looketh on a woman to lust after her hath committed adultery with her already in his heart" expresses a kind of Thoughtcrime; and Boy Scouts in Orwell's day took a famous and much-mocked oath to be "clean in *thought,* word and deed" (my italics).[10] This was precisely the aspect of Christian teaching that the humanist in Orwell detested. There is also a conscious parody of the Catholic church in the text, especially in the meeting and ceremony in O'Brien's apartment. We know that Orwell was anti-Catholic in the 1920s and 1930s, and attacked the antisocialist influence of the church in postwar Europe. Yet this direct satire of the Catholic church in *Nineteen Eighty-Four* can blur the focus. The church may have some totalitarian tendencies, but Orwell is *not* saying that it *is* totalitarian: it is self-evidently a very traditional kind of autocracy, but also a very special kind. So the satire of total power moves ambivalently between totalitarianism proper and any autocracy, with the Catholic church singled out for special mention in the latter category. It is as if the configuration of powers in the novel form an isosceles triangle with a small, ill-defined, but tangible base of Catholicism between the two long, strong arms of totalitarianism and bureaucratic autocracy (or "managerialism").

The treatment of the proles involves this ambivalence. The Party is plainly a totalitarian party, but the proles are anomalous; they seem familiar and closer to home. They are not mobilized or put into uniform marching columns, and "no attempt was made to indoctrinate them with the ideology of the party"—precisely what Orwell had argued in essays and book reviews was the mark of totalitarianism. This can only be because their main function in the story is to serve as a satire of what the mass media, poor schools, and the selfishness of the intelligentsia are doing to the actual working class of Orwell's time. "Heavy physical work, the care of home and children, petty quarrels with neighbors, films, football, beer and, above all, gambling, filled up the horizon of their minds." All that was required of them was a "primitive patriotism" so as "to make them accept longer working hours or shorter rations," and "a vast amount of criminality," including prostitution and drug peddling, was allowed among them. Also "in all questions of morals they were allowed to follow their ancestral code. The sexual puritanism of the Party was not imposed upon them." So the devices of political control most practiced are not indoctrination and terror, as the Inner Party controls the Outer Party or as in Orwell's conception of real totalitarian regimes, but degradation and fragmentation: "even when they became discontented, as they sometimes did, their discontent led nowhere, because being without general ideas, they could only focus it on petty specific grievances." "Without general ideas" implies that the intellectuals have deserted the working-class movement for the security of desk jobs (the Outer Party).

Yet there is something more to the proles than a Swiftian satire on confounded hopes for the socialist ideal of prolitarian man and Orwell's version of the betrayal of the intellectuals. We are told that "they were beneath suspicion" for, "as the Party slogan put it: 'Proles and animals are free.'" And "the Party taught that the proles were natural inferiors who must be kept in subjection, like animals, by a few simple rules." Sir Victor Pritchett once brilliantly described Orwell as "a man who went native in his own country"; and Orwell himself stated in *The Road to Wigan Pier* that he had been led to live among tramps to see if we treated our own working class as he and his fellows had treated the native inhabitants of Burma. So in part at least the proles are "white niggers," a symbol of colonialism: a caricature of the British working class as if they were Burmans or Indians.

Yet despite their degradation, "the proles had stayed human. They had not become hardened inside." "If there is hope," Winston wrote, "it lies in the proles," and the thought is repeated three times. After all, they were "85 percent of the population of Oceania," reasoned Winston (a figure that is repeated in Goldstein's testimony) and "if only they could somehow become conscious of their own strength. . . . They needed only to rise up and shake themselves like a horse shaking off flies." "And yet—!" he adds. For he remembered at once how he had heard a tremendous shouting in the street, had thought that the proles were "breaking loose at last," but it was only a fight in a crowd of women over scarce tin saucepans on a market stall. "But if there was hope, it lay in the proles. You had to cling on to that. When you put it in words it sounded reasonable: it was when you looked at the human beings passing you on the street that it became an act of faith." Of course Goldstein's testimony is absolutely confident that the proles will conquer in the end, and it provides the "general ideas" that both Winston and the proles lack; but it was written by the Inner Party. "Is it true, what it says?" asks Winston in the cells of Miniluv. "As description, yes. The programme it sets forth is nonsense," replies O'Brien. "The proletarians will never revolt, not in a thousand years or a million." Yet, as I will argue, we are not meant to believe all that O'Brien says either: he is mad, and I think we are meant to believe more of Goldstein than we at first believe (even if "as in a glass darkly," and through a subsidiary and rather confusing satire of Trotskyist rhetoric). So the text is perfectly unclear and deliberately ambiguous as to whether we are to believe in an inevitable victory of the common people. "It must be so" wrestles with "impossible if things go so far." If one puts such historical questions to a fiction, the answer can only be, as Winston sees when he looks at the proles, "an act of faith." Commentators are being far too literal-minded, treating Oceania as Orwell's working model of the future, to argue whether rebellion is possible in such a regime and therefore whether Orwell (not Smith) had despaired. And some socialists are being very obtuse or humorless to say that Orwell had either broken with socialism or is unforgivably rude to the workers to liken them to animals: he had already said in *Burmese Days* that white administrators treated the natives like animals and had recounted in *The Road to Wigan Pier* that he had been brought up to believe that the working class smell (not that they do smell, as shocked left-wing activists angrily misread or wickedly distort him).

Leaving the empirical question aside, however, as being irresolvable in terms of the dramatic needs of a satirical story, there can be little doubt that the author intends us to take very seriously the noble passage, already quoted, "the proles had stayed human." And this is repeated in the nostalgic passage about the proles: "They remembered a million useless things, a quarrel with a work-mate, a hunt for a lost bicycle pump, the expression on a long dead sister's face, the swirls of dust on a windy morning seventy years ago." Irrespective of whether "the last man in Europe" and humanity in general is destroyed or not, we are asked to honor the human spirit in its freedom and oddity: the proles have not been fully debased. Immediately after reading Goldstein's testimony and immediately before their arrest, Winston has a vision that the "hard and red and coarse" prole woman, singing while she hangs up her washing in the backyard, is "beautiful."

> The future belonged to the proles. . . . at the least it would be a world of sanity. Where there is equality there can be sanity. Sooner or later it would happen, strength would change into consciousness. The proles were immortal, you could not doubt it when you looked at that valiant figure in the yard. . . . they would stay alive against all the odds, like birds, passing on from body to body the vitality which the Party did not share and could not kill.

Hope in the inevitability of rebellion is, of course, immediately dashed. The irony is dark and bitter indeed. But her "vitality, which the Party did not share and yet could not kill," remains. Orwell is not saying that the only things that are good are those that we believe are bound to succeed, a simple utilitarianism shared, in his opinion (and that of others) by both Marxists and market liberals. He is saying both that the spirit of the common people cannot be crushed and that even when individuals are crushed, memory of their spiritedness is good in itself.

Julia exhibits more of this prole vitality than Winston; or rather, in modern social terms, she seems as if she has risen from the people, whereas Winston has a middle-class intellectual's romantic attachment to the people. Julia is tough and resourceful, she seeks out Winston, trusts her own judgment about Winston's proneness to thoughtcrime, and organizes the complicated separate itineraries to meet and make love in the countryside. She is harsh and unfeeling. She recounts how her first affair was at sixteen with a party member who later committed suicide to avoid arrest: "And a good job too," said Julia, "otherwise they'd have had my name out of him." She does not believe that the rumored Brotherhood exists, and "any kind of organized revolt against the Party, which was bound to be a failure, struck her as stupid. The clever thing was to break the rules and stay alive all the time." She even falls asleep when Winston begins to read aloud to her *The Theory and Practice of Oligarchical Collectivism,* and she shows no interest in or comprehension of his tale of the photograph that gave objective proof that the *Times* was lying about Jones,

Aaronson, and Rutherford, the dissident leaders. "She was 'not clever,' but was fond of using her hands and felt at home with machinery." "She didn't care much for reading," but she quite enjoyed her work "servicing a powerful but tricky electric motor" on the novel-writing machines in "Pornosec, the sub-section of the Fiction Department among the proles." Yet we must admire her sheer vitality. She is not a very deep character, but she is far from two dimensional; and people like her in the real world make life very difficult for the puritanical boss who worries that he doesn't really know what is going on under his nose.

She is consciously nonpolitical, but in fact she challenges by her promiscuity the Party's assumption that "there was a direct intimate connection between chastity and political orthodoxy." And she hates the Party. She "seemed unable to mention the Party, and especially the Inner Party, without using the kind of words that you saw chalked up in dripping alley-ways." When they first try to make love, he fails, but she is splendidly practical: "Never mind, dear. There's no hurry. We've got the whole afternoon." But then what brings him on is not just the vision of "the Golden Country" and the thrush singing its heart out—a very Orwell-like theme of nature undefiled, even if a stylistic lapse into an overwritten piece of purple prose—but also the dialogue of sexual contempt for the Party. "'Have you done this before?' 'Of course. Hundreds of times—well scores of times anyway' " and "always with Party members." Not with Inner Party members though, but she opines that "those swine" would "if they got half a chance. They're not so holy as they make out." And Winston as he "pulled her down" rather surprisingly announces: "Listen. The more men you've had, the more I love you. Do you understand that? . . . I hate purity, I hate goodness! I don't want any virtue to exist anywhere. I want everyone to be corrupt to the bones." Even though Winston plainly does *not* hate goodness and virtue, only the Ingsoc version of them, yet nothing has really prepared us for such a Julia-like cynicism on his part. And of course it ends famously (if a little ludicrously): "Their embrace had been a battle, the climax a victory. It was a blow struck against the Party. It was a political act." One could argue that this crudity is part of the satire, but it is not a well-written passage, though a crucial one.

It's crucial because it leads Julia to break her own rules. For even a short sexual affair in such a regime some mutual trust is needed. Her usual prudent rule is short and sweet or cut and run, but the affair develops into an obsessional entanglement, at the least, on Julia's part, and into love, or seeming love, on Winston's. He tells her early on that "We are the dead," and "Folly, folly, his heart kept saying: conscious, gratuitous, suicidal folly." But they persist with their damning infatuation. When they are tortured, Julia, according to O'Brien, betrayed Winston immediately: "I have seldom seen anyone come over to us so promptly. . . . everything has been burned out of her. It was a perfect conversion, a textbook case." Plainly she has only vitality, love of freedom, and a hatred for the Party, whereas Winston, though physically more frail, can hold out longer because of his passion for truth: two plus two *do* equal four. A whole man is both heart and head, head and heart: for even when he accepts that two plus two can be five, he has the final reservation of loving Julia more than Big Brother, and only the ultimate fear can burn that out. And nothing can ever destroy the fact that they did trust each other.

They even trusted each other in the business of trusting Mr. Charrington and O'Brien, trust betrayed. Now most of us know the story too well. But would any normal first-time reader distrust Mr. Charrington—such a warm-sounding name and such a reassuring description? "His spectacles, his gentle, fussy movements and the fact that he was wearing an aged jacket of black velvet, gave him a vague air of intellectuality, as though he had been some kind of literary man, or perhaps a musician. His voice was soft, as though faded, and his accent less debased than that of the majority of proles." When the arrest comes, "the cockney accent had disappeared." This is a wry joke against Winston (and presumably against Orwell's old enemies, the conde-scending left-wing intellectuals): Winston finds hope in the proles and yet he trusts a man because his accent is better than the majority of proles. More sadly still, Smith trusts Charrington because he teaches him a nursery rhyme about the old church bells of London. This appeals to Winston's dreams of a better childhood. Perhaps the irony is too obvious when he tells Winston, "How it goes on I don't remember, but I do know it ended up, 'Here comes a candle to light you to bed, Here comes a chopper to chop off your head.' " But the familiarity, almost the banality, of the rhyme to the English reader proba-bly masks its meaning or softens the blow on first reading.

Before he rents the room he buys from Charrington the coral paperweight, just as on his first visit he had bought the diary. " 'It's a beautiful thing,' said Winston. 'It is a beautiful thing,' said the other, appreciatively. 'But there's not many that'd say so nowadays.' " Winston even resolved to come back to "buy further scraps of beautiful rubbish." Of course everything becomes per-verted from its natural state in Oceania. As soon as he walks out of the shop he sees that the unknown girl from the Fiction Department has been following him, obviously spying, and so he contemplates smashing in her skull with either a cobblestone or the coral paperweight. Nonetheless, the object is "beautiful rubbish." And "what appealed to him about it was not so much its beauty as the air it seemed to possess of belonging to an age quite different from the present one. . . . The thing was doubly attractive because of its apparent uselessness." He had noted that the proles "remembered a million useless things." So another positive value develops beneath the satiric form:

there is liberty, equality (as the negation of hierarchy), truth, and sociability or mutual trust, but now to these must be added a wholly nonpolitical value, described as useless beauty: aesthetic judgment.

At this stage of the argument I am trying to stay within the text, but the weight that Orwell wants us to give to this symbolic piece of coral is suggested by that most famous passage in his essay of 1946, "Why I Write":

> What I have most wanted to do throughout the past ten years is to make political writing into an art. My starting point is always a feeling of partisanship, a sense of injustice. . . . if it were not also an aesthetic experience. Anyone who cares to examine my work will find that even when it is downright propaganda it contains much that a full-time politician would consider irrelevant. I am not able, and I do not want, completely to abandon the world-view that I acquired in childhood. So long as I remain alive and well I shall continue to feel strongly about prose style, to love the surface of the earth, and to take pleasure in solid objects and scraps of useless information.[11]

He had once teased his fierce *Tribune* readership by devoting a precious wartime column to praise of "sixpenny Woolworth's roses" (a scion is still alive); and on another occasion he told them that though "the atom bombs are piling up in the factories, the police are prowling through the cities, the lies are streaming from the loudspeakers," yet neither "dictators nor bureaucrats, deeply as they disapprove of the process" are able to stop "the earth going round the sun" nor such simple pleasures as "watching the toads mating or a pair of hares having a boxing match in the new corn": "Indeed it is remarkable how nature goes on existing unofficially, as it were, in the very heart of London. I have seen a kestrel flying over the Deptford gasworks, and I have heard a first-rate performance by a blackbird in the Euston Road." His attitude to natural objects, both inanimate "solid objects" and most animals, was almost mystical, pietistic. All this is evoked by the Golden Country episode and Winston's pleasure in possessing the "almost useless" coral paperweight.

Yet, alas, there is nothing in nature that cannot be destroyed, perverted, or tainted by man. The coral is deliberately smashed by the police in the arrest, and the irritation of Charrington of the Thought Police may only be because the smashing is done without his command. And even before this, the spare room is revealed as the trap it really is; its attractions are tarnished. Hardly have Julia and Winston entered when a rat appears. She reacts to "the brutes" pragmatically, but he cries out melodramatically, "Of all the horrors in the world—a rat!" and had "the feeling of being back in a nightmare, a recurrent nightmare indeed." Now, rats are generally admitted to be fairly unpleasant creatures, and rat phobia is common: they eat the dead, they spread disease, they multiply when public order and cities decline and they were once a favorite disguise for the Prince of Darkness. Even in *Animal Farm,* although the animals before the revolution voted "that rats were comrades," the Wild Comrades Reeducation Committee after the revolution completely failed with rats and rabbits. It failed with both, presumably, because Orwell holds that there will always be some evil and some silliness in men. Socialism, he said, could make people better, never perfect. And Orwell's pietism toward nature was mediated by his realism. To be conscious of being part of nature, he implies, is a necessary condition for man to be at his best, but not a sufficient condition: man needs reason, skills, and courage as well for civic action.

Even in his love for Julia, Winston's sense of the importance of a rational politics continues, especially of the question, Does the Brotherhood really exist? The sexual act may by itself be both freedom and rebellion for Julia, but it is not enough for Winston. This leads him to trust O'Brien when he approaches him with "grave courtesy" to congratulate him on his facility with Newspeak and to offer him the loan of the latest edition of the *Newspeak Dictionary,* if he would care to call to pick it up. His readiness to trust is not just linked to the hope to find an active conspiracy, it is also linked to his failure to discover the truth on his own. It is not until part 2, a third of the way through the book, that Winston gets to know Julia, and then O'Brien. The last section of part 1 has dealt with the frustration of his hope to find the truth about the historical past by talking to proles, by evoking their memories. His dialogue with the old man is a marvellous comic invention. The old man is an unreconstructed traditionalist, all right: "A 'alf litre ain't enough. It don't satisfy," but the barman doesn't even know what a pint is—his ramblings are a chronologically jumbled parody of a misremembered and never fully understood *Daily Worker* or Communist-party prolefeed popular history. "A sense of helplessness took hold of Winston. The old man's memory was nothing but a rubbish-heap of details." (So much for oral history.) The significance of the incident is that it makes clear that however important is memory, it is useless without more formal knowledge—in this case documentary verification—and collaborators. The truth cannot be discovered on one's own. So quite apart from psychological need (though this is strongly hinted at too, in O'Brien as surrogate father), Winston needs to trust someone with access to the resources of the Inner Party and the Brotherhood.

Already, in the interview with O'Brien, the text contains forebodings that qualify Winston's moments of hope and should prevent the acute first-time reader from hoping for that happy ending which the British version of the first film of the novel insisted upon. Even the first time Winston speaks to O'Brien, we are told that "when the meaning of the words had sunk in, a chilly shuddering feeling had taken possession of his body. He had the sensation of stepping into the dampness of a grave, and it was not much better because he had always known that the grave was there and waiting for him." "Grave courtesy" indeed. Immediately before he and Julia visit O'Brien they discuss what will happen "when once they get hold of us." Winston stresses that they will be "utterly alone," and they both recognize that they will, everybody does, confess under torture. He says that that doesn't matter: the only real betrayal would be if they could make him stop loving her.

> She thought it over. "They can't do that," she said finally. "It's the one thing they can't do. They can make you say anything—*anything*—but they can't make you believe it. They can't get inside you."
> "No," he said a little more hopefully, "no; that's quite true. They can't get inside you. If you can *feel* that staying human is worth while, even when it can't have any result whatever, you've beaten them."

It is a humanist version of St. Paul's counsel not to fear those who hurt the body if they cannot hurt the soul. And it takes *more courage* (or folly) to mean this if one does not believe in life after death. But it shows that Orwell himself has moved beyond purely political, pragmatic, utilitarian, or hedonistic considerations, even if within the fiction "they" do "get inside" Winston and Julia.

The scene in O'Brien's apartment is tightly constructed and well crafted dramatically, compared to the florid scene in the Golden Country and elements of melodrama and didactic long-windedness in the torture scenes. Despite the very naturalistic setting, the text contains an unexpected symbolism. The door is opened by a little man "in a white jacket." O'Brien initiates them into wine (a privilege of the Inner Party, like being able to turn off the tele), catechizes them, and gives them both "a flat white tablet" (to take away the smell of the wine) before they go. There is certainly more than a suggestion of a communion or even confirmation service, indeed of a black mass, considering the nature of the catechism. For they agree to a list of horrible actions if they would hurt the Party and help the Brotherhood, even "to throw sulphuric acid in a child's face." Only the last question throws them: "You are prepared, the two of you, to separate and never see one another again?"

Julia immediately says "No!," and Winston, only after a long pause and uncertainty, also says "No," (tellingly, there is no exclamation mark). The point is surely that their humanistic reservation is in vain, indeed mere selfishness after what they have agreed to do to a child. Now, of course, the scene has plenty of historic examples to draw on: as Orwell well knew, revolutionary brotherhoods of anarchists and nihilists in the nineteenth and early twentieth centuries had enjoyed such ceremonies and sworn such oaths. He also knew, incidentally, that both individual revolutionaries and police informers were prone to exaggerate the size of such bodies, occasionally inventing (for prestige or employment) huge, totally nonexistent ones.

It is difficult to be sure how consciously the author inserted this symbolism into the text, and if unconscious how important it was to him. No one writing in his tradition can avoid religious metaphor—militant atheistical socialists used to urge us "forward to the New Jerusalem"—but one critic, at least, sees this scene as central to the book and to Orwell's concerns. The whole book is thus about the state replacing God, and Orwell's agonized despair at believing in neither. I find this argument farfetched and missing the multiplicity of satiric targets in the book. It is true that the merging of church and state could be one of them, though it seems more likely that the satire is not on the great question of the impossibility of living without a belief in God (though Orwell saw difficulty, indeed, in the collapse of traditional morality), but more mundanely on the Catholic church as an organization. He had disliked Catholicism as a young man, and he still feared its influence against socialism in Europe.[12] But while the text is charged, it is difficult to take a precise reading on this point. Yet whether or not the church in caricature is like the Party or whether or not it is impossible to oppose such parties without belief in God, Winston and Julia in their negative hatred for the Party have betrayed any possible morality, humanistic or Christian, that could universalize as a principle their experience of mutual trust. In the cells of Miniluv, O'Brien plays back on a tape recorder Winston saying that he would throw acid into a child's face. Such a regime as is imagined would thus corrupt hopelessly even its bravest opponents, just as the concentration camps (as Orwell well knew) did succeed in dehumanizing people before they were physically destroyed.

After meeting O'Brien, Winston is given "the heavy black volume," *The Theory and Practice of Oligarchical Collectivism* by Emmanuel Goldstein. Both mass movements and underground cells have their sacred books. "Goldstein" recalls Bronstein, Trotsky's real name; and "Emmanuel" is the Hebrew name for the Messiah or Savior. Obviously Trotsky is parodied in the general style and the character of Goldstein's book, but the analysis of bureaucracy is the only intellectual point in common. "Oligarchical collectivism" is not Trotsky's phrase. Orwell's Independent Labour Party company had fought in Spain as part of a brigade of the POUM who were Trotskyists so pure that their leader, Andres Nin, had broken with Trotsky (roughly speaking, for being too Stalinist, too dictatorial personally) although he had been Trotsky's confidential secretary in Russia. In 1941 H. G. Wells had called Orwell "that Trotskyite with the big feet," for between 1936 and 1942 Orwell was a bit hard to place politically, as a libertarian revolutionary socialist who hated the Communist party and saw only milk and water in the veins of the Labour

party. However, there is no substance in Isaac Deutscher's claim that Goldstein's book is simply a "paraphrase" of Trotsky's *Revolution Betrayed,*[13] any
more than his dismissive claim that *Nineteen Eighty-Four* is simply a pla-
giarism of Zamyatin's *We.*[14] Even Jeffrey Meyers's assertion that "Orwell's
acute understanding of totalitarianism is most strongly influenced by Trotsky's
The Revolution Betrayed" must be treated with caution: the book is only one
source among many other more obviously important. I share William
Steinhoff's view that Goldstein's testament is much more closely linked to
James Burnham's *The Managerial Revolution* and some later writings.[15]
Burnham had once been a prominent follower of Trotsky, so there is a double
edge to Orwell's parody.

Certainly there is a playful air to Orwell's use of the Trotsky persona and
style to attack Burnham and to convey some truths and some dilemmas,
though it can hardly be denied that the joke becomes labored. There is an
obvious structural clumsiness about the book-within-a-book that must make
one examine with special interest why it is there at all and so important to the
story. It holds up the action at a crucial point, though as Winston reads, Julia
sleeps. Perhaps it is a needed intermezzo, a welcome lull before the storm of
the arrest and the purposeful torturing. Or it could be argued that in this world
of machines, memos, and slogans, such substantial documentation—with a
fair semblance of old-fashioned literacy—suits the atmosphere invoked in the
descriptive passages of part I. But the length is awkward. We quickly get the
point and the joke of Newspeak as it is deftly worked into the general development of the story at several different points, so we can actually welcome the
appendix on "The Principles of Newspeak" as a useful consolidation or a
supererogatory amusement. By contrast, Goldstein's book both is too long
similarly to be threaded in and contains matter that we need to know before
appreciating the final exchanges between Winston and O'Brien; yet its form is
a heavy lump in the otherwise fast-flowing and clear structure of the book. I
suspect that many ordinary readers skip it, and many profound psychological
and philosophical interpreters of Orwell's "message" make little reference to
it (perhaps they skip it too): few people appeared eager to read it in any literal-
minded spirit to see what Orwell really thought. This last would be a mistake,
but not entirely—despite the double difficulty in the text of its being both
O'Brien's invention (though he says that it is true as a description) and a
parody of Burnham's thesis on the managerial elite written in a style that also
parodies Trotsky's style.

Winston begins reading chapter I, "Ignorance Is Strength." This title
sounds more like a satire on fascism than on communism—until now the
incidents or inventions of *Nineteen Eighty-Four* as a whole have been very
balanced in this respect—but most of the rest of Goldstein's book draws more

on Communist than on Fascist ideas and images. The chapter begins to tell us that from the beginning of time there have been "three kinds of people in the world, the High, the Middle and the Low" and that "the aims of these groups are entirely irreconcilable." Mercifully, Winston skips on. We have heard all that before.

Chapter 3, "War Is Peace," is much more novel and intriguing. After relating that the world came to be divided into three great superstates around the middle of the twentieth century (as Burnham had prophesied and Orwell thought likely),[16] the book describes these three powers as having been "permanently at war . . . for the past twenty-five years." War is not "the desperate, annihilating struggle that it was in the early decades of the twentieth century. It is a warfare of limited aims between combatants who are unable to destroy one another, have no material cause for fighting and are not divided by any genuine ideological difference." And "it is impossible for it to be decisive." We are told that "atomic bombs first appeared as early as the nineteen-forties, and were first used on a large scale about ten years later." After hundreds had been dropped on major industrial centers, the three ruling groups without any formal agreement, fearing for their own mutual destruction, ceased to use them; but they continued to manufacture and stockpile them.

> Meanwhile the art of war has remained almost stationary for thirty or forty years. Helicopters were more used than they were formerly, bombing planes have been largely superseded by self-propelled projectiles, and the fragile moveable battleship has given way to the almost unsinkable Floating Fortress; but otherwise there has been little development. The tank, the torpedo, the machine gun, even the rifle and the hand grenade are still in use.

Apart from the fact that mutual fear seems so far to have restrained the use of atom bombs even without that warfare of about 1955, and the minor matter of Floating Fortresses, the analysis is depressingly sensible and close to our own homes in the real world. And if not continuing warfare either, yet hardly peace, or what Thomas Hobbes would have counted as peace: "The nature of War consisteth not in actual fighting but in a known disposition thereto, during all the time there is no assurance to the contrary."[17]

But why, within the story, is such permanent though limited warfare (fought by small numbers of professionals over the former European colonial territories, not their own heartlands) continued at all? Up until now the account might suggest a parody of the Trotskyist, later to be the Maoist, doctrine of "permanent revolution": that constant social upheaval and revolutionary renewal are needed to prevent bureaucratization. Only in the Oceanic world the violence is to ensure that the ruling elites are not challenged politically: to do so would risk giving an advantage to the enemy. The one thing the proles must and do believe in is the malevolence of the enemy. This theory of false or perpetual war could just be, is in part, a sophisticated version of the time-honored tactic for maintaining domestic order that Shakespeare imputed to Henry IV and son. However, a new rationale emerges.

"The primary aim of modern warfare . . . is to use up the products of the machine without raising the general standard of living," Winston reads. The Inner Party has realized that if the general rise in living standards of people typical of the "end of the nineteenth and the beginning of the twentieth centuries" had continued, their own position would have been threatened.

> For if leisure and security were enjoyed by all alike, the great mass of human beings who are normally stupefied by poverty would become literate and would learn to think for themselves; and when once they had done this, they would sooner or later realize that the privileged minority had no function, and they would sweep it away. In the long run, a hierarchical society was only possible on the basis of poverty and ignorance.

So the problem becomes one of "how to keep the wheels of industry turning without increasing the real wealth of the world," and the answer is "continuous warfare. . . . Even when weapons of war are not actually destroyed, their manufacture is still a convenient way of expending labor power without producing anything that can be consumed." The object of war is not to conquer or defend territory "but to keep the structure of society intact"—that is, a hierarchical, antiegalitarian structure.

All this is a parody and critique of the Marxist theories of immiseration and of revolution. Goldstein/Orwell asserts, like de Tocqueville, that revolution is more likely in times of prosperity, of upswings of expectation, not in downswings of hopelessness; and it is a parody of the labor theory of value—for the surplus from exploitation of labor need not take the form of profit and capital accumulation; it can be burned off in war. A parody of Marxism, certainly with a dash of the Nazi "Guns Before Butter" thrown in; but it all now sounds, allowing for Swiftian exaggeration, very familiar and plausible. We now speak a more restrained language imputing a slight suspicion that the military and scientific establishments of the *two* great powers may have a mutual vested interest in the perpetuation of the armaments race, "overkill," and continuance of the cold war. Some of us feel that we've been in 1984 for many years now.

The suggestion that equality can only arise in times of prosperity is also unusual and intriguing. Most socialists have taken the view that poverty creates a desire for equality. But it can be seriously argued that only rising gross national product can arouse expectations that equality (or at any rate a radical diminishment of unjustifiable inequalities) is possible. Did not Marx himself clearly argue that socialism could only follow the undoubted achievements of capitalism and would rise on its shoulders, not pull it down and start again? We are in a fiction, but the argument is startlingly original and could be intellectually in earnest.

When Winston turns back to chapter 1, he quickly reads that "as early as the beginning of the twentieth century, human equality had become technically feasible" with the invention of machine production." Yet a "new aristocracy" had arisen from "the salaried middle class and upper grades of the working class. . . . as compared with their opposite numbers in past ages, they were less avaricious, less tempted by luxury, hungrier for pure power, and, above all, more conscious of what they were doing and intent on crushing opposition." And to do that, of course, they had unparalleled technological resources: not merely print and radio, but television with which to watch, so that "private life came to an end," and to control, so that "complete uniformity of opinion . . . now existed for the first time." So it is not a totalitarian ideology that moves them—this is a fabrication to control public opinion—nor the profit motive, but a desire for power over others. This now pure Burnham.

Goldstein tells us who this "new aristocracy" are: "bureaucrats, scientists, technicians, trade-union organizers, publicity experts, sociologists, teachers, journalists and professional politicians." This makes obvious reference and use of Burnham's thesis in *The Managerial Revolution* that "a new class" of "the managers" would take over the world. Orwell had long shared some of Burnham's key concepts while rejecting his conclusions. When Orwell rashly predicted the coming English revolution in his *The Lion and the Unicorn,* he himself had said that the "directing brains" for the popular movement "will come from the new indeterminate class of skilled workers, technical experts, airmen, scientists, architects and journalists, the people who feel at home in the radio and ferro-concrete age." The last phrase betrays his ambivalence towards this revolution even then, despite his special theory (far from implausible, though very irritating to strict Marxists) that the power of the people needed the leadership of altruistic and patriotic elements of the lower middle class to unleash and direct it. What if they weren't altruistic? What if they were Burnham's managers or "new Machiavellians"? In Goldstein's analysis they are, and all the rest of Oceania's policies follow logically. The people are best controlled by, as it were, "prolerization"—keeping them in poverty, ignorance, and corruption; neither ideological indoctrination nor strict regimentation is needed. The concept of totalitarianism only applies to

36

how the Inner Party controls the Outer Party—a situation astonishingly unlike anything that Orwell himself and his readers would have imagined of the real regimes called totalitarian. The treatment of the proles is old autocracy writ large by the debasing effects of modern communications technology: electronic bread and circuses.

Goldstein's testimony really told Winston very little that he did not know already, only that, fearing to have been a "minority of one" (that is, alone, literally an "idiot"), he now knew that he was "not mad." The account was true. Orwell seems to have intended more of it to be true, or at least speculatively relevant to the dilemmas of our times, than is usually noticed—even if the whole episode somewhat clogs the story and threatens to break the pretence of fiction. The imagined world and the real world become confused—an artistic loss, even if politically interesting.

When Winston faces O'Brien revealed, nothing in Goldstein's analysis is rendered implausible, except, of course, that his prophecy of a proletarian uprising is mocked. When O'Brien tells Winston that the Party can do anything, could easily conquer Eurasia and Eastasia if they wished to, Goldstein's logic seems stronger than his. When he launches into his peroration on "power entirely for its own sake" ("We are not interested in the good of others; we are interested solely in power") this is an impressively plausible stance. We are almost inclined to believe him when he says "we shall abolish the orgasm"; at least it seems plausible that some regime might try, given the plausibility of sexual repression as a device of political control. But what are we to make of O'Brien's claims that "our control over matter is absolute," that "the earth is the center of the universe," and that he could levitate if he wished, just as the Party could reach the stars? They are absurd, as Winston and the reader realize. The good sense of much of Goldstein's testament, at least the congruence of its theories to Winston's solitary perceptions has sustained Winston's belief in his own sanity, despite his nightmare and his physical and mental isolation. It is O'Brien who is mad. Winston only accepts his mad assertions because of torture and only comes to believe them when destroyed and, as it were, reborn. This cannot possibly be a projection of what total power will come to; rather it is a savage mocking of the pretensions of the power hungry in general. At the height of the imagery of total power, totalitarianism becomes a metaphor for something far more general, more common, and not always as pretentious. O'Brien's reference to the regime holding a Ptolemaic rather than a Copernican cosmology must be intended to make us think of Galileo facing the papal inquisition and reveals a religiosity in O'Brien.

So there is a precise link between what Goldstein has to tell us and the interrogation. There may be some flaws in the execution and writing, but the design is most deliberate and well crafted. Certainly many images suggest the fascination and appeal of sacrifice, cruelty, and violence. Orwell had quarreled with H. G. Wells over his assertion that Wells was too much a rationalist ever to understand the appeal of Hitler's irrationality. But the fact that this irrationality did appeal was a descriptive truth; morally he always offered a rational critique of the irrational in politics. His love of oddities and useless things was for private life. So in *Nineteen Eighty-Four* the rational voice (allowing for parody) of Goldstein balances the "mysticism of cruelty" of O'Brien. Orwell was the craftsman who balanced these two forces for literary effect, not, as Deutscher argued, himself the voice of the "mysticism and cruelty."[18]

Consider the structure of part 3, nearly all inside the windowless Ministry of Love. In the first scene Winston is in a common cell, crowded among other prisoners, and images of degradation abound. The ordinary criminals are all proles; but they treat "the polits" with "uninterested contempt." An "enormous wreck" of a drunken woman vomits on the floor. The proles, all "filthily dirty," swear at the guards, even scream back at the telescreen, but the guards treat them with a rough forebearance. Party prisoners, however, are beaten brutally if they even talk to each other. Two acquaintances from the office, Ampleforth and Parsons, are marched in, both arrested for thoughtcrime. Ampleforth, producing "a definitive edition of Kipling" and short of rhymes for *rod*, had left in *God*. (Orwell would certainly have intended the double meaning of humble *rod*, so amid all the horror there is still broad or black humor.) Parsons has been denounced by his little daughter, as he recounts "with a sort of doleful pride," for muttering "Down with Big Brother" in his sleep. (Again, not uncomic.) He uses the lavatory pan in the cell, and "the cell stank abominably." Smell and oppression, as well as dirt, are once more linked.

A man comes in whose face looks like a skull. He is starving. Another prisoner, actually given a name, "Bumstead" (which suggests a decent common man), gives the "skull-faced man" a crust. He is immediately and savagely beaten up by the guards, his head strikes the lavatory seat, and his dental plate is shattered into halves. There is no humor here, and the dental plate is that kind of precise image of the ordinary that Orwell could invest with such terror, like the prisoner in "A Hanging" avoiding the puddle before he mounts the scaffold. The skull-faced man is then told he has to go to Room 101. He screams, "Do anything to me. . . . Shoot me. . . . I've got a wife and three children . . . cut their throats in front of my eyes, and I'll stand by and watch it. But not room 101!" This, alas, verges on the ludicrous, especially because it unconsciously echoes a silly, sadoerotic schoolboy chant.[19] Perhaps it is one of the passages about room 101 that Orwell's friend Julian Symons found "melodramatic" and Orwell himself acknowledged as showing "vulgarity." Then O'Brien comes for Winston. " 'They've got you too!' he cried. 'They got me a long time ago,' said O'Brien with a mild, almost regretful irony." So at the first moment of truth, the minor motif of the Party as a church and the Inner Party as a priesthood is again sounded: O'Brien must have accepted the rule from early youth. Winston is then beaten by fist and rubber truncheon for a long and indeterminable time, softened up before he is taken to the cell where the interrogation proper, or rather his reconstitution or deconstitution, begins. O'Brien has taken over; he "asked the questions and suggested the answers"; he controls the electrical machine that causes graduated pain; and he determines when Winston shall have respite, food, or drugs. It is a long process. "He was the tormentor, he was the protector, he was the inquisitor, he was the friend." And Winston hears him murmuring in his ear: "Don't worry, Winston; you are in my keeping. For seven years I have watched over you. Now the turning-point has come. I shall save you, I shall make you perfect." He is almost fatherly, or perhaps it is big brotherly, to Winston.

Obviously it is crassly literal-minded to protest, as some readers do, that this amount of care by O'Brien for one dispensable individual is implausible, either in a possible totalitarian regime or in a fiction. It is, but the satiric point may be that you would have to go to such lengths against "the last man in Europe" if you were to achieve such results, and if you were so power crazy as to act in this perverse, godlike way. It is a test for O'Brien as well as for Winston. Winston is a difficult case. O'Brien tells Winston that there are three stages in "re-integration": "There is learning, there is understanding and there is acceptance." The first stage is fascinating but relatively easy and clear. Winston learns that the past has no real existence, since all records of it can be destroyed. Another copy of the photograph he thought so important is destroyed before his eyes, reduced to "dust and ashes"—echoing the words of the burial service for the dead in the rites of the Church of England. The Party controls past, present and future. By extreme pain he learns that two and two are not necessarily five, sometimes even four, but always only what the Party says. He is told, to strip down his resistance still further, that there is no hope of martyrdom: "You must stop imagining that posterity will vindicate you, Winston. Posterity will never hear of you." The hope of being remembered has indeed sustained free men in dark times throughout history: the Greeks and the Romans, as Machiavelli and the Italian humanists recalled, believed that immortality consisted precisely in being remembered for civic deeds; and Catholic and Protestant martyrs sometimes used martyrdom or hunger strikes for public example or political ends.

Always the stress is on power for its own sake. O'Brien even takes up Goldstein's at first puzzling point that the new regimes are something different from the totalitarian regimes of "earlier in the century." "The command of the old despotisms was 'Thou shalt not.' The command of the totalitarians was 'Thou shalt.' Our command is 'Thou art.' "

It is in the second stage of "understanding" that O'Brien's famous truth comes out. "The faint, mad gleam of enthusiasm had come back into O'Brien's face" when he asks Winston to tell him *why* the Party clings to power. Winston, though desperate to please, misreads him: "You are ruling over us for our own good."

> That was stupid, Winston. . . . I will tell you the answer to my question. It is this. The Party seeks power entirely for its own sake. We are not interested in the good of others; we are interested solely in power. Not wealth or luxury or long life or happiness: only power, pure power. . . . We are different from all the oligarchies of the past, in that we know what we are doing. . . . The German Nazis and the Russian Communists came very close to us in their methods, but they never had the courage to recognize their motives.

After that he actually declares, "We are the priests of power" and "God is power." Again, certainly there is a satire aimed at totalitarianism, or better the totalitarian mentality; but the greater thrust is not at something that Orwell imagined as going beyond totalitarianism but at something that exists all the time, not necessarily in the form of totalitarianism proper (though in the modern world it helps its growth): power hunger and unprincipled office-holding. Somewhat confusingly, one example of power hunger and hierarchy—the church—which indeed was certainly *not* the most important example in the modern world to Orwell, keeps surfacing in his imagery. Even the name O'Brien, being Irish, may suggest the Catholic.

O'Brien's absurd boast follows. The "mad gleam" has been noted. Yet despite the imagined power of the Party over the universe and the real total power that O'Brien holds over Winston Smith, the "last man" still holds out.

> "Do you believe in God, Winston?"
> "No."
> "Then what is it, this principle that will defeat us?"
> "I don't know. The spirit of man."
> "And do you consider yourself a man?"
> "Yes."
> "If you are a man, Winston, you are the last man. Your kind is extinct; we are the inheritors. Do you understand you are *alone?* You are outside history, you are nonexistent."

Indeed, if we had no memory, no history, and no mutual trust, no respect for truth, no aesthetic sense, our humanity could not exist.[20] O'Brien then breaks down utterly this apparent last resistance of Smith's, not by further solipsistic chop-logic or by torture, but by gently showing him in a mirror his own wasted and broken body: a long and ghastly description then follows, obviously taken from the newsreels of Belsen that were shown in London cinemas in ordinary programs open to children, though with a perfunctory warning (I remember vividly). "Do you see that thing facing you? That is the last man. If you are human, that is your humanity. Now put your clothes on again." But satire holds up a mirror, indeed. While the scene is moving and terrible, to look in the mirror the other way is again to show a human being who has held out so far, so very far.

Winston is willing now to accept everything, yet he still says, "I have not betrayed Julia." And when O'Brien looks down at him and acknowledges thoughtfully, "That is perfectly true," Winston feels a "peculiar reverence" for O'Brien's intelligence and understanding. They both knew that he had betrayed everything there was to betray about Julia, and that she had done the same; but they both know that he still loves her. "You are a difficult case," says O'Brien. "But don't give up hope. Everyone is cured sooner or later."

Then for some time Winston is rested and fed, he even recovers something of his former weight and appearance. He accepts everything he has been told and willingly exercises himself in doublethink and crimestop. Only sometimes our dreams betray our deepest feelings: he wakes up crying aloud, "Julia, my love, Julia." O'Brien knows, and when challenged by him Winston does not deny his true feelings towards Big Brother:

> "I hate him."
>
> "You must love Big Brother. It is not enough to obey him; you must love him."

So it seems that he is a jealous god, one can love no other, not even a fellow human being. To love Big Brother is both to love no other person and to lose any proper love for self, for in loving another human being, both mutual trust and thus a heightened individual identity are asserted in the face of the Party; and when all capacity to love another is crushed, nothing is left to love except Big Brother.

So then in the room "where there is no darkness" Winston meets "the worst thing in the world," for him a rat, the prince of darkness. To Orwell humanity cannot live wholly in the light or wholly in the dark. Both morally and physically we need natural rhythms, not permanent extremes. The good cannot be perfect, and the wicked have some good in them. Imperfect man (here we will all read the parable of "no dark men" differently; perhaps even Orwell was uncertain) can only be saved by God's mercy or can save each other by fraternal love and mutual aid. But no longer Winston. Even he screams, as the teeth come near to his face, that he must be spared and it must be done to her. He is not offered the choice: he just perfectly understands what O'Brien wants. Then he is lost as a man, for that is a sacrifice that one can only make for another: no one can demand another to lay down their life for oneself. So he is spared, cast out as a loyal but empty shell.

The last section shows him back at some kind of meaningless work, drinking the Victory gin again in the symbolic Chestnut Tree Cafe, and even encountering Julia—an empty, meaningless meeting not even bitter, whose only point is to acknowledge "that you don't give a damn what they suffer. All you care about is yourself. . . . And after that, you don't feel the same towards any other person again." If humanity and true individuality are mutual care and trust, Winston and Julia are now both simply the living dead, emptied of humanity.

> Winston, however, looks at the face of Big Brother: Two gin-scented tears trickled down the side of his nose. But it was all right, everything was all right, the struggle was finished. He had won the victory over himself. He loved Big Brother.

THE END

"THE END" is almost certainly part of the author's text. It is there in the final typescript, it was left by Orwell in the proofs, and was repeated in the later nine-volume Secker and Warburg standard edition of Orwell's books, of which only two others use this device. Bad movies and cheap books used to carry this sign. It is "the end" if one actually *loves* any Big Brother. And if this could be thought a tenuous argument against all who consider that the book ends on a note of utter despair, just consider the comic distancing of those two telltale gin-scented tears trickling down poor Winston's nose.

Such great dictators are worthy of such great admirers. For at the end the picture is a comic, grotesque one. And though we must admire Winston Smith for his stubbornness about truth and for holding out so long, he did sell the pass twice. Because of the rat it is easy to understand and forgive his betrayal of Julia. But only God could forgive their mutual willingness to throw sulphuric acid into a child's face, even for rebellion. Rebels who win like that just become the Party all over again. Both *Animal Farm* and *Nineteen Eighty-Four* end in parody transformation scenes.

And, anyway, it is not "THE END"—even that is a little joke. There then follows the delightfully satiric appendix, "The Principles of Newspeak," mordantly written in the past tense. The satire is harsh but good-humored. So the real ending of the book is not on the note of sadomasochistic horror of the scene in Room 101, nor even on the deflating picture of an imaginary dictator being loved by a gin-soaked, broken man, but on the words "so late a date as 2050." That is the date for the final translation of everything into Newspeak— quite a long time after 1984, note. What has held up the final solution so long, we are authoritatively told by the *Times*, is "the difficulty" (that is, the impossibility) of translating the Declaration of Independence and writers like "Shakespeare, Milton, Swift, Byron and Dickens." Conjuring with these names, the reader is led to believe that language can never become purely a method of control and cease to be imaginative and truthfully communicative. So may clear language and good literature sustain us.

NOTES

1. Quoted in Bernard Crick, *George Orwell: A Life* (New York: Penguin, 1982), p. 565. The paperback edition is both revised and corrected, and is to be preferred to the original Secker and Warburg or Atlantic Press editions.
2. Ibid., p. 569.
3. Ibid., p. 550.
4. Ibid., appendix A, "The Nineteen Forty-Three Outline of *Nineteen Eighty-Four*," pp. 582–85.
5. Ibid., p. 546.
6. Julian Symons, Introduction and Appreciation to *Nineteen Eighty-Four*, by George Orwell (London: Heron Books, 1970), pp. xi and 344. Unhappily this excellent essay is little known to critics, since it was written for a book club.
7. Such as George Watson, "Orwell and the Spectrum of European Politics," *Journal of European Studies* 1, no. 3 (1971): 191–97 and Norman Podhoretz, "If Orwell Were Alive Today," *Harper's*, January 1983, pp. 30–37 (with a proper reply from Christopher Hitchens in the following issue). Even Alex Zwerdling, in his balanced and scholarly *Orwell and the Left* (New Haven, Conn.: Yale University Press, 1974) says that "the strongly conservative flavor of [his] belief is unmistakable, and the fact that *Nineteen Eighty-Four* was taken up with such enthusiasm by the right is no accident" (p. 110). But he seems to have an ideal image of socialism and confuses cultural conservatism and skepticism about perfectibility (rather than betterment), typical of English socialism, with political conservatism.
8. Kathleen Nott in her *The Good Want Power* (London: Cape, 1977), argues that "identity . . . entails a principle of mutual recognition." And see my *In Defence of Politics*, 2d Pelican ed. (New York: Penguin, 1982), pp. 234–35.
9. He says so quite explicitly in essays such as "The Prevention of Literature," *Collected Essays, Journalism and Letters*, ed. Sonia Orwell and Ian Angus, 4 vols. (New York: Harcourt Brace Jovanovich, 1968), 4:64–65, hereafter cited as

CEJL; "Writers and Leviathan," *CEJL,* 4:407–10; and in his review of *The Totalitarian Enemy,* by Franz Borkenau, *CEJL,* 2:24–26.

10. Quoted by Jeffrey Meyers, *A Reader's Guide to Orwell* (London: Thames and Hudson, 1975), pp. 178–79.

11. *CEJL,* 1:6.

12. Christopher Small, *The Road to Miniluv: George Orwell, the State and God* (London: Gollancz, 1975) argues that Orwell's "pious atheism" was almost as good as faith itself, and Alan Sandison, *The Last Man in Europe* (London: Macmillan, 1974) shows how deeply Protestant Orwell's assumptions and images were. He may have been closer to Christianity than his nominal humanism suggests, but not to Catholicism: "Both Communist and Catholic usually believe . . . that abstract aesthetic standards are all bunkum and that a book is only a 'good' book if it preaches the right sermon" (*CEJL,* 1:257); and "The Catholic and Communist are alike in assuming that an opponent cannot be both honest and intelligent" (*CEJL,* 4:374). And see Crick, *George Orwell,* pp. 115, 226–29, 254, 273–74, 286; and his introduction to the Clarendon edition of *Nineteen Eighty-Four,* pp. 40–41.

13. In his polemic "1984: The Mysticism of Cruelty," in his *Heretics and Renegades* (London: Hamish Hamilton, 1955). He offers no examples or evidence. The only parallels (apart from the name) are Trotsky's theory of the emergence in the USSR of a "bureaucratic caste" outside normal class relations, and his analysis of Stalinism as "Bonapartism" (more obviously an influence on *Animal Farm*). Most of Trotsky's book is a detailed attack on and analysis of Stalin's policies in the 1920s and 1930s, of relevance to Goldstein's testament. To say "paraphrase" is absurd, wholly of a piece with Deutscher's claim that *Nineteen Eighty-Four* is just a crib (see note 14 below) from Zamyatin.

14. Deutscher so dislikes Orwell for writing a book that could be used as an "ideological super-weapon in the cold war" that he hits him with everything: "*1984* is a document of dark disillusionment not only with Stalin but with every form and shade of socialism. It is a cry from the abyss of despair. . . . He projected the last spasms of his own suffering into the last pages of his last book" (*Heretics and Renegades,* p. 44). That Orwell had reviewed Zamyatin's *We* became "a conclusive piece of evidence that Orwell had "borrowed the idea of *1984,* the plot, the chief characters, the symbols from Zamyatin." Deutscher exaggerates grossly and has no idea of how extensive Orwell's *other* borrowings were, especially from James Burnham. Cf. William Steinhoff, *George Orwell and the Origins of "1984"* (Ann Arbor: University of Michigan Press, 1975). Steinhoff shows how willfully Deutscher conflates *We* and *Nineteen Eighty-Four.* See also Mark Reader, "The Political Critic of George Orwell" (Ph.D. diss., University of Michigan, 1966) for a patient and thorough rebuttal of Deutscher's charges.

15. Steinhoff, *Origins,* chap. 3, "The Influence of James Burnham."

16. "Burnham's geographical picture of the world has turned out to be correct. More and more obviously the surface of the earth is being parcelled off into three great Empires" ("You and the Atom Bomb," *CEJL,* 2:8–9).

17. Thomas Hobbes, *Leviathan*, pt. 1, chap. 13. Orwell had assumed (cf. "You and the Atom Bomb"), writing before the hydrogen bomb, that the world could survive nuclear war.

18. Deutscher, *Heretics and Renegades*, takes it for granted that Orwell identifies himself with *both* the masochism of Winston Smith and the sadism of O'Brien. He interprets fiction somewhat literally and, like others, allows Orwell little inventive imagination.

19. Still current in English public (that is, private) school changing rooms as "Sir Jasper and the Maiden." "*Sir J.* 'The whip, the whip!' *M.* 'Anything but the whip!' *Sir J.* 'Anything?!?' *M.* 'The whip.' "

20. Both Small, *The Road to Miniluv*, and Sandison, *The Last Man in Europe*, use this passage to imply Orwell's feeling of helplessness without God. But Orwell says in his essay on Koestler that belief in God is "the only easy way out," yet "the real problem is how to restore a religious attitude while accepting death as final. Men can only be happy when they do not assume the object of life is happiness" (*CEJL*, 4:243–44). By a "religious attitude" he means something like respecting men and women equally despite their imperfections and respecting nature as if it were a sacred creation.

Robert Coles

GEORGE ORWELL'S SENSIBILITY

ven as Eric Blair became the prophetic voice George Orwell, that pseudonym has in turn become, since January of 1950, when it was stilled forever, an almost mythic presence among many who live in the Western world. The advantages for countless numbers of reflective men and women have been considerable. An intellectual and moral figure of the first rank in English letters (in both the general and the more limited sense of that word) has become a familiar and readily available companion: the books and long essays and shorter, journalistic pieces are much used in schools and colleges, and commonly summoned, still, in the public discourse of the day, certainly in England and America. On the other hand, there are, inevitably, costs to a writer's posthumous celebrity when that writer was so evidently anxious to address controversial social and political matters in a manner that was not petty or frivolous. We have, for instance, recently watched the author of *Nineteen Eighty-Four* claimed by self-avowed conservatives and, in reply, claimed yet again by vigorous socialists or skeptical liberals of leftist inclination. The occasion, of course, was the arrival of that year of years, 1984—and the self-consciousness so many of us felt about that particular year was, needless to say, a measure of the powerful impact one writer's moral and political imagination has had upon millions of readers.

I have for years taught Orwell—in a seminar to college freshmen that couples his literary documentary work (*Down and Out in Paris and London, The Road to Wigan Pier, Homage to Catalonia,* and some of his briefer efforts at social observation, such as "Hop-Picking," or the two quite compelling essays published in 1931 under the name Eric A. Blair, "The Spike" and "A Hanging") with the altogether different writing in a similar genre of James Agee (*Let Us Now Praise Famous Men,* obviously, and a number of pieces written for *Fortune* magazine). There is an obvious coherence and continuity to this side of Orwell—the man of Wigan and the two capital cities and the Spain of the first half of 1937, torn apart not only by right and left but within the left by fateful schisms the nature of which at least one writer immediately knew had enormous significance for all of us in the following decades of the twentieth century. This is the Orwell who wants to wonder and look hard, who has an appetite for factuality and a pen able to render human and social complexity lucidly yet with no sacrifice of narrative subtlety or interpretive depth. This is the Orwell who was an eagerly adventurous hobo or tramp or waiter or reporter on assignment; or yes, a soldier fighting on behalf of a worthwhile cause. This is the Orwell who seemed to notice everything and forget nothing. No tape recorder for him, or other assorted scraps of audiovisual equipment! His eyes and his ears, his scrutinizing intelligence, and his developing writer's craft were quite enough. With persistence and tenacity he watched his fellow creatures and always, through them, learned about himself as well. With a wry skepticism, interrupted on memorable occasions by compelling outbursts of sympathy for certain people, places, or, more generally, human predicaments, he constructed his reports—news from other worlds to the more conventional one (the upper-middle-class intelligentsia) he knew so well. In those reports one does not miss his attentiveness to the accidental, the irregular, the unexpected, the quite odd; and one does not miss a strong mindfulness of the ironies of everyday existence—as in Hardy's phrase, "life's little ironies."

Of course some of them were not so minor in impact, Orwell noticed. Those who have lots of money and enjoy their leisure out, one or another day, with a meal in a fine restaurant may be more vulnerable than they ever realize—because waiters scolded or pushily confronted with demands can always, unobserved, desecrate food with a mouthful of spit, and then enjoy the satisfaction of seeing it downed with everything else on the plate. I mention that not very pleasing discovery relayed in *Down and Out in Paris and London* because it possesses an instructive suggestiveness with respect to the man who chose to set it down in his first book. All through his life Orwell wanted to uncover the conceits and deceits of a given social and economic order. He had little use for things as they were in the England of the 1930s, the time he did his major documentary writing; he was, as well, determined to expose the failings (or worse) of individuals and institutions as he came across them. But he was not given to the broad social statements or economic interpretations some of his intellectual friends favored—or at least, not until he earned such generalizations as he saw fit to earn, through the illumination of particularity. Put differently, he brought to bear upon social reality and the individual psychology or workaday English life (vintage 1930 to 1937, especially) the talents and inclinations usually and correctly associated with the novelist: an eye for detail; an interest in dramatic progression; a knowledge of how willfulness (or the absence thereof) can affect a given life; a fascination with rendering the puzzling mysteries of humankind, not the least of which is the ineffable (at times) yet absolutely determining influence a person's character has upon him or her. Armed with such a stock of perceptual gifts, prompted as well by an obvious yet not greedy (or with respect to others, competitive) ambitiousness, aided upon occasion by that quiet web of privilege which can often be counted on to respond readily and with modest generosity to the temporarily fallen members of the British ruling class, even its "lower-upper-middle class" segment (his social self-definition offered in *Wigan Pier*) Orwell took to the road, quite literally in instances such as he related in *Down and Out*.

The result was not only the nonfiction we all know so well, but moments of sharp, piercing drama that stand on their own, almost—as if the text that surrounds them is, for all its considerable virtues, a mere ornament, or a prelude, then a postlude. One suspects Orwell knew his own literary and sociological might, because in his last summary paragraph of *Down and Out* he reminds the reader of not only what the author has "learned" but what the reader, a stranger of time and space, will surely remember: at least one graduate of Eton, no less, will never "enjoy a meal at a smart restaurant." The appearance, yet again, of this vivid moment is a powerful writer's urgent goodbye to his reader—an embrace of sorts meant to last.

There is, of course, an intrusiveness to such a concluding autobiographical remark. Why need the rest of us, who have already learned pages earlier what revenge can be taken, say, in "Hôtel X" of Paris, find ourselves confronted with *that* scene? This has been a book full of interesting, humorous, and sad events. Without question any number of them might have been used as suitable moral jogs, parting suggestions that money and power cannot control all events, large or small, and indeed can generate their own considerable (or, at least) personal impasses in the course of a day, a week, and longer. But Orwell had Conrad's willingness to link apparent, even gross, success to the seedy destructiveness that both enables it, often enough, and lingers on, commonly, without letup, an echo of the past that won't go away. Even as the fate of Kurz in "Heart of Darkness" is very much connected, we are told, to the drawing rooms of Europe's bourgeoisie, the young Orwell has now come to realize something far more revealing than his witness of one flaw in one Paris hotel: that some resentments are not only abstract attitudes described by the writers of textbooks, to be digested by hungry intellectuals in search of a political position, a social view, but rather evidence of a personal bitterness generated by flagrant and demeaning inequality and vented upon the very people who seem the luckiest, the most·secure, so that they, too, are daily tricked, if not demeaned.

Not that, again, there aren't (there weren't) other ways to make that point stick. But to eat is what all of us who are intent on staying alive must do, and so a seemingly incidental vignette manages to get at our jugular via our palate, our stomach. Orwell is graphic, lest we miss his point. "Everywhere in the service quarters," he says toward the end of chapter 14, "dirt festered—a secret vein of dirt, running through the great garish hotel like the intestines

48

through a man's body." And, alas, it is "mostly Americans" who frequent this place, the saviors of the capitalist order. It is we who are exposing ourselves, at high cost and with great and ostentatious pride to—well, this state of affairs: "When a steak, for instance, is brought up for the head cook's inspection, he does not handle it with a fork. He picks it up in his fingers and slaps it down, runs his thumb around this dish and licks it to taste the gravy, runs it round and licks again, then steps back and contemplates the piece of meat like an artist judging a picture, then presses it lovingly into place with his fat, pink fingers, every one of which he has licked a hundred times that morning. When he is satisfied, he takes a cloth and wipes his fingerprints from the dish, and hands it to the waiter. And the waiter, of course dips *his* fingers into the gravy—his nasty, greasy fingers which he is forever running through his brilliantined hair."

This is by no means the most unnerving of Orwell's offerings in the book, but it contains a representative capacity for causing disgust that won't, one guesses, easily be banished to convenient forgetfulness. Not only is the writing blunt, vivid, and obviously self-assured (this man knows whereof he speaks, *we* know!) but the symbolic language, well executed, clinches the purposes of the narrator's portrait. The themes bring us face to face with: ourselves, our situations as the ones who go to Hôtel X's here and there; and ourselves as the ones who are smart as can be, yet utterly unaware of an entire social reality it is one person's intention to know well and evoke with precision and liveliness. Moreover, even that small section, a part of one paragraph, tells us a lot about not only the cook and the waiter, and, soon enough, the paying customer, but the kind of observer Orwell was. He was ever disgusted by the dirt and filth he was constantly noticing and, later, keeping in mind as he wrote.

One recalls the Brookers, who ran a lodging house in Wigan—the disgust their daily rhythms inspired in Orwell, culminating in "the day when there was a full chamber-pot under the breakfast table." It was then, we immediately learn, that he left, and this dramatic departure, so explained, is purposely made to warn us about the seedy life of minor burghers—in contrast, of course, to the one lived by badly exploited miners, whose own dirt, all over their bodies, worked into cracks and pores in such a fashion that no soap can possibly manage to do its intended job, Orwell finds not at all offensive, quite the contrary: "It is impossible to watch the 'fillers' at work without feeling a pang of envy for their toughness," he tells us. A bit further on he describes their "most noble bodies," observing, too, that "when they are black and naked they all look alike."

The contrast with Hôtel X or the home of the Brookers is edifying and tells us a lot about Orwell's political convictions, true, but also his moral and literary sensibility. That "great garish hotel" is obviously meant to represent the industrial West, whose rot Orwell, like Dickens, intends to survey. In such a place "gravy" gets turned into soiled water, and in such a place the various surfaces (as in "brilliantined hair") lie badly. In *Wigan Pier* the reader is asked to descend from the sick pretensions of the top French places to the foul habits of the English burghers. From haute-bourgeoisie to petite-bourgeoisie it is all unedifying, tainted, contaminated, defiled—except for the bracing condition of the miners, those who are ostensibly the very dirtiest of creatures, yet who (for Orwell, at least) are "noble" not only in body, as he specifically says, but in the direct, vigorous dignity of their working lives.

There was in Orwell a romantic side that he only occasionally indulges in his tough, documentary writing. Where more intellectual socialists would herald all too theoretically the coming ascent of the proletariat, he would select miners, even some tramps, and certainly some ordinary Spanish people, and find in their daily toil, their cheerful persistence against great odds, whatever encouragement there is to be found on this earth. So doing, he abandoned consistency, and even, one suspects, accuracy of observation. Lord knows how many full chamber-pots he might have found in the homes of Wigan's miners, had he been inclined to poke and pry and chronicle his discoveries. Lord knows what those miners' wives served in the way of food, and what their hands looked like as they did the cooking. *Wigan Pier* is indeed about miners and mining. Orwell even descended into the mines. But the book has, too, the ambitious intent of a general statement about twentieth-century capitalism, an intent disclosed even in the first section, meant to set down direct observations, never mind the well-known argumentative second section, so full of cranky and blistering assaults on so many aspects of socialist (intellectual) life.

A writer's tough critical mind spares a few and damns many others, to quite dramatic effect. The reader is, after all, likely to be uncomfortably akin to the people roundly denounced—in a book that, one gathers, so pained those in the Left Book Club (which commissioned the effort in the first place) that Victor Gollancz, acknowledging "well over a hundred passages" with which he took issue, wrote a preface both appreciative and shrewdly admonishing. What had been meant to enlighten a readership ended up also offending a sponsor. Such a result, perhaps, serves to show how original-minded and fussy and feisty and truculently suggestive Orwell was, but also how successful as a writer: no one would be bored or put off self-protectively by this book, and for decades after its topicality was no longer a mainstay of its interest, readers would keep returning to its manner of exposition, reasoning, and contention. That is to say, Orwell the writer and the polemical moralist had triumphed over one moment's political issue.

Orwell the political prophet made his first major appearance in *Wigan Pier,* and this side of his intellect also emerged triumphant—a mix of auto-biographical candor and a bold willingness to examine carefully and censure vigorously the assumptions of his own kind, the 1930s socialist reformers of England. At times, of course, the prophet's self-criticism and the roasting given his ostensible colleagues or fellow partisans sound remarkably similar. "When I was fourteen or fifteen I was an odious little snob," we are told in the intensely confessional ninth chapter of *Wigan Pier*. We learn a bit further on that "at the age of seventeen or eighteen" the author was "both a snob and a revolutionary." Still further on, that word *snob* once again is used, now to describe the "typical socialist," who is "either a youthful snob-bolshevik who in five years' time will quite probably have made a wealthy marriage and have been converted to Roman Catholicism; or, still more typically, a prim little man with a white collar job, usually a secret teetotaller and often with vege-tarian leanings, with a history of Nonconformity behind him, and, above all, with a social position which he has no intention of forfeiting."

There is, no doubt, an Augustinian self-scrutiny at work here; an intellec-tual anti-intellectualism, too, as Victor Gollancz insists in his introduction, which also gives every indication of the offense taken by many who belonged to the Left Book Club. Orwell was able to see his own situation and that of his fellow writers and political activists as one of privilege, with all the attendant risks: self-importance, smugness, arrogance, hypocrisy, pettiness. The "liter-ary world" was for him a "poisonous jungle," and he could be outspoken, to put it mildly: "In the highbrow world you 'get on,' if you 'get on' at all, not so much by your literary ability as by being the life and soul of cocktail parties and kissing the bums of verminous little loins." Such rage, self-directed by implication, was of course a warning to others, lower in station, toward whom Orwell had more affection that he could easily express. Time and again he reaches out to England's working-class people, whose hard work and simple life and unpretentiousness and decency he admires—and may see to the ex-clusion of those warts possessed by all human beings, and all classes of them. After he launches his tirade against the English literati, he turns directly to that working class. He worries about the fate of its bright lads, who might well end up, he is sure, in his terrible world. Orwell is split not so much in opinion as in loyalty. The strenuousness of his assault, when compared with the flimsiness and pettiness of its object, makes one wonder whether he has not cast himself unwittingly in the position of a rather impoverished working man, bright and aspiring but proud as can be and unwilling or unable to make the necessary social gestures that insure success.

The author is in his early thirties at this point, and he is by no means the world-famous writer he became in the last years of his life and, of course, after he died. He is fighting his way up and yet is constitutionally (a matter of character, of principles dearly held) unable to ingratiate himself as he has seen others do. He is tempted enough to turn sour, testy, sardonic; the spleen vented measures the vicissitudes of a promising career. As for the working class, its distance from the intelligentsia had always been a haven of sorts: a population without one's felt vices, temptations, self-serving aspirations, hence a population to contrast with one's own social or occupational kinsmen, and a population to be defended and protected and upheld passionately as a means, really, of holding on to one's own self-respect.

Even as Eric Blair the reserved but determined writer had to make his accommodation to others, to friends who did him favors, arranged for him to get assignments, to receive a loan or two, the writer George Orwell was to the end of his life an uncanny mixture of the idealist and the realist. His idealism obviously accounts for many of his lasting sympathies—for the underdog, for the exiled or hurt or suffering people whose experiences he has rendered to perfection. Nor was this idealism merely abstract. Anti-intellectualism worked against such a development. Orwell's insistence on a concrete knowledge of how others live, endure pain, even die (in a hospital, in the field of battle, or when hung until dead under the auspices of England's glorious empire) is one of his notable achievements. Moreover, it is all the more remarkable that he could convey such a response—a sense of the individual's burdens in one or another difficult or dangerous set of circumstances—within the constraints of the documentary essays that he wrote. Not that he didn't have the space to discuss the particular men and women he'd met; rather, he himself had a sensibility that loved negotiating those two polarities, the concrete and the theoretical, and one wonders that he never lost his balance, succumbed to the temptations of large-scale, ever-so-confident generalizations about, say, the poor, or the Spanish people he met in 1937.

He was, of course, a novelist, which must have helped keep under wraps any overwrought theoretical ambition. But I suspect he was assisted by an interesting writing split he made: the socialists he aimed to parody receive the brunt of his conjectural instincts, and often their excesses; the humble folk were thereby spared, and their vulnerability was not, as a consequence, exploited. Given the number of social scientists who have turned this or that kind of impoverished or tyrannical human being into cannon fodder for one or another all-embracing, ideological analysis, one can only marvel at Orwell's abstinence.

His larger gifts of allegorical prophecy, an aspect of his sensibility, have become worked into an entire (Western) culture's sensibility; hence these lecture-essays, among others surely to be spoken and written in this year, 1984. But in his documentary writings and his literary pieces or strongly personal essays he could demonstrate, in retrospect, a stunning foresight, usually stated so casually the contemporary reader may well miss what he or she has, in fact, happened just to read. For example, in the last chapter of *Homage to Catalonia* Orwell is expressing his affection for the Spanish people and says this: "I have the most evil memories of Spain, but I have very few bad memories of Spaniards. I only twice remember even being seriously angry with a Spaniard, and on each occasion, when I look back, I believe I was in the wrong myself. They have, there is no doubt, a generosity, a species of nobility, that do not really belong to the twentieth century. It is this that makes one hope that in Spain even Fascism may take a comparatively loose and bearable form. Few Spaniards possess the damnable efficiency and consistency that a modern totalitarian state needs."

Here was Orwell the offhand observer, with no academic pretenses—no anthropological caution, no worry that a given remark lacks the justification of proper methodological research. At the time his companions on the left were fighting to the death against Franco, but as well, Orwell had learned, against one another. Those companions, and the writers who were on their side, had scant time for the niceties of cultural reflection—how the people of nations differ and, accordingly, how the fates of particular social and political and economic ideologies vary across the world. Orwell was also a volunteer combatant. Still, he found time for the above passage, and it is, in my opinion, as shrewd and knowing a presentiment of what would obtain in a generation or two as Orwell or anyone else has made during this century. Spain, as all know, has now become a country whose prime minister is a socialist; and even during the Second World War Franco managed to stay clear of fighting, and yes, "comparatively," the brutish excesses of fascism. There are two others whose good judgment matched that of Orwell with respect to the Spanish Civil War, Georges Bernanos on the right and Simone Weil on the left, both of whom spotted the serious misdeeds of even their own side. But Orwell, characteristically, went even further, allowed an almost anecdotal remark to carry within it a sweeping historical prediction.

In the same final chapter Orwell offers his well-known tribute to the essential "decency of human beings," a hymn or praise not as biblical and lyrical in nature as the one James Agee offers in *Let Us Now Praise Famous Men*, but perhaps all the more affecting in its quiet understatement. It is interesting, too, that the remark about "decency" in others is followed immediately by an astonishingly candid and sober moment of self-appraisal: "And I hope the account I have given is not too misleading. I believe that on such an issue as this no one is or can be completely truthful. It is difficult to be certain about anything except what you have seen with your own eyes, and consciously or unconsciously everyone writes as a partisan. In case I have not said this somewhere earlier in the book I will say it now: beware of my partisanship, my mistakes of fact and the distortion inevitably caused by my having seen only one corner of events."

How many others who were writing about the Spanish Civil War at that time were prepared to issue such a cautionary warning? How many social scientists who have returned from their various and sundry "field trips" have felt the requirement for such a modest disclaimer? Orwell could be cranky, irritating, exaggerated in his scorn of one group or admiration of another, but he was never the man of answers for all about everything—nor did he fail to spot that vice in others, especially the social and political theorists of earlier decades of this century who claimed to know so much about so many matters, including the workings of history itself. For Orwell a chance to visit Wigan, or get to know a tramp like Paddy (what a fine job is done in presenting this fellow to the readers of *Down and Out!*) or fight against fascism in Spain was a chance (as he remarked in many ways and on many occasions) to get to know oneself: one's blind spots, animosities, wayward tendencies, limitations of empathy, charity, and, not least, vision. Again and again students of mine who have read *Wigan Pier* or *Down and Out* or *Catalonia* (I've been using *their* common abbreviations in this essay) remark upon the refreshing bluntness in Orwell, and the lack of self-importance, not to mention the down-to-earth honesty. They compare him with an assortment of intellectual authorities or celebrities—and interestingly enough, remark upon the injustice that history has done him, to be in such company! Why? He is, they reply, far too "ordinary" in his approach, meaning without affectation or pretense, and with a surprising modesty of self-presentation, while at the same time, they note, he takes the considerable risks that go with the use of the first person in documentary narration.

For Americans in the 1940s Orwell was a recurring source of exemplary edification—his clean, straightforward prose put in the service of one essay after another for the *Partisan Review:* the "London Letter" he sent, telling of England's wartime struggles, its postwar social and political transformation. Those dispatches were a prize for a quarterly then congenial to a given English correspondent—socialist in spirit, literary in sensibility, a touch anarchist in politics for fear of yet again becoming trapped in the monstrous evil of commitment to an ideology. The *Partisan Review* letters are to this day of great interest; they show a familiar Orwell—spotting the reasons why many of the British disliked American soldiers stationed in England during the war (their enviable salary and provisions, their great self-confidence) or explaining what the prospects of the Labour party were, and why. Orwell is outgoing and friendly, perceptive, even at times didactic, yet able to disarm himself of any preachiness or highhanded assertiveness, both of which, Lord knows, are the besetting hazards of the genre of social comment, especially the kind that aims to facilitate transnational (transatlantic) understanding.

At moments the brilliant polemicist becomes quite the stolid and tolerant educator, anxious to remind Americans why this terribly destructive Second World War is being fought and why they, along with all other democratic nations, have such a high stake in its outcome. At other times Orwell is, quite simply, the marvelously earthy man who is at pains to remind himself how earthy, in fact, his American readers are—they who, he tells his readers in one essay, could long ago read the word *bullshit* without abbreviation, while their English counterparts had to keep reading "b____." Nor should one fail to observe, in connection with America, that Orwell's last notes, meant to help him write a story or two and some literary pieces, reveal him—dying though he was, and so with every excuse for self-absorption or withdrawal of interest—solidly intrigued, still, with matters American: the enormous complexity of our nation, and indeed, the several nations within a nation that we are in several important respects. One also comes across this striking phrase, obviously one of the last he would write: "The big cannibal critics that lurk in the deeper waters of American quarterly reviews." There seems, really, no limit to the spaciousness of his knowledge, nor to the range of his eye for pinpointing exactly the various kinds of meanness and spite so-called educated people can visit upon others.

Orwell was not to be a captive of his own shrewdness with respect to shrewd people. Put differently, he wanted "out" from the world of fashionable slander, rather than "in" as the one, say, who mocks it, detests it, or merely stresses its tawdry nature. His heart was, always, with victims of one sort or another; and there he was, in his final days, an eminently successful writer who took care to worry about how certain writers treat other writers in the name of something called a "critical tradition." Moreover, he was able, in the face of an extremely serious illness, yet again to reach out, take notice of those who easily (in London) went unnoticed—both the comparatively obscure American critics and the quarterlies they favored.

There is in Orwell's sensibility more than a touch of the anger those "cannibal critics" demonstrate to this day among us English-speaking readers. At his worst Orwell can be almost irrationally (certainly inconsistently) belligerent—as in portions of *Wigan Pier,* when his rage at England's socialists becomes not argumentative, or even partisan, but simply spiteful, and only understandable as the response of someone who takes for granted in his readers (those of the Left Book Club, after all) a robust dislike of the kind of brutish and callous capitalism that ruled in the England of the 1930s. If that real enemy of Orwell's is spared—perhaps because there was little hope, then, of budging it, no matter the pitch of one's passionately espoused invective—then a scapegoat of sorts becomes rather tempting, and, given Orwell's satirical gifts and his self-imposed limitations with respect to targets for the exercise of those gifts (the poor, the infirm, the defenseless must be given sanctuary at all costs) the upper-class socialists were, really, his only possible choice.

Orwell can also be (the opposite side of the coin) as hopeful and uncritically adoring, in brief spells, as he was mostly thoughtful and careful scrutinizing and sensibly balanced. The love he felt for his ordinary, working-class English countrymen was, as I've mentioned, considerable, and upon occasion turned wonderfully blinding. I use that last adverb out of delight, I suppose, pleasure in an honorable, sensitive writer's obvious demonstration of his humanity: a strong patriotism that preceded the Second World War, was gloriously heightened by it (and given the enemy, why not!) and was, too, not subdued by the terribly short period of postwar time he was to experience. Indeed, Orwell's love for his country can be considered the greatest source of his writing energy. His novels are, so significantly, efforts at evoking English life. His best essays are similar efforts, as in the marvellous approach to Charles Dickens, an approach which, unintentionally (one dares say) becomes quite autobiographical. Dickens the moralist, the one who disliked much of organized religion but loved deeply Jesus and his disciples, those radical egalitarians and communitarians, becomes so dear to us in the critical piece because Orwell's own anarchic political compassion and social generosity and, yes, spiritual vigor also become eminently clear.

Orwell's sensibility was, to the end, a thickly textured mix of the political, the literary, the moral, and the social—a mind constantly taking notice of how people live, under what constraints, with which degree of uprightness; a mind utterly persuaded that words can make a difference in this life and, very important, that the writing of words bears with it a substantial responsibility. He was with all those words—so many in such a foreshortened life—an exceptionally able craftsman, a wide-ranging commentator, a spirited instructor, an occasional scold, an honorable and lovable author whose message has touched the mind, the heart, the soul of millions with a simultaneity extraordinary in this God-forsaken century of ours. Watchful of this strange life, wary of absolutes wielded to explain away its mysteries, George Orwell has become himself someone all of us watch, himself a source of outstanding mystery —that one man, and for so long a man fighting death, could leave us with so much lasting good sense. He himself, one feels, would tolerate poorly the acclaim that has been his since his departure, and too, the possessiveness toward him of certain writers (indeed, he would have quickly questioned their motives). And maybe that is the highest honor we can pay this singularly literate spiritual wanderer—a determination on our part to strive always for his clear-headed integrity, his big-hearted, open and above-board nature, his frank and powerful manner of expression. One searches in vain for his successor; hence the special necessity of remembering him as someone especially dear and important to us who live in 1984.

Hugh Kenner

THE POLITICS
OF THE PLAIN STYLE

"P roper words in proper places" was what Swift had to say about style, not telling us, of course, how to find the proper words or how to know the proper places to put them into. As so often, the Dean is teasing us. Writing in the century when public consciousness was for the first time alarmed by the norms of printed pages, he confronts his reader with a pervasive bewilderment about what "style" may mean on silent paper, where words have "places" rather than cadences or emphases. He is nearly asking if "style" has become a branch of geometry, or of managing genteel apartment houses.

Styles were long distinguished by degrees of ornateness, the more highly figured being the more esteemed. There was a high style in which Cicero delivered his orations, and a low style in which we assume he addressed his cook. It was to the high style that rhetorical analysis gave its attention. The low style was beneath attention. That was scarcely, save by contrast, a style at all. It is surely obvious that the words *high* and *low* are evaluations passing as descriptions.

It's obvious, too, that evaluation is appealing to the way we judge oral performance. When Cicero spoke with his cook he was offstage; when he addressed the Senate he was in costume and in role and dominating a scene carefully pre-scripted. Of the five parts into which oratory was divided, two pertained to the theatrics of performance; they were *memory* and *delivery*. Here *memory* is a clue to something important. Cicero's intricate syntax, its enjambments, its systems of subordination, its bold rearrangements of the natural order of words, would have been impossible for the orator to improvise. So he worked them out on paper, then memorized them, then performed them in a way that made it seem he was giving voice to his passion of the moment. In fact, he was being careful not to let passion master him, lest it overwhelm memory. And anyone who has studied Latin knows how sentences that, so we're told, once electrified hearers become, on being fixed to a page, mere crossword puzzles, sometimes only to be construed with the help of a teacher, a blackboard, and a diagram. *Quousque tandem abutere, Catilina, patientia nostra?* That's a short and easy example, yet as contorted as anything in Vergil. "How long yet will you abuse, O Catiline, our patience?" It was gesture, and cadence, and pacing, and the emphases of a living voice that once brought it to life, the way they can bring to life the *Aeneid,* which Vergil wrote to be read aloud. The "high style" lives only in spoken delivery. Translated into English to be looked at on a page, the high style becomes Euphuism, and Euphues is dead. Printing, and print's concomitant silent reading, was one thing that killed off its longtime prestige. Yet it had been for centuries the norm of all political discourse.

You will gather that I am approaching Orwell somewhat obliquely. It's important, though, to provide some historical context for the art he practiced. He was a writer, not a speaker, but the tradition in which he wrote had long been shaped by conventions drawn from public speech. Political writing assumed political speaking as its native ground. And a good public speech is something as contrived as a scene by Shakespeare. Even Lincoln, in what is represented as an address of exemplary plainness, launched it with diction he could only have premeditated: "Four score and seven years ago our fathers brought forth on this continent. . . ." The word *style* pertains to the art of contriving something like that. You contrive it by hand. A *stilus* was a pointed tool with which Romans wrote on wax tablets, and what you did with its aid was what came to be called your "style." It seems to follow that a "plain style" is a contradiction in terms. If it's plain, then surely it didn't need working out with a stylus?

But indeed it did. Something so lucid, so seemingly natural that we can only applaud, in Swift's phrase, its "proper words in proper places," is not the work of nature at all but of great contrivance. W. B. Yeats wrote, on a related theme,

> I said, "A line will take us hours maybe;
> Yet if it does not seem a moment's thought,
> Our stitching and unstitching has been naught."

Here's an intricate instance, writing that's saying it was spoken despite the presence of rhymes, writing therefore that's inviting us to ponder its own degrees of artifice. Yeats has in mind poetry that has abandoned the high style and is managing to look not only improvised but conversational, yes, even though it rhymes. That would be poetry contriving to be (in Eliot's later formulation) "at least as well written as prose." And it helps us perceive good prose—a genre that came late in every language—as an art with a new set of norms, the norms of feigned casualness and hidden economy.

It was in a moment of towering self-deception that Molière's M. Jourdain discovered he had been talking prose all his life. Notwithstanding what his bogus instructor tells him, that whatever is not verse is prose, no one talks prose, any more than anyone talks in rhyme. The plainest prose is a counterfeit of natural utterance. As such, it can be the most disorienting form of discourse ever invented by man. It came very late to English. Chaucer hadn't a clue to its workings. Swift in the eighteenth century, George Orwell in the twentieth, are two of its masters.

Bernard Crick has astutely drawn attention to the question of genre that plagues responses to Orwell's writing. His genre seems to be (like that of Lemuel Gulliver) the genre of the reporter, the ingenuous truthteller. And then we discover that he's been saying the thing that was not. Then the fat is in the fire, and his character gets attacked. For what is misrepresentation but a defect of character? A famous example is "Such, Such Were the Joys," the account of prep-school days that drew from one of his prep-school contemporaries such marginalia as "NOT TRUE! You sod!!! LIBEL!" Another is "A Hanging," the eyewitness account of something it's possible he never witnessed; and there's "Shooting an Elephant," his first-person recollection of a deed he may or may not ever have done. And there is much more.

We like to have such things plainly labeled "fiction," if fictions they be. Then we are willing to admire the artistry: so acutely invented a detail as the condemned man stepping round a puddle within yards of the rope, which prompts the narrator's reflection on "the unspeakable wrongness of cutting a life short when it is in full tide. This man was not dying, he was alive just as we were alive." That is like John Donne meditating on a sacred text, and we'd not welcome news that the text was nowhere in the Bible, that Donne had invented it for the sake of the sermon he could spin. We are back in Platonic controversies about poets lying, and may want to note that the dedicated Communists repeatedly announced the banishment of George Orwell from their Republic, on approximately Plato's grounds.

Eric Havelock in a famous essay has explained Plato's rage against poets as an instance of the new literacy (Plato) rejecting the old orality (Homer). For when you'd had to remember what existed only as speech, your only way was to interiorize it, get it inside you, let it take demonic possession of you. That phrase is not too strong; voicing the wrath of Achilles, you *became* Achilles, wrathy. That is not a detached way to be, and what writing encourages us to value is detachment, the cool appraisal, the word checkable against the fact or against other words. It's because Orwell wrote down six words that Mr. Crick can complicate his discussion of "A Hanging" by adducing something from *The Road to Wigan Pier,* "I watched a man hanged once." To be sure, that doesn't prove that Orwell watched a man hanged once; it proves only that he wrote that sentence, which in turn proves only that the author of "A Hanging" (1931) still had such an idea on his mind when he was writing something else six years later. And it's also thanks to writing and printing that Crick can cite a rhythmic parallel from T. S. Eliot—

> Well I left her there in a bath
> With a gallon of Lysol in a bath

—and a semantic parallel from Swift—"Last week I watched a woman *flay'd.*" Such parallels tend to absorb the whole of "A Hanging" into literature, thus into fiction, where questions of veracity can't reach it. For we half-accept the idea that printed words do no more than permute other printed words, in an economy bounded by the page.

We half-accept, that is, the fictive quality of everything we read. That half-acceptance, though, has been long in coming, and many of us still tend to believe what it says here in black and white: what we read in the papers. One tends to believe that because the printed word stays around to be checked, like a stranger with nothing to hide, whereas no one in an oral culture can so much as prove that the village liar ever said what we're saying he said, his wing'd words having vanished forever beyond recall. That was one reason why the whole Platonic controversy about lying, which according to Havelock pertained to the advent of writing, got resumed in the sixteenth century shortly after the coming of printing, to evoke for instance Sidney's "Apologie for a Poetrie" that aimed at a higher truth than merely stating facts you could check.

But print keeps tugging words back toward what persists in being *so* no matter how the words drift about, an ornate way of saying that printed words seemingly require us to believe them. Eighteenth-century readers could savor *The Life and Strange Surprising Adventures of Robinson Crusoe,* who'd been cast away on an island. That's an exotic thought if you live in crowded London, and exoticism fostered the will to believe. The title page, moreover, said, "Written by Himself." The account appealed because it was true. It was a while before "Himself" turned out to be a journalist named Defoe. We now handle the question of deception by saying that Defoe was writing a novel, a genre of which he would have had no inkling. And, knowing that Defoe, not Crusoe, was its author, we still read *Robinson Crusoe* as if it were true. Later, "willing suspension of disbelief" was a formula invented to help us accept what we do.

The next step was journalism, meaning reports you could trust, statement by statement, fact by fact, because they appeared in newspapers. Gradually, newspapers gravitated toward the plain style, the style of all styles that was patently trustworthy: in fact, the style of *Robinson Crusoe,* with which Defoe had invented such a look of honest verisimilitude. A man who doesn't make his language ornate can't be feigning: so runs the hidden premise. "A close, naked, natural way of speaking," Spratt called it in his *History of the Royal Society:* the speech, he went on to say, of merchants and artisans, not of wits and scholars. Merchants and artisans are men who handle *things,* and presumably handle words with a similar probity. Wits and scholars handle nothing more substantial than "ideas." Journalism seemed guaranteed by the plain style. Handbooks and copyeditors now teach journalists how to write "plainly"; that means, in such a manner that they will be trusted. You get yourself trusted by appropriate artifice.

It's a populist style, and that suited Orwell. Homely diction is its hallmark, also one-two-three syntax, the show of candor, and the artifice of seeming to be grounded outside language, in what is called "fact," the domain where a condemned man can be observed as he silently avoids a puddle, and prose will report the observation, and no one will doubt it. "Populist" denotes a style that simulates the words anyone who was there and awake might later have spoken: not literarily, no, spontaneously. But we've seen already that on a written page the spontaneous can only be a contrivance.

So we're piling on a great deal of artifice, beginning with the candid nononsense observer. What if there was a short circuit, no observation, simply the prose? That's what's been suggested, and it's given inappropriate scandal. *The Plain Style feigns a candid observer.* Such was its great advantage for Orwell. He wanted its mask of calm candor, from behind which he could appeal, in seeming disinterest, to people whose pride was their no-nonsense connoisseurship of fact.

I do not want to make him sound like a student of Machiavelli's. The impulse to candor seems to have been a hallmark of his character. But what he needed was a written simulacrum of candor. That was his masterful "plain style," which emerged in full development with the 1938 *Homage to Catalonia,* an effort to supply an account of a war of which the Communists, his one-time allies, were fabricating a boilerplate account. Though their ostensible enemies were the so-called Fascists, much trouble, by their reckoning, was being made when treasonable "Trotskyists" allied themselves with the Fascists, to undo the authentic modes of revolution. It was in Communist so-called "news" of the mid-1930s that Orwell first discerned Newspeak. It penetrated not only the *Daily Worker* but respectable London papers like the *News Chronicle.* It was "the news" and it was believed. How to counter what was believed?

Why, by the device of the first-hand observer, a device as old as Defoe, who used it in *Journal of the Plague Year* to simulate persuasive accounts of things that had happened when he was a child. When Newspeak is indulging in sentences like this—

> Barcelona, the first city in Spain, was plunged into bloodshed by *agents provocateurs* using this subversive organization,

then your way to credibility is via sentences like this:

> Sometimes I was merely bored with the whole affair, paid no attention to the hellish noise, and spent hours reading a succession of Penguin Library books which, luckily, I had bought a few days earlier; sometimes I was very conscious of the armed men watching me fifty yards away.

After you've established your credentials like that, what you say can dismiss the Newspeak utterance as merely academic. And it literally doesn't matter whether you read Penguins in Spain or not.

So I'm suggesting that Orwell's "plain style" was a deliberate contrivance, formed in response to Newspeak? Yes, I am. All his mature life—alas, only about ten years—he was a leftist at odds with the official left; *Masses and Mainstream* saw in *Nineteen Eighty-Four* evidence of "a hideous ingenuity in the perversions of a dying capitalism." The official left's rhetoric is notoriously abstract; "incorrect" remains one of its doughtiest terms of abuse, to grade *Darkness at Noon* like a geometry paper. Orwell's, by contrast, was deliberately concrete. "As I write, highly civilized human beings are flying overhead, trying to kill me." Written in 1941, that cannot be bettered as a statement of fact. The official left would have spoken of Fascists. Orwell even went on to call those deadly fliers "kind-hearted, law-abiding men" who were victims of the form their patriotism had taken. Was that any way to talk of Fascist hyenas? Yes, it was the only useful way to talk of them, to negate the way the official left talked of them.

He was alert to all of English literature, from Chaucer to *Ulysses*. A source for the famous trope about some being more equal than others has been found in *Paradise Lost*. He had studied Latin and Greek, and once, when hard up, he advertised his readiness to translate from anything French so long as it was post–1400 A.D. Yet he is identified with an English prose that sounds monolingual: that seems a codifying of what you'd learn by ear in Wigan. Newspeak, as he defined it in *Nineteen Eighty-Four,* seems to reverse the honesty of all that; War Is Peace, Freedom Is Slavery, two plus two equals five. So he chose a linguistic ground: plain talk versus dishonest. We are dealing now with no language human beings speak, rather with an implied ideal language the credentials of which are moral: a language that cleaves to things, and that has univocal names for them. Cat is cat, dog is dog. That, in Swift's time, had been a philosophers' vision, and Swift had derided, in *Gulliver's Travels,* the philosophers who, since words were but tokens for things, saved breath and ear and wear and tear on the lungs by reducing their discourse to a holding-up of things. Ezra Pound likewise in the 1930s was quoting Confucius, to the effect that you begin ideal government by stabilizing names, calling things by what they are properly called by. In the twentieth century as in the eighteenth, that's the readiest naïve model, word stabilized by thing. It gets invoked by whoever has sensed that words are apt to slide.

Orwell lets it stay tacit, a rhetorical undertow. Examine his famous examples, and you discover an absence of apposite *things.* War is not war the way cat is cat, nor is freedom freedom the way dog is dog. Such abstractions are defined by consensus. A few years ago we found ourselves at "war" on poverty; those of us did, anyhow, who accepted the president's rhetoric. And Orwell's point in *Nineteen Eighty-Four* is precisely that Big Brother's rhetoric exerts pressure on the consensus. As for the sum of two plus two, even that is subject to interpretation. Crick cites Soviet posters that used "two plus two equals five" to help citizens make sense of an aborted five-year plan.

Once we've left behind cat and dog and house and tree, there are seldom "things" to which words can correspond, but you can obtain considerable advantage by acting as if there were. You gain that advantage by employing the plain style, which seems to be announcing, at every phrase, its subjection to the check of experienced and nameable *things.* Orwell, so the prose says, had shot an elephant; Orwell had witnessed a hanging; Orwell at school had been beaten with a riding crop for wetting his bed. The prose says these things so plainly that we believe whatever else it says.

Yet in these respects its statements, as we've seen, have been doubted; and we should next observe that Orwell's two climactic works are frank fictions: *Animal Farm* and *Nineteen Eighty-Four.* In a fiction you address yourself to the wholly unreal as if there were no doubt about it. In *Animal Farm* we're apprised of a convention when we're told of pigs talking to one another. But for the fact that we don't credit pigs with speech, we might be attending to a report of a county-council meeting. (And observe which way the allegory runs; we're not being told that councilors are pigs.)

It is very clarifying to reflect on how, linguistically, fiction can't be told from "fact." Its grammar, syntax, and semantics are identical. So Orwell passed readily to and fro between his two modes, reportage and fiction, which both employ the plain style. The difference is that the fictionality of fiction offers itself for detection. If the fiction speaks political truths, then, it does so by allegory. That is tricky, because it transfers responsibility for what is being said from the writer to the reader. Orwell's wartime BBC acquaintance,

William Empson, warned him in 1945 that *Animal Farm* was liable to misinterpretation, and years later provided an object lesson himself when he denied that *Nineteen Eighty-Four* was "about" some future communism. It was "about," Empson insisted, as though the fact should have been obvious, that pit of infamy, the Roman Catholic church. One thing that would have driven Empson to such a length was his need to leave the left unbesmirched by Orwell, also Orwell untainted by any imputation that he'd besmirched the left. And it summoned Orwell's shade to Empson's side to abet the hysteria he was indulging at that moment. Empson was writing about *Paradise Lost,* contemplation of which appeared to unsettle his mind.

Now this is an odd place for the plain style to have taken us: a place where there can be radical disagreement about what is being said. "A close, naked, natural way of speaking," Spratt had written; "positive expressions, clear senses, . . . thus bringing all things as near to the mathematical plainness as they can." Close, naked, natural, that is terminology to depict a restored Eden, before both Babel and Cicero, when Adam's primal language could not be misunderstood: when words could not possibly say the thing that was not. That was when Adam delved and Eve span, and they had both of them the virtues of merchants and artisans: as it were, Wigan virtues.

But the serpent misled them, no doubt employing the high style, and what their descendants have been discovering is that not even the plain style can effect a return to any simulacrum of paradise. Like any spokesman for political decencies, Orwell desired the Peaceable Kingdom. In *Animal Farm* and *Nineteen Eighty-Four* he showed, speaking in parables, how readily its restoration could go awry. And in his ten years of writing before those two books, he demonstrated that the straight is reflexive if not crooked, that all vision is fabrication, all gain short-term, all simplicity contrived. Yes, he'd have gone on writing if he could have lived; and no, he'd never have subdued the inner contradictions of speaking plainly. These correspond to no defect in Orwell's character. They inhere in the warp of reality, as ineluctably as the fact that the root of two is irrational. Divulging that earned one Greek seer a watery death.

Bernard Crick

ORWELL: A PHOTOGRAPHIC ESSAY

Rarely has a more private and simple man become more famous. His very name has entered the English language. But paradoxes abound: Was he really that simple and straightforward as a writer? The word *Orwellian* conveys the fear of a future for humanity governed by rival totalitarian regimes who govern through suffering, deprivation, and fear, and debase language and people equally. Orwell had first planned to call his book *The Last Man in Europe.* The character Winston Smith was that last man who cared for truth, hoped for freedom, and had the courage to resist; but even he is already less than a man because he agrees, for the sake of the rebellion, "to throw sulphuric acid in a child's face." *Orwell-like* conveys something quite different: a love of nature, a love of plain language, humor, eccentricity, pugnacity, and a contemplative pleasure in ordinary things.

It is arguable whether *Nineteen Eighty-Four* was Orwell's greatest achievement; most critics, and Orwell himself, see *Animal Farm* as his unquestioned literary masterpiece. "What I have most wanted to do—is to make political writing into an art." Orwell was both a great polemical and a speculative writer. As he once wrote, "Liberty is telling people what they do not want to hear." He challenges his readers' assumptions in homely, direct, and commonsensical terms, forces them to think, but often leaves them to reach their own conclusions.

Nineteen Eighty-Four is not a morbid prophecy. It is partly a warning of what *could* happen *if* we don't guard and use our liberties, but more a Swiftian satire against what Orwell thought wrong and dangerous in his world of 1948, and perhaps in ours of 1984.

Among his objects of satire were the division of the world into spheres of influence by the great powers at the wartime meetings at Yalta and Potsdam; the debasement of popular culture by the mass press; power hunger and totalitarian impulses; his belief that the intellectuals were turning into bureaucrats and betraying the common people; the debasement of language by governments and politicians; the rewriting of history for ideological purposes; James Burnham's thesis in his *Managerial Revolution* that the managers and tech-

66

George Orwell at his home in Islington, 1945. (Vernon Richards and the Orwell Archive.)

nocrats are going to take over the world; and the existence of a permanent cold war because of the impossibility of a deliberate atomic war.

Nineteen Eighty-Four may not be Orwell's best work, but it is his most famous. Like *Animal Farm* it has sold millions of copies and been translated, legally or illegally, into every major language. Only with these two books did he achieve his ambition of writing novels which, like those of Charles Dickens and H. G. Wells, would find a mass readership.

He saw the novel as still the popular educator and wished to rescue it from being written for intellectuals by intellectuals. Yet what does one know of Orwell who knows only *Nineteen Eighty-Four* and *Animal Farm?* Fortunately, each year since his death in 1950, the fame of these two books has led more and more people to read his other works, especially his essays and the three prewar documentaries: *Down and Out in Paris and London* (1933), *The Road to Wigan Pier* (1937), and *Homage to Catalonia* (1938).

It is much debated whether his real genius is as an essayist and descriptive writer rather than as a novelist. In "Why I Write" (1946) he said that while "my starting point is always a feeling of partisanship, a sense of injustice," yet "so long as I remain alive and well so I shall continue to feel strongly about prose style, to love the surface of the earth and to take pleasure in solid objects and useless scraps of information." He said he was not able and did not want "completely to abandon the world-view that I acquired in childhood."

Part of his genius was the humor and honesty with which he wrote, when he became politically committed, about his own origins and the English class system. He never hid anything or postured: he described in *The Road to Wigan Pier* how he had been brought up to believe that "the working classes smell"; but he also said that one can never escape, only understand and allow for, one's origins.

Orwell was born Eric Arthur Blair in Motihari, Bengal, where his father, Richard Walmesley Blair, was an official in the Opium Service. His great-grandfather had been wealthy and had married into the aristocracy, but Richard Blair, like his father, had no inherited property and lived by his salary. Eric's mother, Ida, brought him back from India with his elder sister while he was still a baby. Ida's own mother had lived mainly in Burma, where her husband, a French businessman named Limouzin, was in the timber trade. Ida Blair at first took a house at Henley-on-Thames to educate the children and prepare a home for her husband's retirement: they had no family home. Orwell was to describe his parents as being of "the lower-upper-middle class," or "the upper middle class without money."

The Blairs were not "monied," perhaps not even "well off," but they were certainly "comfortable." The mature writer was to exaggerate a little when he

Frank Limouzin, Orwell's maternal grand-
father. (The Dakin family and the Orwell
Archive.)

Ida Blair with her son, Eric.
(Jane Morgan and the Orwell
Archive.)

talked about having grown up in "genteel poverty," or rather it must always be remembered that Orwell when writing about his own past is a writer skilfully using and reshaping memory for both artistic and polemical purposes.

He won a partial scholarship from a village school to a fashionable preparatory school, St. Cyprian's. Sir John Grotrian, who was at St. Cyprian's with Orwell, remembers that "he was an unhappy little boy at prep school. Both my brother and he, as intellectuals, were not infrequently 'mobbed' by the school's gang of Philistines . . . his hair was quite straight and butter coloured, his complexion cream. His face moon shaped and all too often streaked with tears." Later Orwell wrote about the school with great bitterness in "Such, Such Were the Joys." For fear of libel suits, it could not be published in England during the lifetime of the headmaster's wife, and even in America it had to be edited. Some aspects of the school were awful, but it is likely that he exaggerated his own unhappiness. A childhood friend, Jacintha Buddicom, in her book *Eric and Us* raises doubts as to how much "Such, Such Were the Joys" is to be read as autobiography and how much as short story.

Young Eric eventually won a scholarship to Eton, but at Eton, Orwell rested on his oars. After studying so hard at St. Cyprian's, he neglected school work, although he read widely for himself in English literature and books by rationalists, free-thinkers, and reformers like Samuel Butler, George Bernard Shaw, and H. G. Wells.

As a scholarship boy at Eton, he was in the College—a kind of intellectual elite thrust into the heart of a social elite. He found a few kindred spirits, including Steven Runciman (later the historian of Byzantium) and his prep-school friend Cyril Connolly (the critic and writer). In Connolly's *Enemies of Promise* there are good descriptions of Orwell both at prep school and at Eton. Orwell's contemporaries agree that, without being openly rebellious, he cultivated a mocking, sardonic attitude toward authority. The classical scholar Andrew Gow, who as a young man had taught Orwell, in the mid-1970s still remembered him with great irritation and annoyance: he had wasted his opportunities to get to the university. Although everyone expects Eton to produce typical leaders of the English upper classes, it is hard to see what influence it had on Orwell.

Eric Blair, following in his father's footsteps, was sent to a crammers to prepare for the Indian Civil Service exams. He scraped through in academic subjects and in the required drawing and riding, and chose in 1921 to join the Burma Police.

Burma was then governed as a province of India and did not rate high in the pecking order of "The Service." Blair may well have been the only Etonian

Eric Blair at the age of thirteen, with his parents and younger sister. (The Dakin family and the Orwell Archive.)

Eric's childhood friend Jacintha Buddicom, September 1918. (Jacintha Buddicom and the Orwell Archive.)

The Carpenter's Shop.

Physical Exercises.

St. Cyprian's. (Orwell Archive.)

The Swimming Bath.

Mrs. Vaughan Wilkes, the headmaster's wife, whom "everybody in the school hated and feared. . . . Yet we all fawned on her in the most abject way" ("Such, Such Were the Joys"). (British Council.)

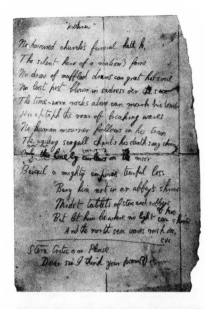

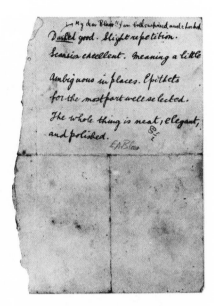

Above left: Cyril Connolly's school exercise poem "Kitchener," written at St. Cyprian's in 1916. (Orwell Archive.)

Above right: Eric Blair's critical comments on Connolly's poem. (Orwell Archive.)

Defiance with a cigarette, 1919. (Orwell Archive.)

Before an Eton wall game, 1921. (Orwell Archive.)
In College at Eton, 1917. (The Master in College, Eton.)

On holiday with Guinever and Prosper Buddicom at Church
Stretton, Shropshire, September 1917. (Guinever Buddicom and
the Orwell Archive.)

ever to pass through the Police Training School at Mandalay to become an assistant superintendent. As the photograph shows, his fellow recruits were all older than he (though none taller); most had gone through the war.

Blair both showed a loathing for the war and for military values but also, not unlike his contemporaries, some signs of guilt at having missed it. He grew to like the Burmese and to dislike the effect of colonial rule on his fellow British. Like Flory, in his first novel, *Burmese Days,* he "learned to live inwardly, in books and secret thoughts that could not be uttered." He was not popular in the police and had poor postings. When he came to write about Burma, both in *Burmese Days* and in two of his finest essays, "Shooting an Elephant" and "A Hanging," his contempt for imperial rule came bursting out. "In Moulmein in Lower Burma, I was hated by large numbers of people—the only time in my life that I have been important enough for this to happen to me" (*Shooting an Elephant*). He resigned at the end of 1927.

To the annoyance of his parents, he resigned his safe and respectable job, and not merely resolved to be a writer but took to making journeys among tramps. He lived as a tramp sometimes for a day or two, sometimes for weeks at a time. He said that he wanted to see if the English poor were treated in their own country as the Burmese were treated in theirs. On the whole he thought they were.

His first book published, *Down and Out in Paris and London* (1933), was an account of his tramping days in England and of the poverty he endured while living in Paris trying to write novels. The sales of the book were modest, but it received good notices. He used a pseudonym, George Orwell, partly to avoid embarrassing his parents and partly because he disliked the name Eric; it reminded him of a prig called Eric in a Victorian boys' story that he deplored as a child.

"I lived for about a year and a half in Paris, writing novels and short stories which no one would publish. After my money came to an end I had several years of fairly severe poverty during which I was, among other things, a dishwasher, a private tutor and a teacher in cheap private schools." So he wrote for an American reference book in 1942. But in an introduction to the Ukrainian edition of *Animal Farm* he revealed more: "I sometimes lived for months on end among the poor and half-criminal elements . . . who take to the streets, begging and stealing. At that time I associated with them through lack of money, but later their way of life interested me very much for its own sake."

Years later Sir Victor Pritchett described him as a man "who went native in his own country." In this period he called himself "a Tory anarchist." At first he didn't know what he wanted to write about. Two early novels, which he destroyed, must have been very bad. The poet Ruth Pitter remembers reading

At the Police Training School at Mandalay, Burma, 1923; Orwell is third from the left on the back row. (Roger Beadon and the Orwell Archive.)

Orwell with an old Burmese sword, a souvenir of his days in the Imperial Indian Police. (Vernon Richards and the Orwell Archive.)

Overleaf:

No. 6 rue du Pot de Fer, where Orwell stayed while he was in Paris. (British Council.)

A bistro in the poor quarter of Paris, "where you could be drunk for the equivalent of a shilling" (*Down and Out in London and Paris*). (British Council.)

early manuscripts: "How we cruel girls laughed. . . . He wrote like a cow with a musket." He stuck to it, however, and taught himself to write.

His first novel, *Burmese Days,* was published in New York in 1934. Victor Gollancz had refused it in London for fear of libel actions: the novel was obviously written directly from experience. Partly while teaching in the "cheap private schools" and partly in vacations at his parents' house (they had now moved to Southwold), he wrote a contrived, "literary pastiche," *The Clergyman's Daughter* (1935). His school teaching ended when in December 1933 he had a bad attack of pneumonia. In October he left Southwold and moved to Hampstead, where he became a half-time assistant in a secondhand bookshop.

Since 1930 Orwell had been reviewing books and writing sketches and poems for the *Adelphi,* owned and edited by Sir Richard Rees, a disciple of John Middleton Murray. Orwell moved to Hampstead partly to see more of Rees and the young writers, who would call at the *Adelphi* office for a cup of tea and to solicit books to review. He became friendly with Jack Common and Rayner Heppenstall, and met Cyril Connolly again after Connolly had reviewed *Burmese Days.* His world, however, was not that of fashionable Hampstead, but of a poor bohemia. The bitter and often jealous intellectuals who lived in one-room apartments feared rent day and knew that the mail brought only rejection slips. All this he portrayed in *Keep the Aspidistra Flying* (1936). At this time he himself, like his book's hero Gordon Comstock, came near to making a cult of failure and to believing that all literary success is selling out.

While in Hampstead he had met Eileen O'Shaughnessy, who had read English at Oxford and, after running a secretarial agency, was taking a postgraduate diploma in psychology. In June 1936, after a short courtship, they married and rented a cheap cottage in a Hertfordshire village, Wallington, hoping to live on his writing, her typing, and running a small village shop.

But that winter he had spent two months in the north, living with working people; Victor Gollancz had given him an advance of five hundred pounds (then nearly two years' income for Orwell) to write a book about poverty and unemployment. Gollancz thus had great faith in Orwell as a writer. He liked

Clockwise from upper left:
At Southwold Beach, 1934. (Dennis Colling and the Orwell Archive.)

Cyril Connolly, who once remarked that Orwell's "friendships were constant, but seldom close." (British Council.)

Reg Groves (at right), Orwell's predecessor at the Hampstead bookshop and a founding member of the British Trotskyites. (Bernard Crick and the British Council.)

Eileen O'Shaughnessy Blair in 1941. (Jane Morgan and the Orwell Archive.)

the clear and unromantic description of working-class life and coalmines in part I of *The Road to Wigan Pier* (1937), but the second part—where Orwell announced both his adherence to socialism and his dislike of most socialists— worried him. Only with great difficulty did Gollancz persuade the selectors of the famous Left Book Club to publish the book. "A writer cannot be a *loyal* member of a political party," said Orwell. Yet he was soon to join a political party.

In July 1936 the Spanish Civil War broke out. Back in Wallington, Orwell was writing *The Road to Wigan Pier,* and also at that time he sent "Shooting an Elephant," one of his finest essays, to John Lehmann for *New Writing.* He was recognized as a considerable minor talent.

When he finished his book in December, he went to Spain to fight for the Republic. Impatient to be there, he made his own way to Barcelona and joined the POUM militia on the Aragon front. The POUM was an independent Marxist movement, hated by the Stalinists and in dispute with the Trotskyites. Because he was on a quiet section of the front, Orwell tried to transfer to the largely Communist International Brigade around Madrid, but he became involved in the May riots in Barcelona. This attempt by the Communists to purge the POUM and the Catalan Anarchists made him bitterly anti-Communist. Upon returning to the front, he was badly wounded in the neck, then hunted by the Communists while still convalescent. With the help of his wife Eileen, who had come to Barcelona to work for the Independent Labor Party (ILP), he escaped from Spain at the end of 1937.

Orwell went back to Wallington and wrote *Homage to Catalonia,* a supreme description of trench life—lice, boredom, and all—but most of all a brave and precise exposure of how the Communists risked the whole Republican cause in their lust for power and in their zeal to suppress all other socialists. Victor Gollancz refused to publish it, so Frederick Warburg— known as the Trotskyite publisher simply because he had books from the left that were critical of Stalinism—bought it.

Orwell now saw himself as an anti-Stalinist revolutionary socialist; he joined the ILP, and he attended and spoke at their summer schools. *Homage to Catalonia* was much abused and much defended. Its literary merits were hardly noticed, and it sold few copies. Some now think of it as his finest achievement and nearly all critics see it as his great stylistic breakthrough: he became the serious writer with the terse, easy, vivid colloquial style.

In March 1938 he collapsed with a tubercular lesion in one lung and was removed to a sanitorium. Thanks to help from an unknown admirer, the Blairs spent the winter of 1938–39 in the warmth of Morocco, where he finished *Coming Up for Air* (1939). It is a novel of a foreboding of war and an ironic nostalgia for a lost past.

The Tripe Shop, Darlington Road, over which Orwell lodged for
a brief period in 1936. (By permission of Smith's Books
[Wigan], Limited.)

Eileen Blair visiting her husband in the International Labour Party contingent on the Aragon front, at Huesca, March 1937. (Orwell Archive.)

Orwell (second from left) with members of the ILP contingent in Spain, 1937. (Orwell Archive.)

The streets of Barcelona during the May uprising, 1937. (British Council.)

In his ILP days Orwell claimed that "the coming war" would be merely a capitalist struggle for the control of colonial markets. As late as July 1939 he wrote "Not Counting Niggers" (a title of savage irony), claiming that British and French leaders did not ask the vast majority of their colonies about whether they were in favor of fighting the war. But, when war broke out, he immediately declared that even Chamberlain's England was preferable to Hitler's Germany. In his essay "My Country, Right or Left" he stated a left-wing case for patriotism that he developed in his book of 1941, *The Lion and the Unicorn.*

Orwell was several times rejected for the army because of his tuberculosis. A friend said: "He tried harder to get in than many tried to get out of the Army." All he could do was move back to London and join the part-time Home Guard; for a while he seemed to think that it could become a Catalan-style revolutionary militia. That hope soon faded.

In August 1941, after a period of painful underemployment, he became a producer with the Far Eastern section of the BBC, tolerating the unaccustomed and uncongenial restraints until November 1943.

Orwell had published a volume of essays, *Inside the Whale,* in 1939. His powers as an essayist went from strength to strength. During the war he wrote regularly for Cyril Connolly's *Horizon* and for *Parisian Review* in New York. But some of his best writing came after November 1943, when he was made literary editor of the *Tribune,* a left-wing weekly directed by Aneurin Bevan. His weekly column, "As I Please," ranged through a vast number of topics, some serious and some comic, some political and some literary.

"George Orwell" became a character, hard-hitting and good-humored, a quirky socialist but with a love of traditional liberties and pastimes. The private man was, however, very reserved and a compulsive overworker. Both his and Eileen's health became very run down, partly through wartime conditions and partly through physical neglect; yet he persuaded her to adopt a child, Richard.

Early in 1944 he finished writing *Animal Farm* but at least three publishers (Gollancz, T. S. Eliot for Faber, and Jonathan Cape) turned it down as being inopportune while Russia was an ally. It was only published shortly after the end of the war. Several critics called it the greatest satire in the English language since Swift's *Gulliver's Travels. Animal Farm* brought Orwell instant fame and a huge new and international readership. Harcourt Brace took it after many New York firms had turned it down, and it was a Book of the Month Club selection: it sold 250,000 copies in one year.

Before *Animal Farm* appeared Orwell had gone to France for the *Observer* to report on the liberation and on to Germany to try to see the opening of the concentration camps, but Eileen died and he came hurrying home. He told

SIGNALEMENT

Taille **1.82**

Front **moy.**

Nez **rect.**

Bouche **moy;**

Menton **rond**

Visage **ovale**

Cheveux **cht.**

Barbe **rasée**

Corpulence **moy.**

Yeux **cht.**

Teint **clair**

Marques particulières apparentes

Nom et prénoms de la femme :

Ellen Maud O'SHANGHNESSY

Prénoms des enfants âgés de moins de 18 ans :

Certificate of registration, Marrakesh, September 1938. (Orwell Archive.)

At Marrakesh, September 1938 to March 1939. (Orwell Archive.)

The cottage at Wallington, circa 1939. (Peter Holt and the Orwell
Archive.)

Feeding Muriel at Wal-
lington. (Dennis Colling
and the Orwell Archive.)

people that her death was through the anesthetic in a minor operation. In fact she had cancer. She may well not have told him, but it seems obtuse of him not to have seen that something was badly wrong. Outwardly he bore her death with the stoicism of "Orwell," but Eric Blair was deeply hurt and shaken—though by now the public mask had taken over almost entirely. Only a few very old friends called him Eric; new friends, as diverse as Julian Symons, Arthur Koestler, Anthony Powell, and Malcolm Muggeridge, called him George.

He stuck to young Richard, first on his own, then with the help of a housekeeper. He began writing regularly again for the *Tribune* and the *Observer* and also for the *Manchester Evening News*. And he visited Scotland to see a farmhouse on the northern tip of the remote island of Jura, where, even in Eileen's lifetime, he had resolved to move to escape from the distractions of London and to begin work on *The Last Man in Europe*.

Barnhill, on Jura, was eight miles from the nearest house with a telephone, which in turn was twenty-five miles from a small village with a shop where steamers came twice a week. The journey from London took two days, and the island was very remote and primitive. At first Orwell reveled in the difficulties and seclusion, although his younger sister followed him, froze out the young housekeeper, and became herself both housekeeper and "gatekeeper" against unwanted visitors. Brother and sister did not always see eye to eye on who was unwanted or welcome. He worked hard, perhaps too hard, in a small room with a smoky stove, and chain-smoked. In a notebook he wrote that in all his writing life "there has literally been not one day in which I did not feel that I was idling, that I was behind with the current job, and that my total output was miserably small. Even at the period when I was working ten hours a day on a book, or turning out four or five articles a week, I have never been able to get away from this neurotic feeling, that I was wasting time."

He collapsed with tuberculosis with only a first draft of his long-planned new book finished, which as always "to me is only ever halfway through." In a Scottish hospital the new drug Streptomycin, obtained from America with the help of David Astor and Aneurin Bevan, was tried on him. The ghastly side effects, however, could not yet be controlled, and the treatment had to end.

Rested, he returned to Jura, but he drove himself hard again and when his agent and his publisher failed to find a typist who would go to Jura, he sat up in bed and typed the second version himself. He collapsed again when he finished.

From January to September 1949, Orwell lay in an old-fashioned sanitorium in Gloucestershire. Then he was transferred to University College London to be under one of the best chest specialists in England, who had also once treated D. H. Lawrence. The doctors, as was then customary, gave him

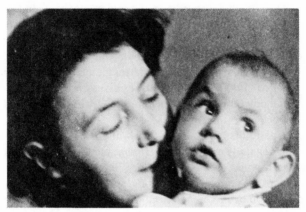

Eileen Blair with Richard, circa
1944. (Orwell Archive.)

Orwell's union card, dated 29 December 1943. (Orwell Archive.)

Pushing Richard in his pram in
Canonbury. (Vernon Richards and
the Orwell Archive.)

Malcolm Muggeridge. (British Council.)

Anthony Powell. (British Council.)

Arthur Koestler. (British Council.)

Orwell at his work bench; he enjoyed carpentry and made toys for Richard and furniture for their house. (Vernon Richards and the Orwell Archive.)

some hope. In fact they knew that there was none. But Orwell was not told, nor was Sonia Brownell, a former editorial assistant on Connolly's *Horizon* to whom he had proposed without success in 1945. When he asked her again, however, she accepted, hoping to help him and nurse him back to health. In a letter to a friend he wrote: "As I warned you I might do, I intend getting married again (to Sonya) when I am once again in the land of the living, if I ever am. I suppose everyone will be horrified, but apart from other considerations I really think I should stay alive longer if I were married."

On the one hand, he married and began work on a new novel, as if he thought he might live; but on the other hand, he made his will and left precise instructions (fortunately ignored by his widow) about which of his writings to reprint and which to suppress. He read the first reviews of *Nineteen Eighty-Four* and dictated notes for a press release to correct some American reviewers who saw it as an attack on all forms of socialism, not on all forms of totalitarianism. He reminded them that he was a democratic socialist, that the book was "a parody" and that he only meant that something like the iron regime could, not would, occur, if we didn't all guard and use our liberties. Orwell died suddenly on January 21, 1950. Unexpectedly (he was an avowed non-believer) he had asked to be buried not cremated, and according to the rites of the Church of England.

If George Orwell of *Animal Farm* was already a famous writer of plain, simple English, and someone who believed passionately that no meaningful idea was too difficult to be explained in simple terms to ordinary people, yet something is odd and perpetually disturbing about *Nineteen Eighty-Four*. Serious critics have variously argued that it is basically a pessimistic and deterministic prophecy; a conditional projection—what could happen if . . . ; a humanistic satire of social conditions and events contemporary with Orwell; a religious allegory on the impossibility of staying human without God; an anti-Catholic diatribe, in which the inquisitor, O'Brien, and the Inner Party are really the Church; a world-hating act of nihilistic misanthropy; a deathbed renunciation of any kind of socialism; or a humanistic and libertarian socialist (almost anarchist) satire against totalitarian tendencies in both his own and other societies. Isaac Rosenfeld saw it as "mysticism of cruelty, utter pessimism"; and Anthony Burgess as "a comic novel."

Despite the many targets of the author's satire, it cannot be all things to all men. But it is the most complex piece of writing Orwell attempted, and it is a novel and not a tract or a forecast; thus it is more open-ended than most people suppose. Jenni Calder has called it a "well-crafted novel"; part of the craft is dramatizing dilemmas and fears of humanity today, not offering easy solutions.

Any work of art is greater than the planned and literal intentions of the

Barnhill, on the island of Jura, 1947. (Orwell Archive.)

Sir Richard Rees, Orwell's friend and patron, who visited him on Jura and in the Scottish hospital. (Orwell Archive.)

Sonia Brownell (foreground), Orwell's second wife, on her last day at *Horizon,* October 1949. (Orwell Archive.)

author. We must all read *Nineteen Eighty-Four* differently. Perhaps it is too complex for its own good, but it stimulates a lasting debate. Some dismiss it because in 1984 we in the West are not living under the iron rule of Big Brother and the Party of Oceania and Airstrip One, but they should at least recognize that if it is a satire (and Orwell said it was) and not a prophecy, many of the things that he hated in 1948 and mocked with imaginative and grotesque exaggeration are still with us.

Some things are clear, however, in all the possible interpretations of this rich, worrying, complex, and congested book: that this novel was not his last will and testament but simply the last book the great ordinary man happened to write before he happened to die; that it is not a work of unnatural, psychotic intensity dashed off by a dying man riddled with the death wish and regressing to memories of childhood traumas but in fact long planned and premeditated coolly; and that it is not a conscious repudiation of Orwell's well-known political position.

Czeslav Milsoz in his *Captive Mind* (1953) reported that in Poland some of his party colleagues had read smuggled copies as a manual of power but that the freer minds had seen it as "a Swiftian satire," and "the fact that there are writers in the West who understand the functioning of the unusually constructed machine of which they are themselves a part, astounds them and argues against the 'stupidity' of the West." Orwell indeed succeeded in "making political writing into an art."

Enclosed with letter dated 14.2.49 in envelope postmarked
Gloucester 16 Feb 1949; so Tuesday must have been Tuesday
15th February 1949.

Cranham
Tuesday

Hail and Fare Well, my dear Jacintha,

You see I
haven't forgotten. I wrote to you yesterday but the letter isn't
posted yet, so I'll go on to cheer this dismal day. It's been a day
when everything's gone wrong. First there was a stupid accident to the
book I was reading, which is now unreadable. After that the typewriter
stuck & I'm too poorly to fix it. I've managed to borrow a substitute
but it's not much better. Ever since I got your letter I've been remembering. I can't stop thinking about the young days with you & Guin
& Prosper, & things put out of mind for 20 or 30 years. I am so wanting
to see you. We must meet when I get out of this place, but the doctor
says I'll have to stay another 3 or 4 months.

I would like you to see Richard. He can't read yet & is rather
backward in talking, but he's as keen on fishing as I was & loves working on the farm, where he's really quite helpful. He has an enormous
interest in machinery, which may be useful to him later on. When I was
not much more than his age I always knew I wanted to write, but for the
first ten years it was very hard to make a living. I had to take a lot
of beastly jobs to earn enough to keep going & could only write in any
spare time that was left, when I was too tired& had to destroy a dozen
pages for one that was worth keeping. I tore up a whole novel once &
wish now I hadn't been so ruthless. Parts of it might have been worth
re-writing, though it's impossible to come back to something written
in such a different world. But I am rather sorry now. (" 'An w'en I
sor wot 'e'd bin an' gorn an' done, I sed coo lor, wot 'ave you bin
an' gorn an' done ? ") I think it's rather a good thing Richard is such
an entirely practical child.

Are you fond of children ? I think you must be. You were such a
tender-hearted girl, always full of pity for the creatures we others
shot & killed. But you were not so tender-hearted to me when you abandoned me to Burma with all hope denied. We are older now, & with this
wretched illness the years will have taken more toll of me than of you.
But I am well cared-for here & feel much better than I did when I got
here last month. As soon as I can get back to London I do so want us to
meet again.

As we always ended so that there should be no ending

Farewell and Hail

Eric

A letter from Orwell to his childhood friend Jacintha Buddicom,
who had only recently discovered that "George Orwell" was Eric
Blair. (Jacintha Buddicom and the Orwell Archive.)

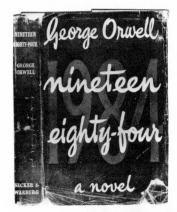

Book jacket for the first edition of *Nineteen Eighty-Four*. (Orwell Archive.)

Telford New Town taking shape. (British Council.)

At any rate, spring is here, even in London N.1, and they can't stop you enjoying it. This is a satisfying reflection. How many a time have I stood watching the toads mating, or a pair of hares having a boxing match in the young corn, and thought of all the important persons who would stop me enjoying this if they could. But luckily they can't. So long as you are not actually ill, hungry, frightened or immured in a prison or a holiday camp, spring is still spring. The atom bombs are piling up in the factories, the police are prowling through the cities, the lies are streaming from the loud-speakers, but the earth is still going round the sun, and neither the dictators nor the bureaucrats, deeply as they disapprove of the process, are able to prevent it.

Tribune, 12 April 1946; *New Republic,* 20 May 1946; SE; OR

Sheldon Wolin

COUNTER-ENLIGHTENMENT:
ORWELL'S *NINETEEN EIGHTY-FOUR*

o an age whose appetite for textual interpretation has been fed on the subtleties of critical hermeneutics, structuralism, and deconstruction, no text might seem less challenging or more ingenuous than George Orwell's *Nineteen Eighty-Four*. It is, most everyone agrees, an object lesson about the dangers of totalitarianism. Most everyone knows, too, what totalitarianism is. The reading public of 1949, the year of its publication, would doubtless have retained many of the images of Nazism established by the literature and Allied propaganda of World War II; the reading public of 1984, the patronymic year of the novel's title, may have had only a dim memory of Nazi totalitarianism, save perhaps for the Holocaust, but nearly four decades of cold war rhetoric would have created a near-automatic association of totalitarianism with the practices of the Soviet system.

Certainly the society described in *Nineteen Eighty-Four* was intended by Orwell to represent a totalitarian system. Many of its general features corresponded to those associated with Hitler's Germany and Stalin's Russia. Oceania (to use the name Orwell gave to the regime of Big Brother) was ruled by the dictatorship of a single party that ruthlessly suppressed all forms of opposition, maintained constant surveillance over the entire society, indoctrinated and manipulated the mind of the population, and produced a steady flow of lies, distortions, and falsifications designed to promote a conception of reality useful to perpetuating the regime.

All this seems straightforward until one asks whether it was Orwell's intention to redescribe the main features of totalitarianism or to present a picture of totalitarianism that, while presupposing the historical existence of German Nazism and Russian communism, would try at the same time to represent a system which differed from its predecessors in ways that would be critically relevant to nontotalitarian societies. It has been obvious to most critics that Orwell was concerned to warn nontotalitarian societies about the evils of totalitarianism. They have generally not taken seriously the notion that a future

98

totalitarianism would build upon the experience of Nazism and Soviet communism, that it would incorporate that experience and go beyond it. Instead interpreters have tended to give what might be called a "horizontal" reading of *Nineteen Eighty-Four,* claiming that it was an attack upon the policies of the postwar British Labour government,[1] or that it was a veiled exposé of Stalinism and a "diagnosis of the totalitarian perversion of socialism,"[2] or that it was a warning about the threat to individual freedom posed by the new technology of surveillance available to the modern state.[3]

What has been mostly overlooked by the horizontal interpretation is the carefully constructed "history" that Orwell furnished for the world portrayed in *Nineteen Eighty-Four.* For the history Orwell uses a long analysis of the totalitarian regime that is purportedly the work of Emmanuel Goldstein, a half-mythical leader of the underground opposition who is patently modeled upon Trotsky. *The Theory and Practice of Oligarchical Collectivism* sets down the principles that constitute the totalitarian system as well as the historical events that enabled it to come into existence. By outfitting it with a history and by deliberately choosing the title *Nineteen Eighty-Four* Orwell was signifying that the regime being depicted was not the result of a revolutionary takeover but rooted in a history immanent and imminent in Western societies. "The main outlines" of the new totalitarianism, according to Goldstein's testament, "had long been obvious." The Nazi and Communist systems, he remarked, had "foreshadowed" it, but in its essence, as O'Brien the Party leader explains to Winston Smith, the antihero of *Nineteen Eighty-Four,* this later system looked upon its predecessors as benchmarks to be surpassed when it came to identifying the distinguishing mark of the new. If, then, there is a difference between the new totalitarianism and the old in respect to their distinctive principles, the lesson of *Nineteen Eighty-Four* is not to reaffirm what is known and has been realized but to identify what is possible but unrealized.

From the beginnings of political theory in ancient Greece it has been commonplace to associate the emergence of a particular kind of political regime with a particular social stratum or class and its distinguishing characteristics, skills, and values. Orwell specifically identifies the regime of *Nineteen Eighty-Four* with the appearance in the late nineteenth century of a cohesive social stratum whose members have in common certain practical skills of organizing men and manipulating symbols. The "new aristocracy"

> was made up for the most part of bureaucrats, scientists, technicians, trade-union organizers, publicity experts, teachers, journalists, and professional politicians. These people, whose origins lay in the salaried middle class and the upper grades of the working class, had been shaped and brought together by the barren world of monopoly industry and centralized government.

The new aristocracy crystallizes in opposition to socialism and to its ideals of equality and "human brotherhood." This new "Middle" is fearful that socialism will end the status distinctions that the group prizes. But the Middle stands for more than an antisocialist movement. The various *technai* of its members represent skills in creating artificial, abstract worlds. They are skills of organization and of persuasion through the manipulation of symbols that build up structures of "reality" to intervene between the individual and the natural realities and continuities of everyday life.

The possessors of *technai* represent a dissociation from the vitality and concreteness of life; they come, as Orwell put it, from the "barren world" of corporate and governmental bureaucracies. They are at once practical and abstract, or rather they are skilled at making a practice of the abstract. They are, finally, themselves abstract; for other than wanting to preserve their power and the privileges of higher status they have no social or political values. They are "less avaricious [than previous ruling groups], less tempted by luxury, hungrier for pure power, and, above all, more conscious of what they are doing and more intent on crushing opposition."

The strain of asceticism is crucial to the nature of the new ruling class. It signifies, literally, a kind of disembodiment, a loss of contact with physical being and natural processes. It will be reflected in the harsh sexual prohibitions in Oceania and the puritanism that prevails generally. Appropriately, when Winston and Julia defy the regime, their defiance is sexual, and when the regime captures them it is their bodies that are cruelly punished. What happens to the bodies of Julia and Winston is a metaphor for what has happened to the body politic. It has been destroyed in the specific sense that the regime rejects what was possibly the most fundamental of all political commonplaces since antiquity, that power emanates from the community to political authority and that political authority is an embodiment of power, the power of the body politic. The contrast between the traditional and totalitarian conceptions of power suggests a paradox: power that issues from the body politic cannot by its nature be brutal; power dissociated from the body politic must be brutal and must turn its brutality against the body and depoliticize it.

The classical totalitarian regime of the interwar years was distinguished by its rejection of the principle that state power ought to be limited both by its objects and by its means. The ideal of unlimited power was the expression of a dynamic conception of society as in a permanent state of total mobilization. The Nazi dictatorship was organized for military conquest, the Soviet system for the creation of a new socialist society and, to some uncertain degree, for the propagation of Communist ideology and the expansion of Soviet power abroad. Both regimes were revolutionary in the very specific sense that both were in revolt against the recent past of their societies, Nazism against Weimar Germany, bolshevism against Tsarist Russia.

Orwell's totalitarianism aspires to total power; indeed, it sees itself as dedicated more absolutely to that end than its predecessors had been. But it is not organized for conquest, although it is organized for continual warfare, or for social reconstruction in the conventional sense. Insofar as it has a revolutionary impulse, that impulse is directed against the future rather than the past or, more precisely, against a certain conception of the future that was worked out during the late seventeenth and the eighteenth centuries and that can be roughly characterized as the Enlightenment or progressive conception of the future. Yet while Orwell's regime would reject the futurist orientation of communism, it would not embrace the utopianism of the reactionaries and seek to reinstitute some golden age in the past. It would be in a fundamental sense atemporal.

For the modern sensibility despair is rooted in attitudes toward history. The Enlightenment looked to history to record human progress, to project human possibilities. Modern utopian as well as antiutopian literature has perpetuated the historical outlook of the Enlightenment. Utopias such as Edward Bellamy's *Looking Backward* or antiutopias such as Huxley's *Brave New World* were projective in that they extended selected tendencies in existing society so that certain human dreams—for example, of space travel or of material plenty —were imaginatively realized. In the case of negative utopias, certain possibilities were drawn to a conclusion that turned against the benign hopes that they had originally inspired. Science, for instance, is enlisted to control human behavior rather than to make life safer, longer, and more agreeable. Although *Nineteen Eighty-Four* represents the realization of certain developments that Orwell located in the nineteenth century, it is not a projection of them. Much less is it a warning about the dangerous potential inherent in the technology of surveillance. The peculiarity of life in "1984" is its retrogressive character, which is deliberately accomplished by its rulers. They had resolved "to arrest progress and freeze history at a chosen moment."

This decision to renounce the historical commitment to progress represented a heresy against the central article of faith that had inspired not only middle-class liberalism but most forms of socialism as well. This was faith in "the economy" as the force that would propel mankind to ever higher levels of material and spiritual progress. The economy was conceived as a great rational structure for efficiently allocating resources, maximizing the productive power of machines and men, and increasing human well-being. Liberal thinkers believed that a "free economy" would assure a steady rate of social progress because it stimulated the human drives for wealth, status, material satisfactions, and possessiveness. For the socialist theoretician rational planning by public agencies would take the place of entrepreneurial self-interest in promoting a dynamic, efficient, and progressive economy. "The economy" was the ultimate showcase of modern rationality: a structure in which means and ends were in perfect accord.

In Oceania this vision is totally rejected in favor of what might be called an "antieconomy." Instead of increasing abundance, efficiency, and quality the antieconomy is designed deliberately to produce shortages, shoddy goods, and a general condition of dreariness. A clue to the antieconomy is provided by Orwell's remark that "the primary aim of modern warfare . . . is to use up the products of the machine without raising the general standard of living." The aim of the antieconomy is to prevent "an all-round increase in wealth" that might make life easier for the many and perhaps encourage them "to think for themselves."

The conscious perpetuation of poverty was the corollary to the perpetuation of "a hierarchical society." The goal was not the maximization of wealth but "to keep the wheels of industry turning without increasing the real wealth of the world. Goods must be produced, but they need not be distributed. And in practice the only way of achieving this was by continuous warfare." The result is not a static economy but a retrogressive one. "As a whole the world is more primitive than it was fifty years ago." It is "a bare, hungry, dilapidated place compared with the world that existed before 1914. . . . Experiment and innovation have largely stopped."

The trauma reflected in *Nineteen Eighty-Four* is not only that "the earthly paradise" of "human equality" was rejected just when it was "technically possible" but that economic rationality, the most general standard for the practice of individual and social rationality, had been destroyed. The depth of the trauma for the modern liberal and socialist mind may be gauged by comparing the destruction of economic rationality portrayed by Orwell— "nothing is efficient in Oceania except the Thought Police"—with Schumpeter's classic claim about the contribution of economic thinking to human rationality generally:

> Now the rational attitude presumably forced itself on the human mind primarily from economic necessity; it is the everyday economic task to which we as a race owe our elementary training in rational thought and behavior—I have no hesitation in saying that all logic is derived from the pattern of economic decision.[4]

The antifuturism of the regime is connected with other characteristics that set it off from the two major forms of twentieth-century totalitarianism. Unlike communism or Nazism, Orwell's regime is without vitality. Its economy is without growth, there is virtually no scientific advancement, and international relations consists of an endless military stalemate. At the same time, it is a totalitarianism without a significant ideology, no racial myth, no myth of economic abundance. It is, in fact, a condition of pure nihilism whose Nietzschean mood would have been perfectly captured had Orwell retained a title he had seriously considered, *The Last Man in Europe*. It was not a nihilism inspired by a fierce hatred of modernism, as might have been the case with the Nazis, who might be said to have represented the revolt of vulgar, even muscular realism against effete intellectualism. It was, instead, a nihilism of the intellect driven by a determination to reduce the world to mind. The new totalitarianism, like the old, renounced the notion that state power should be limited: "All competing pleasures will be destroyed. But always . . . there will be the intoxication of power, constantly increasing and constantly growing subtler."

The totalitarianism of mind is, as we shall see, more totalistic, not because it is more efficiently mobilized but because the line between subjective and objective has been obliterated. It has discovered what neither Nazism, with its fetishism of blond muscularity, nor communism, with its reification of productive forces, ever grasped: the potential power in the collective exploitation of mind: "Reality exists in the human mind, and nowhere else. Not in the individual mind, which can make mistakes, and in any case soon perishes; only in the mind of the Party, which is collective and immortal." Because, literally and figuratively, it is singleminded, the new totalitarianism disdains the simple liquidation of its opponents or unleashing holocausts against "alien" elements. There will be neither gulags nor Auschwitz. This will not be because the reign of mind is more benevolent than the tyranny of *Blut und Boden* or the dictatorship of the proletariat, but because the potential of mind is fulfilled differently: "We are different from the persecutors of the past. . . . We do not destroy the heretic because he resists us; so long as he resists us we never destroy him. We convert him, we capture his inner mind, we reshape him."

Oceania is ruled, then, by disembodied reason—no one knows for certain whether Big Brother actually exists—which is reason dissociated from all reality save that of its own de-signing. What kind of regime, then, results from the reign of reason, and what is the nature of reason when it is sovereign and unembodied?

Perhaps the word that best describes the regime is *endlessness,* a condition that is sustained indefinitely and with no end in view except the preservation of the system. O'Brien, the party leader who is at once Winston's confessor and Grand Inquisitor, declares, "Power is not a means; it is an end." Inequality and class privileges are maintained not as ends but for their functional value in serving a system so singlemindedly devoted to power that its rulers confuse the utter pointlessness of the system with an abstract purity. The Party, O'Brien continues, is not interested in promoting the "good of others," or in wealth, luxury, or happiness. "We are interested solely in power . . . pure power."

At one stroke this conception of power dissolves the instrumentalist conception that had permitted most modern thinkers, Hobbes excepted, to mystify power. Power, so the modern argued, was neither good nor bad in itself but neutral; its moral or political status depended on how it was used. Questions about the genesis or accumulation of power tended to become secondary. The perfect illustration of the mystification of power—perfect because accomplished by the illusion of transparency—was early modern social-contract theory. Somehow power is made to materialize after each individual consents to be bound by the authority established by the contract. Authority, in turn, agrees to exercise power in accordance with the terms of the contract. Preexisting forms and accumulations of power are first ignored, or fantasized away by inventing the state of nature, so that the covenanters may focus solely on the question of consent to authority. Then the various forms of power—political, social, economic—are silently allowed to resume their place in society. Yet these various forms of power and the values that became accessible to those who possessed them were usually identified as the ends that authority was supposed to use its power to protect and encourage. Lockean man, for example, enters society in order to secure his life, liberty, and property. These are the ends that political power is supposed to preserve. The point of the entire system rested upon a presupposition about the objective status of ends: life, liberty, and property were "natural" rights, not objects of subjective preference or of custom or convention. They were rational objects in the sense that they were considered to be necessary conditions for a genuinely human life. One could not live a human life, Locke asserted, if one was an object that another could do with as he pleased.

The rational status of ends made it possible to conceive of society as a complete system of rationality in which certain means appeared to be rationally necessary rather than pragmatic or historically arbitrary choices. Thus, as Locke argued, the rights of life, liberty, and property required a system of known, standing law, an impartial judiciary and executive, and a sovereign representative body. Later liberals believed that the rational ends of progress, freedom, political equality, and material plenty could be achieved by the rational means of private property, market economy, universal suffrage, civil liberties, representative government, the rule of law, the encouragement of the natural sciences, and universal public education. Socialism merely shaded some of the ends—"real" or social equality instead of just "formal" political equality—and substituted some different means—planning for the market—but without surrendering the hope that society could be shaped into a rationally perfect system of ends and means operated by rational actors, in this case the rational planners of socialist economics rather than the rational egoists of classical economics.[5]

When Orwell has O'Brien assert a conception of power pursued for its own sake and unconditioned by ends, totalitarianism appears as a system in which ends disappear into endlessness and means into meaninglessness. O'Brien attempts to spiritualize power by saying of the Party elite, "We are the priests of power" and by adding "God is power." This is, however, to confuse abstinence with purity of motive. The Party is a simple illustration of what Nietzsche referred to as the "ascetic priesthood" for whom self-denial is the form in which its will to power is embodied.

The regime of abstract power in which endlessness has rendered means meaningless is essentially a mechanism for recycling power so that the system can be maintained in a steady state. Its most vivid illustration is in the way that the societies of *Nineteen Eighty-Four* have institutionalized warfare. The world is envisaged as divided among three "superstates," Oceania, Eastasia, and Eurasia, who are constantly at war with each other. The wars are fought on a tacit understanding that no state will gain a clear advantage and that no final victory will be won. Although there are occasional moments where the wars are fitfully fought so that one side or the other may rid itself of excess population or may seize a needed labor force, the sole purpose of war is to perpetuate the rule of disembodied mind-power.

Toward the end of the brainwashing and mind-conditioning sessions O'Brien remarks that "power is in tearing human minds to pieces and putting them together again in new shapes of your own choosing." The obsession of mind with mind, the narcissism of the intellect, is accompanied by an almost complete indifference to the external world. Nature and society are no longer the domains where human ambition, energy, and skill seek to make their mark. Mind is totally absorbed in itself as an object of power: "The real power, the power we have to fight for night and day, is not power over things, but over men. . . . Over the body—but, above all, over the mind. Power over matter—external reality, as you would call it—is not important." Liberated from any stewardship for society, history, or nature, the mind can focus on purifying itself. "It is intolerable to us that an erroneous thought should exist anywhere in the world, however secret and powerless it may be. . . . Everyone is washed clean. . . . But we make the brain perfect before we blow it out."

The horror of *Nineteen Eighty-Four* rests on a paradox. It portrays a regime demonized by mind that has become divorced from reason. If we ask, What would it mean for mind to become dissociated from reason? we would be asking an essentially historical question: What historical understanding of reason was Orwell's totalitarian mind rejecting? The answer has been hinted at earlier.

Nineteen Eighty-Four is about the end of the Enlightenment, the great historical project begun in the late seventeenth century and dedicated to creating a society based upon reason. The idea of reason developed over the next two centuries was many things: critical, logical, and instrumental. But it was more than these formal qualities. Reason was typically assumed to be "embedded" in a context of political and civilizational values from which it took its reference. This meant, among other things, that the advance of reason was to be measured not by reference to reason but by the extent to which other positive values (literacy, for example) were increased, or negative values (ignorance) diminished. One of the most fundamental Enlightenment convictions was that the advancement of science and technological innovations would be accompanied by the rapid reduction in human suffering. Ever since Francis Bacon had prophesied early in the seventeenth century that the union of scientific knowledge with state power would bring dramatic "relief" to man's "earthly estate," the reduction of pain and the cumulative advancement of science had been accepted as important criteria for measuring human progress. The eighteenth- and nineteenth-century preoccupation with the reform of prisons and of legal punishment was a practical expression of the belief in an inverse relationship between the application of scientific knowledge and the incidence of brutality.

Curiously enough, Huxley's *Brave New World* incorporated the Enlightenment faith that social engineering, that is, the political, social, and psychological applications of science, would reduce physical suffering. Huxley was intrigued by—even playful about—the diabolical possibilities of scientific ingenuity for achieving such a total degree of control that crude physical torture seems atavistic, inefficient, and hence superfluous. Orwell, however, refused that vision of totalitarianism. The regime of Big Brother relied heavily upon torture and brutality, and Orwell insisted upon describing its most minute details as though to parody the mistaken notion that a totalitarian future would be simply an inverted triumph of technological rationality brought to perfection. The icon of the new totalitarianism was not represented, as some have imagined, in the two-way television screen that allows for perpetual surveillance by the state of the most intimate details of human life. "If you want a picture of the future," O'Brien carefully explains to Winston, "imagine a boot stamping on a human face—forever."

The icon is shocking because it signifies the complete reversal of the Enlightenment faith that as mind advances, suffering diminishes, and as suffering lessens, progress is increased. "Progress in our world," O'Brien declares, "will be progress toward more pain." The project is to compel the mind to conform to an ideal of absolute oneness. O'Brien's "mind *contained* Winston's mind." To achieve that ideal or, rather, to work toward it forever means "inflicting pain and humiliation" and creating "a world of fear and treachery and torment. . . . not less but more merciless as it refines itself."

Torture is directed at the body, but its aim is to separate mind and body, or mind and senses, so that the mind loses its grip on reality. Reality, for Orwell, was basically physical; truths about reality were truths about physical reality of which bodily truths were an instance. Mathematical truths were not essentially logical truths but truths about physical reality. The basic axiom to which Winston clings throughout the torture sessions— "Freedom is the freedom to say that two plus two makes four. If that is granted, all else follows"—is precious because it is a statement about the real world: it is cruelly illustrated when O'Brien holds up four fingers and demands that Winston agree that five fingers are being shown. To believe that mathematical statements derive their truth from mind-created conventions alone would be to share the philosophy of O'Brien. "If one is to rule, and to continue ruling," Goldstein had observed in his memoir, "one must be able to dislocate the sense of reality."

Orwell illustrated his view about what constituted a truthful relationship between mind and reality by the example of warfare. Although the history of warfare is commonly presumed to be a chapter in the history of human irrationality, Orwell makes the opposite point by contrasting the traditional practice of war with warfare in Oceania. Traditional conceptions of war, he argued, were comprehensible because one side was in fact trying to defeat the other. The deeper meaning was that traditional warfare preserved a certain form of rationality which, as we shall see shortly, Orwell regarded as peculiarly precious and specifically marked out for extinction by totalitarianism. In the old days rulers understood that wars could not be effectively fought if certain illusions or fantasies were fostered that impaired "military efficiency." At the most elementary level, therefore, even the most benighted Bourbon recognized that if the weapons of his army were to work effectively, certain principles of reality had to be respected. "Physical facts," as Orwell put it, "could not be ignored." Moreover, some rulers also believed that useful military lessons could be learned from the past, and so they encouraged the preservation of historical truths and, indirectly, the idea of historical truth itself. Orwell summed it up by saying, "War was a sure safeguard of sanity."

The connections between sanity, things that work, and facts about the concrete world point to an Orwellian preoccupation with the relationship between knowing and reality that goes beyond an attempt to establish a straightforward epistemological model. It is an effort to discover the reality principle that might crack "the sealed world" of endlessness and meaninglessness created by mind: "In philosophy, or religion, or ethics, or politics, two and two might make five, but when one was designing for an airplane they had to make four." Against O'Brien's vision of a totalitarian world governed by collective mind—"We make the laws of nature. . . . Nothing exists except through human consciousness"—Winston clings to the belief that, as O'Brien puts it in his helpfully schoolmasterish way, "reality is something objective, external, existing in its own right." Ultimately, however, torture forces Winston to assent that "two plus two equals five" and to declare his love for Big Brother. In the end, perhaps, O'Brien is right in describing Winston as a "poor metaphysician" because on the plane of philosophy alone the twentieth century has heard too many ingenious arguments against transcendental assumptions, or an ultimate ground to things, and too many arguments in favor of truth as simply a linguistic convention or an agreement among philosophers to converse in accord with the rules of a particular language game, to believe that the problem of totalitarianism comes down to the respective claims of philosophical realism versus philosophical conventionalism. Perhaps we need to ask whether in the end Orwell was not suggesting certain values that were more important in warding off or weakening totalitarian tendencies than any strictly philosophical appeals.

There were, I would suggest, two in particular that mattered to Orwell. One was personal privacy, the other was shared experience. Leaving aside for the moment Orwell's treatment of them, let me characterize them generally and place them in a broad context. Incontrovertibly, the value of privacy is at the center of most modern and contemporary defenses of individualism, and the invasion of it is regarded with abhorrence. Privacy is the expression of an ideology in which the individual is the ontological center, the basic reality whose needs and well-being are best realized and most accurately expressed when people are free to define and pursue them for themselves. Individual human beings are private not in the hermetic sense that they enjoy no relationship with others. Individualism is a celebration of private life and private life is typically associated with family, friends, religion, personal relations, possessions, and what has come in recent decades to be called "life-styles," patterns of personal preference, especially in matters of consumption (clothes, food, drink, dwellings, cars, and the like). Privacy originates in a need to shut oneself off from the outside in order to have space for self-definition. Privacy is a decision for a certain form of deprivation: it is to be deprived willingly of the public world.

The value of shared experience, on the other hand, takes the individual toward others, not as a matter of social necessity (as in the division of labor) or simple sociability, but because it is confirmation of a common condition in which we all dwell, which is constantly in jeopardy and which therefore requires that the body politic be continually tended by its "members." Unfortunately, the modern and postmodern sensibility is distinguished as much by its intense resentment of "invasions of privacy" as it is by its lethargy in responding to threats and injuries to the common world.

Privacy, or rather the absence of it, haunts most of Orwell's pages, but its pathos is most poignant when Winston Smith happens upon an unused room hidden above an antique store which, as it turns out, is a trap set by the dreaded Thought Police. Winston and Julia fall into it as they stubbornly insist on treating it as their private hideaway, determined to find some refuge from the omnipresent Big Brother and the state's efforts to penetrate every aspect of their lives, even though they both know at some level that it will be only a matter of time before they are caught, as of course they are. Orwell's point is that totalitarianism cannot permit private space where individuals can do as they please. All space must be "publicized." Private space poses the threat of nonconformity; public space connotes uniformity, abstract and deadly.

The status of shared experience in *Nineteen Eighty-Four* has nothing to do directly with concern over a public world, or even, as we shall see, with nostalgia for a vanished public world before Britain became Airstrip One, a mere province in the empire of Oceania. Instead, shared experience takes its meaning from the desperate plight of the totally atomized and isolated individual in the surveillance state. Shared experience is a value because it testifies to the existence of a common reality and so gives each of us confidence in our minds as well as our senses. Shared experience and perceptions are a rough proof of our sanity, and, at the same time, a justification of our freedom that might otherwise signify nothing more than subjective preference and so be hardly worth the defense of it. As Winston concludes, the Party was logically compelled to claim that "two and two made five" and to deny "the validity of experience" and "the very existence of external reality." As Orwell takes pain to show, the most fragile elements of shared experience are not common sense or the intuitive truths of arithmetic, but some event that we may have witnessed or that we have good reason to believe really did happen. The totalitarian state of *Nineteen Eighty-Four* is fanatically determined that history shall be made to suit the changing needs of state power, and accordingly it organizes a huge bureaucratic industry devoted to rewriting the past.

It is possible to see the reasoning that led Orwell to depict the state of Oceania as compelled to eliminate both privacy and shared experience—totalitarianism's conception of order depends upon central control, and central control is achieved through uniformity, while privacy implies the possibility that diversity and shared experience may posit a world that differs from the official version of reality. But it does not follow that because privacy and shared experience are likely to be at odds with state authority, they are compatible with each other.

Both the furtive liaison of Winston and Julia and Winston's desperate attempts to salvage something of a dimly remembered past reduce ultimately to gestures of helpless defiance that lead nowhere except to Winston's betraying Julia and, with "his soul white as snow," composing his own valedictory: "He had won the victory over himself. He loved Big Brother."

Is there, however, some further meaning to the (literally) grotesque ending of *Nineteen Eighty-Four*, with its tortured bodies and mindless minds, that relates to the two values of privacy and shared experience? I want to suggest that because shared experience is imperfectly realized in Orwell's work, and the connection between it and privacy is left undeveloped, the novel is inadequate, not as an account of the evils of totalitarianism but of the dangers emerging within liberal societies.

The inadequacy develops because Orwell understood shared experience and historical memory individualistically rather than politically. When Winston reads Goldstein's exposé of the nature of the new totalitarianism, his first response is to say that now "he knew better than before that he was not mad." It is revealing that when Winston conducts a frenzied search into old newspapers in the hope of discovering the causes for the reign of Big Brother, it does not take him back into what might be called a "civic past." Throughout the entire novel there is virtually no reference to a past of parliamentary institutions, free political parties, local institutions of self-government, or the ideal of the citizen-participant. The possibility is never suggested that the true betrayal that might threaten nontotalitarian societies would be not if "the earthly paradise" promised by science and technology were snatched away just "when it became realizable" but if those societies chose to vest their identities in the performance of their economies while allowing political life to languish from corporate and bureaucratic centralization and from the steady corruption by commercial television of public perceptions of a public world.

The apolitical quality of Orwell's understanding of shared experience is most powerfully illustrated in a scene in which Winston and Julia, in all of their innocence, return from an exhilarating evening with O'Brien, who gives them Goldstein's testament, *The Theory and Practice of Oligarchical Collectivism*. Scarcely able to contain himself in the thought that now he possesses the key that will unlock all of the mysteries to the horrors around him, Winston assumes that Julia will also want to share the political revelation. He begins to read aloud, but Julia is soon asleep, for she does not need, as Winston does, to have her mind confirm what her body has already told her, that a regime that represses sex will repress all else—which is, again, an appeal to knowledge gained in the context of privacy rather than of shared public experience, however, as in this case, pedantically represented by Goldstein's memoir. It is as though the common and the public keep reaching out to the private, only to find that they are not needed. Even Winston concludes that Goldstein "had not actually told him anything that he did not know; [the pamphlet] had merely systematized the knowledge that he possessed already."

No one of a liberal persuasion, let alone a democrat, would be tempted to denigrate the values of privacy and private space after pondering the phenomenon of totalitarianism. But does that knowledge help toward understanding a different question, one that does not so much concern the evils *in* totalitarianism as the tendencies of liberal capitalism? The question is, What kind of regime might liberal capitalism turn into, not if it were suddenly to adopt methods specific to totalitarianism, but if it were to accentuate tendencies, even virtues, peculiar to itself? There is within liberal capitalism a potential for a regime which, as yet, has no name and no prior embodiment. It could be described as a form of domination without terror, brutality, and thought police. The notion was captured best, although imperfectly, by Alexis de Tocqueville when he envisioned the possibility of "democratic despotism." The name he chose was misleading, for what he meant by democracy in this context was a regime based upon an acquiescent population that had been leveled into uniformity. Above society would be, Tocqueville imagined, "an immense tutelary power" that would govern men in a manner that would be "absolute, minute, regular, provident, and mild." It would be a society run by paternal administration, not by violence. But it would keep the citizens "in perpetual childhood," that is, dependent. This would not be difficult because the democratic age produces "an innumerable multitude of men, all equal and alike, incessantly endeavoring to procure the petty and paltry pleasures with which they glut their lives."[6]

Tocqueville's dark vision was based on exactly the opposite reasoning from Orwell's. Despotism was made possible by the extreme privatization of life, not by the absence of privacy. It thrived because the individual was encouraged to retreat to a private cocoon where he could huddle in the warm intimacy of family and acquaintances, and devote himself to the pursuit of his own interests. The despotism would welcome the cult of privacy because it distracted men: "Private life in democratic times is so busy, so excited, so full of wishes and of work, that hardly any energy or leisure remains to each individual for public life."[7] The denial of public life was a denial not only of shared experience but of a qualitatively different kind of experience. Public life meant venturing outside the family circle to encounter difference and multiplicity, contrasts and strangeness, and to attempt, nonetheless, to arrive at collective decisions. Tocqueville called this venture "freedom." He meant by it the right to participate in a free civic life. Only participation can deliver men from "isolation" and put them "in touch with each other, promote an active sense of fellowship. In a community of free citizens every man is daily reminded of the need of meeting his fellow men, of hearing what they have to say, of exchanging ideas, and coming to an agreement as to the conduct of their common interests."[8]

Tocqueville's argument was essentially an attack upon individualism, that is, upon the doctrine that society should be organized so as to insure the right of the individual to make his own determinations about what he values and what his interests are. Although Tocqueville placed a high value upon individuality, that is, upon the individual's developing his own manner of self-expression, he believed that individualism was merely a more sophisticated version of selfishness. It disposes the individual "to sever himself" from all but his familiar acquaintances and it "saps the virtues of public life."[9] What made individualism so powerful a force in America, he thought, was that it had become allied with the principle of self-interest. Self-interest was, Tocqueville concluded, "an irresistible force." It could not be abolished or overcome; yet if its tendencies toward self-absorption went unchecked, the society would evolve toward despotism. No one would come to care about public things and would feel relief to be rid of the burden, especially if those who offered to assume it were benevolent.

The main hope, as he saw it, was in the qualification that Americans introduced, "the principle of self-interest rightly understood." This was the simple recognition by the individual that it would be in his interest to be virtuous in a civic way. Americans had learned through experience that "an enlightened regard for themselves constantly prompts them to assist one another and inclines them willingly to sacrifice a portion of their time and property to the welfare of the state."[10] Although Tocqueville never claimed that this principle would produce a society of altruists, he did believe that if men became accustomed to participating, made it an integral part of their lives, and insisted on their right of access to a world of public experience, they would gradually come to view it as natural and be prepared to defend it.

In the century and a half since Tocqueville wrote *Democracy in America* the forces making for privatization have increased in power and legitimacy. The most dominant of these is the capitalist economy, which has evolved from an economy of small-scale producers to one dominated by huge corporations and oriented increasingly toward competition for control of the international economy. Its evolution has also extended its requirements and mentality into the whole range of life: education, science, culture, and politics have all come to serve the needs and to live off the bounty of the capitalist economy. For a portion of the population large enough to assure support, it offers a comfortable existence on certain terms. One of the most basic terms involves the depoliticization of life in all domains, not by abolishing politics but by first trivializing its commonality and then claiming that it is represented by the public opinion poll and mass elections dominated by the powers big money can buy. That is how political power is recycled and a mild despotism legitimated.

NOTES

1. The basis for this attack was Orwell's description of the main ideology in Oceania as "Ingsoc," which he admitted was Newspeak for English Socialism. Yet in a well-known letter he denied the charge of being anti-Labour: "My recent novel is *not* intended as an attack on Socialism or on the British Labour Party (of which I am a supporter) but as a show-up of the perversions to which a centralized economy is liable and which have already been partly realized in Communism and Fascism (*The Collected Essays, Journalism and Letters of George Orwell*, ed. Sonia Orwell and Ian Angus, 4 vols. [New York: Harcourt Brace Jovanovich, 1968], 3:502).
2. Philip Rahv as represented in Jeffrey Meyers, ed., *George Orwell: The Critical Heritage* (London: Routledge and Kegan Paul, 1975), p. 270.
3. See the remarks by Daniel Bell in Meyers, ed., *George Orwell*, pp. 264ff. See also Walter Cronkite's introduction to the New American Library edition of *Nineteen Eighty-Four*, p. 2.
4. Joseph A. Schumpeter, *Capitalism, Socialism, and Democracy* (New York: Harper, 1942), pp. 122–23.
5. Marx and Engels had envisioned a society where "the anarchy of social production [would be replaced] by a socially planned regulation of production in accordance with the needs both of society as a whole and of each individual" (Frederick Engels, *Herr Eugen Dühring's Revolution in Science*, trans. E. Burns, Marxist Library [New York: International, n.d.], p. 314).
6. Alexis de Tocqueville, *Democracy in America*, ed. Phillips Bradley, 2 vols. (New York: Knopf, 1945), 2:318.
7. Ibid., p. 293.
8. Alexis de Tocqueville, *The Old Regime and the French Revolution*, trans. Stuart Gilbert (Garden City, N.Y.: Doubleday, 1955), p. xiv.
9. Tocqueville, *Democracy in America*, 2:98.
10. Ibid., p. 122.

Robert Solomon

ANT FARM:
AN ORWELLIAN ALLEGORY

'm not an Orwell scholar, and won't pretend to be. I'm not a political scientist, or a literary critic. I'm a philosopher, which might mean something very different to many of my colleagues, but, to me, it means being an anti-specialist, a writer whose discipline is dilettantism. Philosophers entertain theories and entertain thoughtful people with theories—the more abstract and unusual, perhaps, the better. In a symposium on George Orwell and *Nineteen Eighty-Four*, therefore, being a philosopher puts one at a certain disadvantage.

George Orwell was not at all abstract; indeed his few lapses into abstraction inevitably tended to be paradoxical, not unlike the willfully insidious paradoxes that emerge in *Nineteen Eighty-Four* and *Animal Farm*. He was a curiously heroic, pathetic, remarkably moral human being who sincerely believed that the salvation of the world was to be found only in, as he put it, "individual values," precisely those values—staunch if not heroic—that were so de-spairingly absent from *Nineteen Eighty-Four*. He believed himself to be, para-doxically, a man of principle who was not subservient to principles. Like many Enlightenment thinkers—and that, I believe, is what he was—he dis-dained abstraction and theory. He believed instead in the virtues, moral and intellectual. Class preferences aside, I would compare him most of all to Voltaire.

Orwell had an enormous impact when we read *Animal Farm* and *Nineteen Eighty-Four* during the previous cold war. Like most of my peers, I dreaded the coming of the year 1984 as the prophesied apocalypse; I never could think of that number as a mere literary device ("84" as an inversion of "48"). The current question, Have we made it to, if not yet through, 1984?, gets mixed answers. Some say, with a hint of hidden disappointment, "Yes, we have." Others have said, with a sense of relief, "No—things are just as bad as Orwell predicted they'd be. In fact worse, because we don't know they are so bad."

In between those rather dramatic extremes, of course, there were the dozen unrepeatable because simply tedious responses: "In some ways yes, in some ways no," and "Not us, but look at Russia and Chile," and "Wait until 1994." It is as if the very number—1984—precludes any response other than qualified gloom.

What do I think? I think that Orwell got it wrong, at least as prophecy. Some of it is a question of temperament. At least some of it is the unredeemed pessimism of a dying man, saying goodbye to a world he never did find very hospitable. But I think some of his error is, he would hate to hear, philosophical. I believe that he misunderstood the scope and variability of totalitarianism, much like Hannah Arendt, who was writing about the subject at the same time. And, I think that, more than Arendt, a philosopher (and a woman), his view of the world was too dark, too angry, too resentful, if not downright cranky. 1984 may not be a good year for civil liberties or enlightenment, but it is hardly the overture to the apocalypse.

More philosophically, I have great trouble coming to grips with the admittedly attractive contrast between "individual values" and totalitarianism that permeates so much of his political writing and, of course, defines *Nineteen Eighty-Four*. It is a dichotomy that is too easy—and false. There are no individual values, in that sense. There are only shared values, including the mores, the morals, and the ideology (or ideologies) of a culture. Perhaps—but just perhaps—there are universal human values too. But Orwell, like Voltaire, was too suspicious, too hostile to ideas, as if all ideology were nothing but falsification and subterfuge. The positive role of ideas gets left out, and some other critical ingredients of culture and morality as well. It is worth noting once again that Orwell never felt as if he *belonged* anywhere. His indisputably enlightened moral opinions—and I do not say that sarcastically —share the enigmas of all Enlightenment views—detachment, resentment, and sometimes insidious philosophical perplexity about human nature, its differences and identities—his love of English breakfasts and the impossibility of communication in Burma notwithstanding. It is not surprising that Orwell, like Voltaire before and E. B. White after him, created his most powerful work by casting animals as his ideological spokescreatures and characters.

For all of its horrors, I find the world still more amusing than Orwell did or could. In a symposium on *Nineteen Eighty-Four,* however, I am afraid that the amusement in politics—the human circus—tends to be forgotten. I shall try to correct that here, and so turn to *Animal Farm,* not *Nineteen Eighty-Four,* which is relentlessly unamusing (not that *Animal Farm* has many light lines).

Orwell's concern in *Animal Farm* is not just Russia, of course. However exactly the plot and characters of the book may follow the Russian revolution from 1917 to 1943, the book far transcends that as an allegory and as a morality tale. It is a book about gullibility, manipulation, hypocrisy, and deception. My thesis—if I have one—is that these issues are more intricate than vigilante paranoia makes them seem. Orwell objected when *Time* magazine tried to use *Nineteen Eighty-Four* as cold-war propaganda; we can assume that he would be similarly indignant about the use to which his books have been put in this past year. The threat of totalitarianism is not limited to countries of Communist or "classical" totalitarian persuasion. In fact, one of the questions that has come more and more to disturb me in my philosophical reflections is the inherent dangers in the liberal Enlightenment tradition, and its defenses as well. The political and psychological dimensions of these dangers have been and will be discussed by the other symposium contributors. I would like to toy, in a manner that I hope is befitting to Orwell, with certain philosophical perplexities: the vocation and the isolation of intellectuals in America; the continual Enlightenment blindness to history which in *Nineteen Eighty-Four*, at least, required an elaborate set of deceptions from the top; the obsession with a paradoxical and extremely ill-defined concept of "freedom"; and what Philip Slater has often attacked as the simply ridiculous sense of individual uniqueness that is the heart of one brand of contemporary liberalism. This coexists, strangely comfortable, with the Enlightenment pretense of a universal humanity, and it leaves out, apparently without a sense of loss, a full appreciation of the communal, the social, the cultural, even the emotional (the inescapable truths of greed and pride, for instance). Consequently, but not surprisingly, enlightened thinking often ends up indulging itself in an orgy of self-doubt, entertaining charges of Laschian if not Kohutian "narcissism" and warnings of the impending collapse of civilized society, if, indeed, this has not already happened, as Alasdair MacIntyre has recently written.

In tribute to Orwell, and in part in criticism of him, I too would like to descend the phylogenetic ladder, not to look at the emerging dictatorship of the mammalian proletariat but rather to look at a more amusing subject—us. I admit that my anthropomorphic allegory has little of the charm or the subtlety of *Animal Farm,* and certainly none of the genius or originality. It is, however, in the spirit of Orwell, and it has an equally unsettling if not so gloomy ending. Of course, I too would like to set my tale among the domestic pettables—furry or at least fuzzy characters make any story more palatable from the beginning—but Orwell has exhausted the political role of pigs, horses, and donkeys, even if he meanspiritedly denigrates dogs and cats, who in any case already occupy an enviable position in the attention of the popular reading public. A few rungs farther down the ladder, pettability diminishes but sociability and efficiency increase. What might surprise you, however, is that the amount of philosophizing remains more or less constant throughout the animal kingdom. (Plants, on the other hand, prefer deconstructionist criticism.) With this confluence of biology and philosophy, I bring you, as a tribute to Orwell, *Ant Farm,* an allegory about liberalism, the Enlightenment, freedom and individualism, keeping in mind Orwell's belief that only individual values can protect us against totalitarianism. (My apologies to E. O. Wilson for taking such entomological liberties.)

ANT FARM: AN ORWELLIAN ALLEGORY

Ants are so much like human beings as to be an embarrassment. They farm fungi, raise aphids as livestock, launch armies into war, use chemical sprays to alarm and confuse enemies, capture slaves. . . . They exchange information ceaselessly. They do everything but watch television.

—Lewis Thomas, The Lives of a Cell

I

The revolution at Harvard Farm was ten generations ago. Though no one remembered the details, everyone knew the story. One night, in Professor Wilson's laboratory, an absentminded graduate student had forgotten to fasten the lid on the terrarium. The queen, her escorts, and the better part of the relatively small nest poured out across the shelves, devouring a couple of cockroaches but otherwise meeting little resistance. At the corner of the cabinet the graduate student had come up suddenly on their rear, recaptured a few dozen workers and, in the frustration of defeat, killed a great many others. But the queen and her escorts had already escaped, even if at a considerable cost.

A few weeks later, no one remembered why they had left the terrarium. The names of the murdered workers were forgotten, but it was remembered that there had been a revolution. The ants had won. There had been terrible losses, but now the nest was once again flourishing, in liberty rather than in slavery. Ants might not have much by way of memory, but they have a keen sense of freedom.

Freedom is what life in an anthill is all about. Thousands of ants die for freedom, virtually every day. They all work for and in freedom, and it is the topic of daily conversations, especially among the males, who have nothing else to do. Their role in the nest, in addition to their occasional sexual favors to the queen, is to keep memory of the revolution and its heritage alive. Since ants have minimal memory, the constant reminders of their liberty are essential.

The males of Harvard Farm were the curators of freedom. "There is no freedom without vigilance," they insisted, though they were never quite sure what it was they were to look out for. They all knew that "freedom is fragile and easily lost," the unspoken presumption, of course, being that they all were free. But, nevertheless, they feared for their freedom, and a few unhappy pessimists argued that they had lost it already.

What you have to understand—what you would certainly think that everyone already understands—is that every ant is different from every other ant. Every ant is unique, with her own personality, her own smell, her own abilities, her own needs. The freedom of the hill was precisely the freedom to develop personality, to smell as one likes (that is, as one is), to realize abilities, to satisfy needs, to help oneself, and, at the same time, to serve queen and colony. The most important thing in life for an ant is self-esteem—which means status in the hill. What ants despise most is dreary uniformity and the banal altruism of most other species. Contrary to certain opinions outside of the hill, every ant works, first of all, for herself, and in competition with every other ant. Indeed, how could it be otherwise? And the collective effort of this competitive selfishness—if you want to call it that—is the energy and efficiency you see in every channel of the nest. (It has been suggested that there is "an invisible antenna" in the colony, a wisdom of organization in the whole that is not necessarily found in any individual ant. But ants, at least, are smart enough to know that this is a suggestive metaphor, nothing more.)

II

Every nest is different from every other nest, and not just in the trivial sense that they are in different places, made of and in different materials and so on. Witness the inevitable warfare that even the most casual contact initiates. And the reason is not hard to discern—smell. A simple, basic difference in smells. Every ant colony has a different smell, a difference in pheromones secreted by the queen. As an ant approaches the nest, that smell means the difference between life and death. Every ant knows every other ant in the colony, not by name of course (only males have names) but by smell. It has been suggested by certain liberals, inside and outside the hill, that the uniqueness of antsmells is merely trivial, that all ants are, "deep down," fundamentally the same. That is a piece of nonsense and is considered by all ants to be both insulting and dangerous. Anyone who smells can smell that every ant is unique, even if some smells are clearly distinctive (not to say superior) to others. Of course one can and sometimes must think in terms of anthood in general, but the beginning and the end of anthood is the unique individual ant. Indeed, the very notion of "anthood" has recently been called into question, for instance, by that ant'ropologist Claude-Levi and by the ant philosopher Jean-Paul. There are no "ants," writes Claude-Levi, there are only drivers, reds, carpenters, "bulldogs," leaf cutters, spider eaters, aphid herders, fungi farmers, and the Disney version. "Ants make themselves," writes Jean-Paul; "whatever is true of us as biological organisms en-soi, every ant has her (or his) autonomy as an ant-pour-soi, the dreadful duty of taking responsibility for our instincts and making them our own (*eigentlichkeit*)."

You will notice that these two great thinkers are males, in a colony that is otherwise entirely made up of females. It is true that all productive roles in the colony are female roles. Yet there are, occasionally, and for brief periods of time, males in the hill. They are the oldest and therefore the wisest members of the hill, having arrived with the queen before any of the workers or soldiers were born (obviously, since one or another of those males was also the father of every ant in the hill). The winged males usually die before the anthill is even founded, but when they live, and they are not needed for food, the colony gladly makes room for them.

Inevitably, an easy life surrounded by hard-working females produces no small number of oddballs among the males. For example, there is Jean-Jacques, who had fought with and alienated every male ant in the hill, and though he frequently mingled with the female workers (often having to run from the soldiers at the same time) he found those relationships equally frustrating and on a number of occasions he had injured female workers in his biologically if not ideologically confused amorousness. Jean-Jacques was forgiven—from a distance—only because of his inspiring vision of natural anthood. In fact, when he was away from the hill—walking through the woods usually—he was in absentia the most popular ant in the hive, favored especially, surprisingly, by the queen.

Then there is Orwell, who also spent most of his time with the females, not wooing but working, in fact, doing the hardest work in the hill, digging new channels and hauling cockroach carcasses from one end of the nest to the other. Consequently, he often found himself on the brink of exhaustion and starvation and extremely bitter toward ants generally, whom he often compared, unfavorably, to aphids and other domestic insects. And yet, Orwell too was generally admired, even liked, by the other ants. He could often be heard to say that he felt inferior to every worker, and he despised the other males, among whom he found "not a single rebel, only cowards, spies and betrayers." Accordingly, Orwell's visions for the future of the colony were dreadful, but they were taken very seriously by a large majority of ants. Indeed, if ants had a calendar, they would readily set a date for the Orwellian apocalypse.

Anthistorians have suggested that the very soul of the colony is to be found not in the queen or the workers but in such odd characters as Jean-Jacques and Orwell. Curiously, we thus find that the celebrities (not heroes or heroines) of antculture often turn out to be those ants who are least part of the colony, least intimate with the activities and loyalties that define the colony, farthest in their thinking from the thoughts and ideals that actually define ant nature (however they try to redefine nature to suit themselves). And, most curiously, they are males, in a culture that is defined by females. But the only ants who can or bother to write anthistory are males, not soldiers or workers. Indeed they are usually odd fellows at that, whose similarities and sympathies with Jean-Jacques and Orwell are obvious. And, of course, the articulate oddball is a convenient vehicle for the symbolism (if not the expression) of individualism, which every ant holds dear. But can you imagine a colony filled with ants such as Jean-Jacques and Orwell?

We might also mention, just in passing, two other such celebrities. There is Franz, a particularly pathetic case, who awakens every morning thinking that he has overnight turned into a human being. Then there is Henry David, who disappeared one day to go into Boston, insisting that a prudent ant in the city did not need a colony to support him. But they are the stuff of literature, hardly of note in the hardworking antworld.

I do not want to give the impression that males are useless. Most males, because they have nothing whatever to do, tend to become the brains of the hill, so to speak. (In fact their brains are no larger than anyone else's.) They provide symbols, amusements, plans for the ultimate revision of the colony. Their job is to design the future, no easy task among animals without a sense of time. They see the "big picture"—not only the colony as a whole (which no other ant, including the queen, has a moment to do), but the entire world of ants and nonants, the world defined and controlled by ants—the antworld. (The history and variety of religions among ants is a fascinating topic that we cannot go into here.) But because of their leisure and their larger view, the males have the awesome duty of defining and protecting freedom, since most of the ants, having little time and no memories, would simply forget that they are free, were not the male ants there to remind them. (When there are no males, it is usually necessary to invent them.)

III

The competitive individualism of ants and their constant concern with status often caused problems within the colony, however "classless" ant society might seem to those who have no place in it. The fact that ants have no concept of "class" and no criteria for status only makes the competition more anxious. Ants were running into and all over one another. Self-proclaimed "realists" (that is, cynics) insisted that antlife is a "jungle," not unlike the truly bug-eat-bug world of some spiders. The competition often divided the hill into de facto groups, usually based on nothing more substantial than some minor matter of smell. Josephine, the queen, routinely worried about questions of class and conflict in the hill. (It is worth remembering that almost all of the ants were immediately related, but competition was no less ferocious for that.) She tried, with some absurdity, to present herself as "one of the girls," her enormous size and singular importance to the hill notwithstanding. In news conferences she always insisted on the equality of all ants. (Ants don't need television, as they are telepathic.) With her public Josephine went out of her way to use popular smells and touches. But this emphasis on equality, unfortunately, only seemed to highlight differences in status, even when it did not diminish the efficiency of the hill.

Among the surviving males, status was a special problem. However ludicrous the queen's egalitarianism, the males had to contend with an even greater absurdity: from the definitive point of view of efficiency and productivity, they were utterly useless and totally expendable. They were well fed and much honored, if also ignored, and virtually nothing was expected from them in return. Accordingly, they found it necessary to continually proclaim the utility of their activities. Consequently, the male ants themselves developed a highly refined and rigid code of "standards" for their behavior, which they used (instead of the more obvious facts of their sex and nonproductivity) to distinguish themselves from all other ants in the hill. (There was considerable uneasiness about the status of the queen in this scheme of things.) This led to a certain tension in the males' ideas and their attitudes toward the colony —a keen sense of their own integrity and superiority to the run-of-the-hill ants mixed with a humiliating sense of their lack of utility and removal from the mainstream of ant activities. Orwell's contempt and Jean-Jacques's resentment were symptomatic. They couldn't deny the importance of the workers without rejecting the life of the colony, but they couldn't praise the workers without at the same time being painfully aware of their own shortcomings. So even while praising the hardworking females in the hill, they were disdainfully aware of their deficiencies, according to the strict if abstract standards canonized by the males.

This confusion of attitudes always surfaced in the vicious politics among the males, which, though concerned with great questions, had no effect or influence whatever on the rest of the colony. The much-disputed leader of the males—and probable father of the colony—was Napoleon, an unusually small but virile ant whose vitality was something of a legend among the workers and the soldiers. Napoleon, like Josephine, talked about equality all of the time, but unlike the queen, he wore an imperial air. He spoke of the duties of every ant to the hill, and of the better-off ants to help the worse-off ants.

"Noblesse oblige," he called it, thus infuriating the more consistently egalitarian ants, particularly Jean-Jacques and Orwell.

Jean-Jacques resented Napoleon's imperial posturing because it seemed to him to be a corruption of natural anthood, made possible by the artificiality of anthill society. It was the individual virtues of the ants that counted, not the false manners of the male ants, whose lives centered on pleasing a too-busy queen and—what was utterly impossible but nevertheless their constant effort—impressing each other. Orwell, on the other hand, despised what he called "the class racket," and though his admiration was directed at the worker ants his contempt was aimed at the informal class divisions among the males themselves, so well symbolized by Napoleon (whose ancestry was reputed to be an ancient and particularly powerful ant farm in Hyannis Port). "All ants may be equal," Orwell would sarcastically comment to whoever would listen, "but some ants are more equal than others." This was generally received as wisdom most profound, summarizing in a phrase both the ideal and the paradox of colony-wide equality. Equality is in evidence, it seems, only to the extent of its absence.

IV

It is often thought that ant colonies are the very paradigm of busy, unreflective, unphilosophical activity. Grasshoppers, for example, who are known for their philosophical opinions but not their prudence or hard work, have long promulgated this misunderstanding. This is, of course, not at all the case. The ant way of life is deeply ideological, whether or not most of the ants have ever thought through their ideology and whether or not they have the time or the interest to talk about it. It is an ideology of service, but service in the name of enlightened self-interest, predicated on the indisputable proposition that all ants are both equal and different. They are different in their abilities. Their tastes and needs are different. Their need to be equal is unequal. This indisputable proposition, however, provoked a perennial dispute about power in the colony. Some ants insisted that there was no power in the colony, apart from the powers of each individual ant. Other ants argued that the power in the hill was concentrated in the pincers of a few ants surrounding the queen, though no one knew exactly who they were. More knowledgeable ants thought that both of these opinions were naïve but had no better suggestions themselves.

At the founding of the colony, Queen Josephine had insisted confidently that she knew what "her girls really wanted." Whether or not that was so, the resentment of her maternalism was so great, and not only among the males, that she ceased saying that altogether and, instead, expressed her confidence in the individual judgment and choice of each individual ant. Many ants still suspected Josephine of somehow determining the tastes and needs of the colony, but as every ant seemed to be making her own decisions, this suspicion could not even be articulated, much less confirmed. Every ant had her job, did her job, enjoyed her job, and if it was not true that ants chose their tasks this was, of course, dictated by the necessities of the hill. Free choice was the right of every ant in the realm of religion, art, and private life, and it was one of the pillars of the hill that every ant had the right to speak as she chose, without fear of punishment. But since ant life was defined by one's tasks in the hill, these rights—though all-important—did not make much practical difference. When an ant is defined wholly in terms of her skills and contributions to the efficiency of the colony, the question of rights, and of power, would rarely arise, except in the conversations of the males.

Part of the problem, of course, was the dual optics of antlife. The individual was everything, but the life of every ant was defined and made possible by the colony. An ant alone, it was sometimes said, is not anything at all, a pitiable creature without a place, without an identity, without a meaning for her miserable existence. On the other hand, it was obvious that the colony itself, and anthood in general, were abstractions and nothing whatever without the multitude of individual ants that populated them. What made this all the more confusing was the logical fact that the colony possessed features not attributable to any individual ant or group of ants. Consider, for example, the much-discussed "roachleg problem": the simple transporting of a roachleg across the hill: no ant would carry it more than an inch or two, and no ant had any idea—usually—where the leg was coming from or where it was going. (The communal fabrication of rumors about such matters was one of the most enjoyable aspects of antwork.) And yet, the transported load clearly had a destination that was never in question, whether or not it was known by any individual ant. Thus it had sometimes been suggested that the truth is the whole, the activities of the colony and not the individual activities of the ants. But this was almost always dismissed as "totalitarianism." Nothing could be more of a threat to freedom than planning from the top, even the wisest, most benign and uncorrupted planning. Even if individualism failed to explain the rationality of life in the hill, it was preferable to the horrors of totalitarianism. (Ants are very wary of slippery slopes.)

The other side of this argument, however, was best expressed in the morbid view, falsely attributed to Jean-Jacques and Orwell, that ants are irrational and ant life essentially meaningless. This theory preserved the integrity of individualism, but at a terrible—if still acceptable—cost. Except when they are very busy, which luckily is virtually every minute of the day, ants are prone to depression and despair, a matter which some of the males attributed to the degrading nature of most antwork. Whether or not it was planned (and this was a subject of considerable debate) the work of the hill was such that every ant had her inescapable role and place. No one was quite clear whether this was an infringement on freedom, but virtually all of the workers simply accepted it as necessity, indeed, defined what they called "the invertebrate condition" in terms of it. (A popular tale told of a celebrity named Sisyphant, a worker who had spent every day of her life pushing a pebble up a mole hill, only to have it always roll back down again.)

The seemingly inescapable system of things to do was also explained by naturally suspicious ants by reference to an unnamed coterie of powerful ants surrounding the queen. Those who had more faith in anthood proclaimed the system of necessities to be nothing other than the expression of all the collective antwills, guided, as we mentioned before, by "invisible antennae" for the good of all ants. But there was another hypothesis, which dated (as far as anyone knew) back to the earlier incarnation of the colony in Professor Wilson's laboratory. This outrageous hypothesis suggested that the behavior of each individual ant—and consequently the behavior of the colony as a whole—was determined (or at least 78 percent determined) by instincts and "hard-wired" connections in the ants' brains, which in turn were wholly determined by genetics. This would explain the integration of behavior, of course, but the view, popularized as "socioentomology," had one fatal flaw: it left no room—or at any rate too little room (22 percent)—for free will. It was a fact that ants made their own choices. It was a fact that ant society was the result of generations of experimentation and antwisdom. And so the socioentomological hypothesis was treated with utter contempt by virtually every ant. If it could be applied at all, it was suggested by a few sympathetic ants, the socioentomological hypothesis might be appropriate to some of the larger social vertebrates, particularly to those whose large brains and mechanized lives suggested an extraordinary dependence on calculating ability and other complex computerlike functions.

V

As an allegory, the story of Ant Farm lacks several critical ingredients. There is no history, apart from the naked fact of an ancient revolution. And there are no heroes, since, in an important philosophical sense, nothing ever happens. Of course, the ants go on with their work, the queen continues to lay eggs by the hundreds, the males go on arguing. Almost daily, of course, the hill is invaded by wasps and damaged by dogs. Thousands of workers are born and die; new sources of food are discovered and trails are secreted where no ant had ever stepped before. A recent war with the red ants claimed some twelve thousand soldiers, but it was a romantic human observer, no ant, who rhapsodically proclaimed, "For numbers and carnage it was an Austerlitz or a Dresden. Concord fight! . . . I have no doubt that it was a principle they fought for, as much as our ancestors, and not to avoid a three-penny tax on their tea." That human fellow was right, as a matter of fact, about the battle being for principle (more on that in a moment). But he was wrong about its historical importance, for ants have no history. And when the same casual observer declared that "the results of this battle will be as important and memorable to those whom it concerns as those of Bunker Hill, at least," he was clearly anthro- (not ant'ro-) pomorphizing. Ants don't have histories, and so they don't have heroics or heroism.

Ants may not have heroes, but they do have, as we have seen, celebrities—Jean-Jacques and Orwell, for instance, though no one really takes them seriously. This is extremely important to ant life, for where heroes might have some claim to superiority, celebrities do not. Indeed, celebrities are notoriously at the mercy of the most whimsical whims of the most ordinary ants, constant reminders that no ant is really superior to any other ant. (The queen, it is important to note, is never counted as a celebrity.) Most of the current celebrities are male, most of them admired for the sheer sensuality of their bloated abdomens. Only a few, like Jean-Jacques and Orwell, are famed for their ideas, though most ants talk on about their odd personalities. It is one of the peculiarities of antlife that fame and fortune are most often granted to those who contribute *least* to the needs of society. Otherwise, after all, they would not be so readily replaceable.

The emphasis on celebrity should show, once and for all, that ants are not mere utilitarians, concerned with food supplies, colony security, productivity and surplus value and the expansion of their domain. This would be an empty life indeed, and no ant could possibly be satisfied with it. Accordingly, the celebrity system is a vital concern, for it enriches the life of every ant—vicariously, of course—while at the same time keeping everything exactly the same. (Their lack of historical sense notwithstanding, ants tend to be extremely conservative by nature.) One might argue with some persuasiveness that ants live to work and prosper—and to be entertained. (It has even been suggested—most inappropriately—that the queen is too dull for her central place in the hill; accordingly she surrounds herself with antclowns whose sole function is to keep the politics of the colony entertaining.)

VI

It would seem that there are only the brute exigencies of the present moment, and distractions from them. This conclusion, however, is not quite right. In fact, it is entirely mistaken. It is true that ants don't have a sense of historical time; but therefore their sense of the eternal—the timeless—is all the more keen. Ants don't fight for history or tradition (at least, not knowingly) but they do fight for eternal principles. Indeed, if you were to ask any ant—from the soldier whose sole job it is to use her head to plug up an opening to Napoleon, who supposedly coordinates the battle plan of the colony from his cell deep in the hill—she (or he) could not imagine anything else worth fighting for. "For queen and colony." (It has been suggested that the principle of patriotism should be stated, "My colony, right or wrong," but the very idea that one's colony might be wrong is—we should say—deeply unintelligible.)

Antethics is not an ethics of utility, nor even of selfishness, the self-interestedness of ants notwithstanding. Antethics is an ethics of principle. However cynical ants may be about politics, however foolish they may seem in their choice of entertainments and celebrities, one must never underestimate the ultimate importance of antmorality. Ants may not have history, but they do have their eternal principles. "For queen and colony," for example (since there is no conceivable time before, or after, the life of the queen). Some ant principles are extremely general, such as "all ants are equal," and considerable effort is required by the males to state the seemingly endless qualifications, presuppositions and exceptions that such a principle requires. Others are adjustable to the times, such as "Six legs good, eight legs evil," which once was the reigning principle in the days of the spider wars. (We might note that a more recent battle with the centipedes caused considerable confusion, as not even the numbers-minded defense minister, Caspar, had been able to make up a number sufficiently high.)

The essential role of principles in antlife is sometimes misunderstood because, in the hard work of daily life, little time can be spent examining or explaining principles as such, which are usually reduced to simple slogans that every ant is expected to master. Even the brightest ant soon gets perplexed trying to unravel the meaning of "All ants are equal," for example, but not even the dumbest would ever make the mistake of saying that some ants are better than others. So too every ant could be expected to insist that no ant kills another ant without reason, even though in practice this was rather a limited prohibition since the smell of an ant was always a good enough reason to kill her.

Termites and other utilitarian insects do not understand this profound sense of morality shared by all ants. They suggest that such principles are contrary to the ethic of efficiency, but they do not understand that there are values which, to an ant, are more important than mere efficiency. They point out that obedience to moral principles may be contrary to the self-interest that motivates every ant, but any ant can tell you that the interests of the colony and the interests of every ant are one and the same (though no one has ever succeeded in actually proving this). In fact, since every ant desires the well-being of the colony above all else, self-interest and ethics do indeed turn out to be the same. But let us quickly emphasize that this does not mean that ants are ethical "by instinct" or without proper choice in the matter. Ants are free and autonomous creatures who choose as they will as well as choose as they ought to. To insist that ants are "naturally" ethical would be to rob ants of their all-important sense of self-respect and pride.

It seems as if principles have always been the heart of anthood. Indeed, being an ant was even *defined* as acting on principle—working because one believed in the hill, eating because one knew that it was good to eat, cooperating with the other ants in the colony and following the rules because one always knew, according to the great philosopher ant Immanuel, that one should always "act in such a way that the maxim of one's act could be generalized as a universal law for all ants, indeed, for all rational creatures" (presumably that last phrase was meant to include the "lower" insects, if indeed any were rational). If it was pointed out to Immanuel that most ants never thought of such principles, he had simply pointed out that *implicitly* they did so. When it was argued that most ants simply followed a natural, instinctual pattern of behavior, Immanuel angrily retorted that rational anthood and natural inclination were quite distinct, and though instinct might be quite adequate—even necessary—to explain the behavior of less complicated creatures, one had as a matter of rational necessity to assume that every ant was free to reason and rationalize her behavior according to principles. No one in the hill understood exactly what this was supposed to mean, although the queen had evidently considered it very carefully. But the influence of Immanuel in the hill was so great that even those ants who never heard his name believed in the slogan that he had defended: "A good ant is an ant that acts on principle."

VII

The Immanuelian emphasis on principles was intimately tied to the overall emphasis on freedom in the colony and elegantly resolved the paradox of necessity and individual freedom that had plagued some of the more thoughtful ants. It was generally understood and accepted that the safety and well-being of the hill required that every ant adhere rather closely to her (and his) established duties, and that minor transgressions of the natural order of the hill must be punished severely, usually with death and dismemberment. But these restrictions were no limitation at all on individual freedom, which, after all, was not a matter of license and permissiveness but rather of free will, that is, the ability to decide to do one's duties in the colony as a rational creature. Very few of the ants understood this—or had thought about it at all—but they all agreed that they did indeed carry out their duties as an act of their own free will and, therefore, were free. Of course, this was only rarely a topic of actual conversation, and then usually among the males. Most of the time, the ants simply enjoyed their freedom, and on collective impulse paraded in long lines along the length of an old log in joyful celebration.

It was this happy harmony of efficiency and freedom, ironically, that formed the foundation of the current crisis in the colony. Ants have two over-whelming fears. They live in fear that they will lose their comfortable life-style, and they work themselves to death to make sure that this does not happen. And they fear that they will lose their freedom. No ant can imagine anything worse than an unfree life—a life in which no one had a choice about what to do, a life in which one could not go where one wanted, wear what one wanted to wear (if, that is, one wanted to wear anything), say what one wanted to say. As there was no authority in the hill who threatened such unfreedom, one might think that the ants would be quite content and assured. But the very opposite was the case. Deprived of evident threats to their freedom, they felt compelled to invent them. Indeed, the most radical of the male ants even went so far as to suggest that the affluence and efficiency of the colony—on which ant freedom was based—was itself the source of an insidious unfreedom, an argument which by its very logic turned the ants against themselves. The mood in the hill turned to gloom. Accordingly, Orwell became enormously popular, and Jean-Jacques came to be viewed as an unrealistic optimist by comparison.

Self-deprecation became the ideology of the day. An ant sociologist accused the hill of becoming a "colony of aphids" and a popular writer chastized a whole generation of workers as the "me-decade." The queen herself made a comment about the colony-wide "malaise," and "sickness" became the ruling metaphor for self-perception. An ant historian rumbled the conscience of the hill again with an accusation of "ant narcissism," which just happened to coincide with an unprecedented population boom in which, for the first time, there were more ants than necessary jobs. Thousands of ants saw themselves and their colony as "narcissistic"—though only an ant or two knew what this meant or what was wrong with it. Most recently, a rebellious ant named Alasdair set most of his fellow ants in a tizzy when he declared that civilization had already broken down long ago—indeed, long before the queen and her escorts had even arrived at Harvard Farm. He reminded the ants of their unresolvable disputes; he pointed to the simple-minded phrase making that constituted the supposedly "principled" life of the workers; he lambasted the isolated self-importance of the male ants, who supposed that they directed life in the colony when in fact they supplied at most an otherwise unheard commentary which they argued amongst themselves. Alasdair spoke rhapsodically of the good old days, when every ant knew her place and her virtues, when it was not pretended that every ant had her own unique personality and needs and tastes, when a single spirit of unity held the colony together through even the worst of times. The shame of dubious motives became replaced by the embarrassment of inner emptiness—and the sense of impending doom.

Such talk saddened many ants, while infuriating a few. But no one remembered those good old days, and so life and work went on as usual. Nevertheless, even the most productive ants felt as if they were missing something, as if the truth of life—and freedom—had sneaked by them.

VIII

Harvard Farm still exists, though it has recently moved to the garden behind Kresge Hall of the Business School. The males died, but other males did and would always take up their places and their ideas. Intellectual life too goes on as usual, although the philosophy of the hill now tends to speak more in terms of costs and benefits instead of the older, more idealistic terms of Immanuelian ethics. Cynicism has replaced despair, though it is difficult to tell the difference. *Freedom* is a word that is used more than ever, though its meaning has become increasingly obscure and it has been suggested by the ant songster Kris that it is just another name for "nothing left to lose." Yet even the most cynical ants remain rightly convinced that talking about freedom, no matter how confused, remains the most essential condition for having freedom.

The colony prospers, but it must be said that the ants are not happy. Cyril Connolly caught their plight with an ironic sympathy: "Why do ants alone have parasites whose intoxicating moistures they drink and for whom they will sacrifice even their young? Because as they are the most socialized of insects, so their lives are the most intolerable."

Joseph Weizenbaum

THE COMPUTER
IN THE ORWELLIAN YEAR

▌▌read Orwell's *Nineteen Eighty-Four* soon after it arrived in America in the late forties. My exposure to it coincided roughly with my first exposure to computers. I don't remember whether I noticed it then, but on rereading *Nineteen Eighty-Four* within the last year or so, after spending most of my professional life fiddling in one way or another with computers, I discovered that, although Orwell invented the ball-point pen in his novel and although Winston Smith's work in the Ministry of Truth could really not be accomplished without the computers we in 1984 actually find all around us, Orwell failed to mention the computer. The computer existed while Orwell was writing; indeed, it was further developed than television technology. And he made much use of that.

Why Orwell failed to include computer systems in the world he imagined could exist in 1984 is a question I gladly leave to those literary scholars who make their living answering such questions—without fearing, by the way, that their explanations will be falsified. But I do want to defend the thesis that the computer has become *the* technical instrument which, more than any other single device or technology, is symbolic of, is to some extent a contributing cause of, and is an index of the extent to which our world (in America) has been transformed into Orwell's world of *Nineteen Eighty-Four* (a world which, I would say, is insane).

I don't have to argue here that *Nineteen Eighty-Four* is, among other things, an essay on language. Somewhere Orwell said that to change the universe it is sufficient that we speak differently about it. The computer has changed the English language—perhaps I ought to restrict myself to America, however— and with that has changed the world we inhabit.

Let me illustrate this by attending to the word *problem*. First I suggest we think about an experiment we might carry on in our imaginations. Suppose we transcribe the American novels written between, say, 1920 and 1940 on computer-readable magnetic tape A, and the American novels written between

130

1960 and 1980 on tape B. A would then contain novels by Hemingway, Faulkner, J. T. Farrell, Dos Passos, and many other authors. B would contain works of Bellow, Mailer, Asimov, Clarke, and so on. Now we enter these tapes into computers and ask them to count for both bodies of text how many times the word *problem* occurs and how many times it occurs in the neighborhood of the word *solution* or some synonym of it. We don't really have to make the experiment; the answer is obvious to any American my age or older. The word *problem* occurs quite rarely in the American novel of the period between the world wars, while it occurs very frequently—particularly in the near neighborhood of the word *solution*—in the American literature of the 1960s and '70s.

What can we infer from that, and what does it have to do with computers? The computer introduced the concept of "problem solving" *massively*—into modern consciousness—not that it wasn't present before, say, 1950. Of course it was. But the computer was hailed as the great problem solver, the machine to which one gave one's problem, an algorithm for solving problems and which, once the start-button was pushed, produced a solution to one's problem. Just as the question, If we can put a man on the moon, why can't we do *X*?, where *X* might refer to solving the problem of poverty or the problem of racial or world peace, just as that question became a cliche in the sixties, so a form of speech developed—and by some form of Gresham's law, became dominant—in which it was no longer possible to say, for example, "I feel dizzy"; in which one would have to say (if one felt dizzy) "I have a problem with my space perception," or some such thing. People with reputations as great problem solvers were imported into the American government: the likes of Robert McNamara, McGeorge Bundy, Walt Rostow, and so on. When they saw that the struggle in Viet Nam was developing against the interests of the United States (as the president and the people with whom he surrounded himself determined those interests) they saw that the United States *had a problem* with the North Vietnamese (among others) and that proven *problem-solving methods* had to be invoked. Without going into details here, let me just say that this view of the clash of conflicting interests in Southeast Asia, created an abstract world, very like the world of a computer model or simulation, in which it became quite natural to talk of scenarios, scripts, and so on; in which, in other words, a totally disembodied problem set could naturally be attacked by equally disembodied algorithms (strategies), with equally disembodied measures of success, such as the infamous body count that was broadcast to all America daily much as the nearly equally abstract Dow Jones stock index is broadcast these days. A logic was induced in which the statement "We had to destroy the village in order to save it" seemed perfectly sensible, not at all absurd. I remember too that at the time of the Watts riots in California, Gordon Brown, then dean of engineering at MIT, asked angrily, "Why didn't they tell *us* [at MIT] that they had problems out there? With our technology, we could have solved them!" In the society generally, people talk of "giving their problem to the computer." Computer talk has invaded, I would say corrupted, the English language in many other ways as well: people speak of themselves as being programmed, the human brain is, to quote the artificial intelligence pioneer Marvin Minsky of MIT, a "meat machine," that is, a computer in organic form.

To speak of it differently is to change the universe! The modern universe then consists of people whose brains are fundamentally computers, whose behavior one modifies—as in schools—by programming them, whose every discomfort and misadventure is a *problem* that can be solved by suitable applications of logical rules. From this perspective it makes sense to ask what were Christ's problems with authority! I myself wrote a computer program many years ago which some psychiatrists, who were already speaking of their patients' and their own thoughts as being "rule governed," hailed as the dawn of automatic psychiatry. This January a paper in the professional psychiatric literature carried a long article reviewing the growth of this idea and forecasting that soon a psychiatry machine could "treat" over a thousand patients an hour! A program to simulate a priest in the confessional was written long ago. Machines already administer the physical functions of the dying. How soon will they enforce "correct" thoughts on the dying and, in a remarkable triumph of computer technology, begin to administer the last rites (of whatever faith the computer judges the—what shall I say?—"client" to be) at the precisely computed optimum microsecond, that is, I suppose, just before the client's soul leaves the body. I was going to use the phrase "real time" here. It reminds me of some of the many new terms the computer and other forms of high technology have imported into our vocabulary: real time, "live" means the recording of real people doing real things in real time. But then there are variations such as "live on tape" and "live on stage" (as opposed to "simulated on stage" I suppose). We have people on television presented "live" mouthing songs being played on tape machines in the background. The voices of famous singers on recordings are "improved" by computational and other electronic means: there may not be a Pavarotti! (I think he exists—but has any audience heard his voice not mediated by electronics?)

I perceive George Orwell—in much of his writing, not just *Nineteen Eighty-Four* and *Animal Farm*—as searching for moral meaning in a patently unjust world. He was a story teller and, as such, meant his stories to be understood. What, under the impact of computers, has become of the notion of understanding? What does it mean, say to graduate students in that branch of computer science known as artificial intelligence (AI, for short) to understand a story? How does one test a computer program designed to understand, say, children's stories? It is said to understand if it can answer questions about the story—and not merely about what was explicitly said in the story, but also (and more important) what is implied to have happened. If, for example, a story says that a little girl ate ravenously until she could eat no more, a computer should be able to know that the girl was hungry before she ate and not hungry for a while after she ate. This requires that a computer that is to understand stories would have to have access to a large amount of world knowledge. Computers can in fact be given much such knowledge in many different domains. They can then answer quite tricky questions about stories they've been fed—even newspaper stories. Under that definition, understanding becomes being able to say what happened. Understanding *King Lear*—or, for that matter, *Animal Farm*—means being able to list all events in those stories, being able to compare a college outline of them with the help of which college tests such as the SAT can be passed. From this perspective it becomes absurd to think one can understand *Lear* in different ways as one gets older. From this perspective a *Reader's Digest* condensation of *War and Peace* is just as good as, even better than, the original. It is, after all, shorter.

Artificial intelligence is another index of the insanity of our world. This is true in two respects, both of which would, I think, have caught Orwell's attention had he lived longer. First, there is the absurd doctrine that essentially no difference exists between human beings and machines, that in principle the computer can realize or be made to embody every aspect of the human mind. That absurdity is the basis of entire graduate education in such elite universities as Stanford, Carnegie-Mellon, and MIT. Entire faculties believe this nonsense and its corollary, that every aspect of human experience is representable in some formal notation—say bit strings or diaries of letters of the ordinary alphabet. No wonder then that graduates of such an education—I am tempted to say victims—can solemnly assert that "the brain is merely a meat machine" (notice the *merely* and, more important, the word *meat* where ordinary people might have expected *flesh*!—I leave it to the reader to think about what this signifies.) No wonder that they can conceive of machines that serve as psychiatrists or as clergy and of machines that can compose poetry. The point is that meaning and understanding have been reduced to purely syntactic (grammatical) concepts. In a universe spoken about in this language there can indeed be no differences between human beings and machines.

The second matter that would have caught Orwell's attention is the use of high technology, particularly of the computer, in warfare. Goldstein, the Trotsky figure in *Nineteen Eighty-Four,* explains that there really isn't any war among the superpowers. It is simply in the interests of the three major powers to maintain a permanent *state* of war. Only in such a state can the three governments maintain their holds on their respective populations. I suggest it isn't very different here at home and—I dare say—in the Soviet Union. *We* are in a permanent war economy. Our government justifies the spending of our treasure in terms of national security, that is, defense against the alleged fountain of all evil, the Soviet Union. When our President uses the word *enemy* we have no doubt who he means. Under wartime conditions, it seems right that military considerations should determine limits on what we can spend on social programs such as education and health and welfare, and that military "requirements" should shape the very definition of scientific progress, as indeed they do in the United States.

The computer was born in warfare, that is, to serve attempts to make mass killing more effective at less cost, and it, like virtually every other high technology, has been in the service of death ever since. Few modern weapons, from military aircraft to cruise missiles to aircraft carriers, can be imagined without computers, let alone could "progress" on such weapons be imagined.

Recently the military leadership (I prefer to speak of "the military" as opposed to "the Department of Defense"—everyone should try to substitute the word *military* wherever the word *defense* is now used, as in "military budget," for example) announced it would spend six hundred million dollars in the next five years on research on artificially intelligent computer systems that can navigate a tank, for example, and automatically target and operate its ordnance, guided only by its "built-in" intelligence. Another such system is to act as a copilot and assistant to a fighter pilot in combat. It is to receive its commands in spoken form. Finally, a computer system that can manage sea battles involving aircraft carriers, airplanes, submarines, and the like, is to be constructed under this program. An enormous amount of military money is flowing into the research centers of the United States, particularly into the few laboratories (such MIT's Artificial Intelligence laboratory) that have the technical competence (and the requisite moral attitude) to carry out such research. I ask you to consider what effect the influx of so much military money will have on the scientific experience and education of student researchers, that is, graduate students, as well as on young professors.

Computers are increasingly looked to, in almost every sector of life in America, to keep track of things. I mean school grades, the flow of money among banks, inventories of every conceivable kind, airplanes in the sky, the migration of people—especially the movements of people of interest to the police—and so on and on. A subtle side effect of this pervasive phenomenon is that gradually the only things that count (in *any* sense) are those things that can *be* counted, quantified, put in machine-readable form. In the end, the artificial intelligencia will win: people will have been reduced to machines—

as Winston Smith was reduced to loving Big Brother—and there will be only one understanding of *King Lear.*

Perhaps the most telling computer invasion of our thought and language is the introduction of the term *computer literacy* and its almost hysterical adoption by school professionals and parents of school children—this in a time in which ordinary literacy can no longer be routinely expected from the millions of young people our schools are pouring out in what one government study called "a rising tide of mediocrity." Clearly, masses of Americans have come to believe that the ability to communicate with a computer is more valuable than is the ability to read and write even only a few paragraphs in one's everyday language, to make oneself understood to fellow human beings. Indeed, Professor Feigenbaum of Stanford University hails the advent of computer networks and of electronic mail as a liberation from the "trauma" of face-to-face communication! In reality, computer illiteracy is like "tired blood," a disorder invented after its cure was put on the market.

The March 12, 1984, issue of *Time* magazine reported on the "sales campaign that computer manufacturers have been waging at educational institutions": "Behind the company promotions is some simple arithmetic. According to Market Data Retrieval, a Connecticut research firm, the average grade school in the U.S. now owns 3.6 computers, while the average high school has ten. But those figures are likely to double annually for the next several years. . . . More is at stake than merely a place in the schoolroom. By installing their computers in classes or on campus, the manufacturers hope to ensure after-school success. 'The education market is not all that profitable, but it is highly strategic,' says Clive Smith, an analyst at Boston's Yankee Group, a market research organization. 'School use turns out to be absolutely key to establishing brand loyalty.' . . . Students working on Apple, Commodore, or Radio Shack computers in school often lobby parents to get the same brand at home" (p. 62). A most remarkable phenomenon, by the way, is the enthusiasm with which educators—who may be expected to know better and even to regard themselves as guardians of children's interests—have embraced this development.

Finally, I anticipate the question, Isn't there anything positive and good to say about the computer? In response I remind my readers that the title of this volume is *Reflections on America, 1984.* The computer, like so many other things one might discuss, is a mirror in which certain aspects and qualities of contemporary America are reflected. It isn't my purpose to say anything good or bad about the mirror. I am talking about what it reflects.

Ivar Berg

DEREGULATING THE ECONOMY AND REFORMING WORKERS: THE ECLIPSE OF INDUSTRIAL DEMOCRACY

No subject among the many contemplated by those who have pondered over the nature of social relationships has been accorded more attention than the matter of social control. The nature of social controls and their correlates, among members of groups, associations, communities, and states, have been among the explicit or implicit concerns of philosophers, social scientists, novelists, biographers, historians, legal scholars, playwrights, and even painters. The fact that the general subject has been examined by so many creative minds does not, however, mean that we have anything like a satisfactory paradigm for the multitudinous pieces in a voluminous literature.

It would, of course, be a tall order to develop an intellectual model that would help us synthesize the ideas about controls that may be found in the Mayflower Compact, the Declaration of Independence, the Federalist Papers, the Constitution, John C. Calhoun's speeches in the House and Senate and perhaps a dozen landmark Supreme Court decisions, to take just a few widely celebrated native statements about control in our own society.

It would be an even taller order to incorporate such statements about controls in social systems as have been made by de Tocqueville and by his forebears during the French and English Enlightenments; by such self-conscious theorists as Adam Smith, Wilfredo Pareto, Sigmund Freud (especially in *Civilization and Its Discontents*), Roberto Micheles, Emile Durkheim, Friedrich Nietzche, and Raymond Aron; such often implicit but lucid statements on the subject as those in novels by Tolstoy, Dostoyevsky, Sinclair Lewis, and John Steinbeck; in Elizabethan plays; in early films by Fritz Lange and Serge Eisenstein; in reportage like that by Edgar Snow (about China) and William L. Shirer (on Germany); and, finally, in a series of paintings, about the trial of Sacco and Vanzetti, for example, by Ben Shahn.

It would be desirable to have such a paradigm; the terms of a well-constructed one would help us to clarify and join the issues in endless debates conducted about the differential legitimacies, especially, of controls pertaining to the rights, privileges, and immunities that apply to natural in contrast with those applying to "corporate" persons in a society in which corporate persons have come to figure so prominently. Such a paradigm would also help us to hypothesize, a bit more confidently than we now can, the consequences to a society's members of adjustments in one or another of many mechanisms of social control that are urged upon us by partisan groups.[1]

In the absence of a satisfactory paradigm for the analysis of a multivariate problem we often turn to the efforts of those who have at least tried to sort out the themes relating to a critically important topic and to classify them in suggestive ways. In the next section I outline one such effort, by a sociologist, and in subsequent sections I make some observations about preferences among Americans about social controls suggested by his taxonomic exercise.

SOCIAL CONTROL: FRAGMENTS OF A SCHEMA

Fortunately, though our theoretical claims must continue to be staked out with very considerable modesty, sociologists have been very productive in the derivations of "ideal types." One such typology is especially helpful not only because of what its architect more or less succeeds in doing but because the limitations inhering in the typology and in the applications thereof are also instructive. Thus, the late Alvin Gouldner has come closest to reducing the literature on social control to manageable proportions.[2]

Gouldner's objective was to make a contribution to what became a seminal collection of papers assaying the state of the sociological art in the late 1950s, a contribution in which he sought to identify and discuss what he argued were the most fundamental differences in scientific studies of organization; it is one of the strengths but also an instructive weakness in the piece that he exceeded his editors' mandate by addressing not just controls in organizations but controls in their parent societies as well.[3]

The strands he drew, two of them, are more than evident in the literature on social control; indeed they describe quite adequately two more or less organized analytical schools whose foundations were laid down by three social philosophers whose names I deliberately omitted from the aforementioned allusions to "the literature": Henri St. Simon, "the last of the gentlemen and the first of the socialists"; his sometime student and collaborator, August Comte, "the father of modern sociology"; and Max Weber, the lawyer, economic historian, and philosopher of science par excellence, for whom legitimacy and authority were major subjects of intensive study.

Gouldner first traced a long line of studies and theoretical statements deriving from St. Simon's convictions about the superiority of social orders organized around scientific-rationalistic principles.

Among those in what Gouldner terms the "rational systems" school are the legions—economists, administrative science types, and social engineers, for example—bent on discovering efficient new ways of bending means to ends. Adam Smith's pin factory, F. W. Taylor's "scientific management" movement, early political scientists' urgings about city-manager forms of municipal government, the Hoover Commission Report on Government Reorganization, modern-day "operations researchers" and the new "management science" fraternities are among many subdivisions of a school that owes a great deal to the tradition first staked out in some detail by St. Simon.

The major alternative approach, Gouldner suggests, is a "natural systems" school with its own legions. This approach was originally developed by Harvard Business School investigators who endowed us with the celebrated studies of the Western Electric Company's Hawthorne works, an approach we have come to know as the human relations tradition. In recent years we have witnessed updated versions of the work by Elton Mayo, Fritz Roethlisberger, and their students in the 1930s; by a corps of investigators who have added sociotechnical systems, organizational development (OD), and the work reform–participative management perspectives to the earlier one by consultants on "union avoidance"; by social scientists manqué (especially among business-school professors); and by a few who, somewhat more ingenuously, sincerely hope and work for more humane and "self-actualizing" organizations. Gouldner traces these natural systems ideas to the early nineteenth century, to August Comte's enthusiastic elegies to voluntarism in social relations and to "spontaneous, emergent social forms," and, closely related thereto, to Comte's misapprehensions about St. Simon's endorsements of expertly planned, rational social systems.

Weber's followers, meanwhile, have recognized the need for syntheses of these two sets of conceptions of order and control, with their very different emphases on the virtues, variously, of planning and spontaneity in social systems. They have also commented on the degree to which Weber himself nearly linked the two bodies of thought in his widely celebrated discussions of the ideal typical bases for the legitimation of authority, legal-rational structures, charismatic appeal, and tradition. Weber noted, furthermore, that there clearly are admixtures among these ideal types in "real" social systems. As Gouldner suggested, Weber also made many references to phenomena in social systems, pertaining especially to members' loyalties, that are closely akin to what today's natural systems writers call "informal organizations," and that Weber might indeed have incorporated his recognitions of these unplanned arrangements in planned organizations in his evolving theoretical apparatus, had he lived longer.

Space does not permit a detailed treatment of Gouldner's explications of these two basic schools of thought; it must suffice to state that adherents to the first school's perspectives are very much taken with the prospects for organizing social relationships, given agreed-upon ends, in accord with scientific principles, empirical investigations, and experimentation. The idea, as proponents of rational planning view things, is to develop ever more refined divisions of labor, to reduce the play of whim and the margins for the members of social systems to exercise preferences and to make choices. These rational systems students stress the needs for predictability in social exchanges, and for the applications by leaders of techniques that reduce exploitable ambiguities in social systems, if economic efficiencies are to be realized therein.

Proponents of the natural system school, almost in reverse, emphasize the advantages, to both the leaders and the members of complex social systems, of ad hoc structures that inevitably emerge as the actors therein accommodate either to inadequately or to excessively ordered relationships often found in legal-rational structures. The members of organizations not less than citizens generally thus inventively bend rules and procedures in order to adjust or fine-tune them as they seek to gain psychological as well as economic benefits from their participation and to add their initiatives to the initiatives of those who have designed and planned the structures and procedures in which the organizations members or citizens are obliged to operate.[4] In their most familiar forms these efforts are undertaken when we "fight city hall," "beat the system," and otherwise "finesse," "evade," and so on.

Knowledgeable readers will recognize Gouldner's key distinction as akin to that between *gesellschaft* and *gemeinschaft,* an illuminating two-fold typology that refers to many of the basic differences highlighted by students who have tried to distinguish economically from non–economically driven social relationships. Adherents of both of Gouldner's schools are well equipped with empirical evidence of the correlates—productivity, satisfaction among workers, and conformity, especially—of emphasis on one or the other of the natural and rational structures to be found in social systems.

Not many of either school's members, however, have tried very hard to define the conditions under which natural and rational admixtures occur. Nor has much effort been expended to discover the limits on the returns to sponsors (or members) of relaxations of "bureaucratic" principles on one side, or of contractions on opportunities for "voluntaristic" adaptations on the other. Gouldner's classification, meanwhile, is useful precisely because it is comprehensive: the two traditions, in either "pure" or "mixed" forms, are clearly discernible in the literature on social control.

The limits on the utility of Gouldner's typological exercise and of the conceptualization in the bulk of the innumerable studies that his typology comprehends are equally instructive. Indeed, they are, in the immediate context, of very considerable significance. These limits do not leap to a reader's consciousness. As a matter of fact, the limits I have in mind have been overlooked, generally, not only by Gouldner and Gouldner's readers but by most of us who aspire to discuss and to do research on social control. The limits, I would like to suggest, inhere in widespread tendencies in the social control literature, broadly defined, to skip up and down from micro- to macrocosmic levels of analysis without pausing to assay the consequences thereof and to switch in the skipping process from one to the other of the naturalistic and rationalistic modes.

Max Weber, for example, spoke about capitalist societies in the same breath with firms, in his numerous discussions of legal rationality; Comte wrote about families and whole societies without missing a beat; Durkheim spoke, back and forth, about clans, moeities, and nations in his works on symbols, on the division of labor, and on suicide rates; St. Simon wrote about economic organizations and about Western society, head upon heel. And Gouldner, in his own effort to stake out the main lines that a synthesis would have to incorporate, borrows from St. Simon's, Comte's, and Weber's multilevel analyses, but he is writing a chapter on organizational analysis.

In preparing to write this paper I reviewed well over one hundred formal studies and an equivalent number of somewhat less specific discussions in which the writers, whatever their main interests, at least touched on both the levels, macro- and microcosmic, at which control issues arise. Thus, some writers write about the nation or the "economic system" but make more than just passing comments about interest groups, industries, or business firms. Others will be occupied with organizations—a business takeover or a local union—but will make allusions, for example, to capitalism, to the two-party system, or, in A. A. Berle's fine phrase, to "the American economic republic." While conducting this review I made a mental list of the implicitly or explicitly positive and negative dispositions of authors toward Gouldner's two schools and, in the process, found what may be a significant clue to the lamentable absence of the synthesis concerning social control I noted at the outset.

The fact is that proponents of natural systems, *typically without ado*, transform themselves into advocates of rational systems when they move from macro- to microcosmic phenomena. In like manner, rational systems ap-

140

proaches to macrophenomena are replaced in their proponents' writings—quite precipitously—by natural systems approaches to microcosmic phenomena. Gouldner's own conceptual notions skip from one to the other of these levels of analyses, as do those by Weber, Comte, St. Simon, and many others who write as though movements may be made from macro- to microcosmic levels of discourse without explanations for (or warnings about) the discontinuous conceptual shifts they make in the process. These discontinuous shifts, meanwhile, obscure what are just plain *ideological* preferences, and in their unexamined fashion they get in the way of synthesis. The two principal parties to debates about control, moreover, seem to realize that they are both offering us a kind of intellectual version of the bait-and-switch game; since both sides tergiversate, neither is obliged to call the other to account. The exchanges, in print and on television, between John Kenneth Galbraith and William P. Buckley are among the more familiar examples of a widespread and chronic disposition both to eat and to have one's cake.

Consider, for example, that present-day neoclassical economists, that is, economists who most often deplore economic planning, "industrial policies," "incomes policies," and Keynesian conceptions of the so-called positive state, almost never apply these misgivings when they move to what is known as the theory of the firm; that is, when they move from macroproblems to management practices in organizations. At the latter level they strongly favor rational planning, hierarchical structures, highly differentiated divisions of labor, and all manner of devices that are identified with bureaucracy, in the least pejorative sense of the word. I recently heard a manager enrolled in an academic degree program for practicing executives object during a class that he had never plotted any of the curves favored in discussions of price theory. The lecturer responded with an astoundingly simple statement: "You do, even if you don't realize it, and, besides, it works out, in accord with price theory, precisely that way in our aggregated data."

These economists' liberal antagonists, similarly disposed to employ a two-valued logic, often support vital local union activity as well as energetic human relations and "organizational development" programs, targeted on the "humanization" and "democratization" of the workplace. When they turn to their macroanalyses, however, they urge that we temper merger-happy managers, apply limits to capital mobility, and embark on national policies and programs designed to reindustrialize the republic through rational "declarative" planning, guided investment, "fine tuning" of monetary and fiscal policy, rationed credit, and the rest.[5] It is perhaps not to be expected that intellectuals who are busy grinding axes will attend to discontinuities in their logics. But there are more than disquieting imperfections in the marketplace of ideas when competitors contrive to accord each other concessions therein.

As an example, Samuel Huntington has recently written a masterful volume on the near-universal misgivings among Americans since the republic's infancy about strong central government, against which, he argues persuasively, there have been cyclical periods of "creedal passion" stirred by one or the other of two camps.[6] His sympathies for the two groups' hysterics about the matter of strong central authority—closely reasoned and well defended—become attenuated, however, when he moves from his main thesis, about the American polity, to discussions about its subsidiary components. The reasons for the collapse of the discipline our two leading parties exercise over their erstwhile constituents and their candidates-in-office are very competently and persuasively sketched, for example. But Huntington implicitly deplores the misgivings many Americans have about hierarchical arrangements and controls at these lower levels of sociopolitical life. Indeed, his volume appears to have been inspired to some degree by the revolt against authority of many young Americans in the late 1960s and his misgivings about the effects of this rebellion on the Democratic party, especially. Some readers will be reminded of Karl Marx's wry comment in *Capital* that "the enthusiastic apologists of the factory system have nothing more damning to urge against a general organization of the labor of society than that it would turn all society into one immense factory."

The point is that ideological preferences regularly affect virtually any writer's efforts to come to grips, explicitly, with issues attaching to questions about social control, and, as is the case with ideologies, almost by common definition, they do so in self-servingly selective ways. And if writers' and investigators' concerns with social control are implicit or indirect ones, it is even easier for them to bypass the fact of their compartmentalization of levels and, understandably, for the reader to overlook these discontinuities as well.

Martin Luther, devout defender of the Fifth Commandment to honor parents and reputedly a tyrant around the house otherwise, was the founding theologian of the Protestant tradition in opposition to papal authority; his name comes readily to mind as the prototypical religionist-compartmentalist. Indeed, in his last writings, Luther acknowledged his pride both in shattering the hegemony of the Vatican over Western Christendom and in having been the greatest supporter, ever, of secular authorities in the German principalities.

Other examples abound: captains of industry, not less than corporals of economic bureaucracies, who raged at the Kennedy brothers' forceful initiatives against steelmakers' price increases in 1962 while energetically defending the doctrine of "fire at will"; proponents of right-to-work laws at the state level who want to circumscribe the rights of pregnant women in low-income groups to have abortions by placing constraints on federal health programs; opponents of federal gun-control legislation who urge that community standards should not be subverted by entrepreneurs who peddle X-rated entertainment.

Beyond the near-universal disposition to compartmentalize but to suffer little, thereby, of what psychologists unfelicitously term "cognitive dissonance," lies another problem in Gouldner's twofold characterization. Thus one can detect a theme in the writings to which he refers and in popular conceptions of controls otherwise that "rational" controls are all the more frightening when they are "societal" in scope; "natural" controls at micro-levels, somehow, are less threatening. On the one hand, for example, Samuel Huntington's explanations of the near-unanimous resistance of Americans to centralized "rational" controls, in the aforementioned volume, are rooted historically in what he persuasively argues is the continuing American version of the Puritan Revolution in England. He is not quite certain which implicitly misguided masters in history led youths to rail so vehemently against party apparatuses in the late 1960s.

I would like to suggest that our vaguer if not more modest misapprehensions about the power of smaller groups' powers—well demonstrated in the literature on group dynamics, peer-group pressures among adolescents, organization men, conspicuous consumption, status seeking, and community norms—are probably related to the belief that it is far easier to escape from a work group that sends uncooperative members "to Coventry," or from among bigoted suburban homeowners, than it is to escape from the untoward consequences of belonging to a group that has been enumerated on an attorney general's list, or of refusing to answer questions put by one or another Congressional committee supposedly concerned with loyalty and security problems, or from the bureaucratic reach of SEC or FTC commissioners.[7]

My own disposition, for the moment, is not so much to insist that both conservatives and liberals underestimate lower-level tyrannies—though I believe, as a sometime member of several different university faculties, that there is much more to be learned about small-time despotisms in the academy than we have distilled, to date, from the lessons offered us in books on *The Organization Man, Middletown,* Norman Mailer's and James Jones's novels about army rifle companies, Solomon Asch's experiments on conformity in small groups, C. Wright Mill's study of community leadership, and recent articles in business slicks on "corporate cultures"; and in such other micro-cosmic intellectual and aesthetic exercises as Eugene O'Neil's and Tennessee Williams's dramas on the family, films like *Twelve Angry Men* and *Cool Hand*

Luke, and biographies of James R. Hoffa, Mafia leaders, and urban machine politicians.

Rather, my disposition is to retrieve, first, the neglected agenda items in conservatives' enumerations of the threat to American society (and to such economic arrangements as they seek to protect) of macrocosmic public social controls, especially public regulatory arrangements; and, second, the neglected agenda items in the chorus of paeans to microcosmic workplace measures targeted on work participation, quality circles, and organization development.

I would like to suggest, first, that conservatives seek not to deregulate the economy at all but simply to reassign controls to actors in markets that are and will continue to be far more imperfect than those we discuss in the empirically vacuous versions of the doctrines reviewed in our essentially theoretical economics journals, business-school courses, and in other mansions of the House of Adam Smith.[8] Second, I submit that controls exercised by private parties, at microcosmic levels, are more difficult to resist or otherwise contend with than is commonly supposed by either conservatives or liberals. They are so principally because we barely see them as controls, in the literal sense, at all. Indeed, we almost never speak of the initiatives and referenda of super- and subordinates in organizations (in the usefully suggestive language of politics) but in squishier, more innocent, if not laundered terms, as in innumerable social scientific studies of corporate culture, management by objectives, theories x and y, status systems, and group norms. These and a host of other terms that distract us from questions about control are favored by social psychologists, sociologists, and others whose ranks are essentially dominated by consultants to business and government leaders who have difficulties with manpower management or human resources and who operate on organizations as agents of change. Finally, as the first two propositions imply, the exercises of what can more usefully be called private power and control gain no more delicate bouquet for being expediently relabeled private initiatives.

Concerning perspectives about controls at microlevels, I would like to suggest that there are ample reasons for believing that the newest look in human-resources management owes more to employers' longtime dreams of being unfettered in their unilateral management (control) of human resources than it does to widely articulated hopes for a new era of truly bilateral labor-management collaboration, to envy of the putative human-relations skills of Japanese foremen and plant superintendents, or to the counsel of well-intentioned consultants in the social sciences who issue recommendations to their corporate clients urging that they restructure their organizations in their own and their employees' interests.[9]

CONTROL IS AS CONTROL DOES

The debates in the United States over deregulation have historically been conducted as if our choices are between the applications, to economic enterprises, of more or fewer *public* controls. For example, state and federal agencies are charged by the electorate's representatives to administer controls that preserve competition; protect workers, consumers, and investors against risks that, judging by emergent social standards, are excessive; and protect, otherwise, ratepayers of all types against potentially predatory behavior by those, like utilities, who have been granted monopolies.

In these debates words like *power* and *wealth* have, of course, been used regularly to describe the targets in the private sector of sundry public controls. But critics of public controls have long argued that the controls in question have far more often undermined than augmented the healthy effects of free market competition, as though private sectors can manage but do not control. Markets left to their own purifying ways, according to conservatives' arguments, would effectively but impersonally control (that is discipline) most economic agents because miscreants in the marketplace can do mischief, under competitive conditions, only over the shortest of runs. Parents, they seem to suppose, will happily learn, quite by themselves from stories about a few scorched babies, to buy safe pajamas for their tots without interference from the FTC bureaucrats and Naderites who collected data on inflammable textiles. And sales of Ford Pintos will eventually decline as auto buyers learn about explosively hazardous gasoline-tank designs from news reports of highway incinerations and photos of grieving relatives. Ford engineers who protested the Pinto's design in the planning phases were disciplined for their organizational sins. The need to protect consumers, according to opponents of consumer-protection laws, is exaggerated, while manufacturers' freedoms are needlessly compromised by would-be regulators.[10]

In these debates little has been said about *private* controls, as such; while there have been academic antitrusters and a few other cottage-industry progressives who have written about private controls, their findings have been fed into debates, in and out of the houses of Congress, as data relevant only to whether *public* controls should or should not be used to tame or restrain one or another supposedly powerful private agent. In the process, few efforts have been made to identify and understand the controls, as such, that are exercised by private agents themselves.[11] The notion of control is lost in discussions of market power, concentration ratios, predatory pricing, unfair competition, per se illegalities, and such like.

Over the past ten years the remarkable progress of America's foreign competitors and the shocking effects of initiatives undertaken by the OPEC countries has encouraged would-be deregulators literally to turn the tables on even the relatively small groups of observers favoring public regulations. The tables have been turned, especially, on those liberals who see antitrust laws as regulatory anchor points.

These laws, free marketers are really telling us, are obsolete; trustlike arrangements are desirable precisely because they afford American managers opportunities to exercise more effective controls over their corporations. As they see things, these keystone regulations are obsolete because of the social not less than the private returns that flow from the economies of scale; the growing importance of nonprice issues in many markets, given the growing significance to purchasers of suppliers' services, suppliers' dependability, and especially, these days, the quality of suppliers' products; the interchangeability of many different industries' products, which is ignored in *industry*-related antitrust proceedings; and the benign attitude of many foreign governments toward American corporations' large, integrated corporate competitors from abroad.[12]

The facts, however, are more complicated than deregulators would have us believe, because the problems of concentration addressed by antitrust laws are those attending vertical and horizontal integration and are focused on industries. But the waves of mergers and acquisitions occurring in recent times are of the conglomerate variety. "Conglomeration" does not much add to a conglomerate parent's controls in an industry, perhaps, but it does contribute to the *aggregate* concentration of manufacturing wealth in fewer and fewer corporate hands. The aggregation of manufacturing wealth by conglomerates is in no way seriously limited by existing regulations, although some in Congress feel we should at least be looking at the need to regulate conglomerates.

The mention of conglomeration and concentrations of manufacturing wealth is not an idle one in the present context. Consider that one of the main issues in discussions about mergers and regulations, in and out of Congress, relates to the question of whether costly dollars become costlier and less productive (thus fueling inflation) when borrowed dollars are used to make speculative acquisitions of existing plant, equipment, and resource supplies rather than for investments in new plants, equipment, and explorations for resources; and when tax-free transfers of equities to stockholders pick up where borrowed funds leave off in making payments for acquisitions. If so, the owners and managers of merged companies, in virtue of benign and seemingly neutral laws, gain strategically important controls over the degree of inflation both directly (vis-a-vis their prospectively unproductive use of borrowed funds and tax "loopholes" in acquisitions) and indirectly (to the extent that the production of new, efficient physical capital is foregone). We may leave aside here the question of whether the investors who reap benefits from takeovers use their gains to greater social purpose than do their hired managers-employees.

At some point the Congress may generate proposals to develop new regulatory arrangements designed to curb mergers. If so, however, the debate thereupon will most assuredly be conducted entirely in keeping with the terms of the familiar one: attention will be directed to the pros and cons of government *controls* versus private *initiatives*. This, despite the fact that the concerns of those political leaders who are the critics of conglomerates will actually have been sparked, in the first instance, by the de facto regulatory roles of large corporate aggregates in the allocation of credit, the deployment of physical and human capital, and in their investments, around the world, of their financial wherewithal. [13]

No reasonably knowledgeable person expects that the merger waves of recent decades will be rolled back; indeed, there has not yet occurred even a successful third-party suit against a would-be conglomerator, essentially because the courts have no clear legal guidelines for making judgments about these ventures.

Note too, meantime, that the Reagan administration has been cutting back on the enforcement capacities of the SEC (by cutting its budget); that Mr. Shad, the chairman of the SEC, believes that large mergers are a net gain; and that in his first weeks in office he spoke of the need for "reducing excessive registration, reporting and other regulatory burdens." He stated, very early, that "the SEC is moving toward more self-regulation by the securities industry" (*New York Times,* July 13, 1981). His colleague William F. Baxter, head of the Antitrust Division of the Justice Department until December 1983, signaled a few weeks later that he would "ignore . . . 'clear judicial precedent' from the Supreme Court that manufacturers cannot set the retailer's price," describing such precedents as "rubbish" (*New York Times,* October 18, 1981, p. 2F). Baxter also made it clear that he would ignore even unambiguous Supreme Court rulings against mergers and other arrangements affecting the chain of production or distribution of a product. The tables are turning, no one may doubt it: *public* officials, charged with *public* mandates to exercise *public* controls (and to follow longstanding legal precedents) simply and, in their own words, quite literally intend to transfer control functions from what they call public bureaucracies to a number of leaders of what we may, reciprocating the spirit of their criticisms, term *private bureaucracies.* In the process, the term *private sector* must be viewed in analytical terms as a de facto politicolegal jurisdiction to which controls, in constitutional terms, can be delegated.

At about the same time that other administration leaders were transferring regulatory functions, AT&T entered into a consent decree with Reagan's attorney general to restructure a large segment of the communications industry. The most basic aspects of the AT&T case were thus not hammered out by a judge within the framework of antitrust law. We are accordingly speaking, once again, less of deregulation than of private versus public regulation. Similar developments have taken place in the FTC, the Department of the Interior, and elsewhere in executive departments.

In the fiscal area we have moved, though in de facto fashion, to distribute taxes so that we end up with an equally de facto "new industrial policy," while our national leaders tell us that under no circumstances should we embark on such a legal-economic journey on what their mentor, F. von Hayek, termed the road to serfdom. Only a hopeless illiterate could fail to identify such a policy, however, once one examines the effective rates of corporate taxes, industry by industry, or the percentage of research and development funded by the federal government, again industry by industry, as Robert Reich reminds us (*The Public Interest,* Fall 1983, pp. 3–17). Reich's tables make a mockery of our leaders' protests, but, one must add, no reputable conservatives have protested the distributions in Reich's tables.

As Reich points out, "A nation's industrial policy is the sum of its microeconomic policies—like tax rules, research and development grants, credit subsidies, and import restrictions—as they affect the pace and direction of industrial change." The disparities in his tables, however, as Reich adds, "are due not so much to tax breaks targeted [by the public's representatives in government] to particular industries as [they are] to differences in the ability of industries [or subclusters within them] to take advantage of superficially neutral deductions and credits." These abilities are controls by another name,

TABLE I. Effective Rate of Corporate Income Tax, by Industry

Automobiles	48%	Airlines	16%
Trucking	46%	Metal manufacturing	10%
Pharmaceuticals	36%	Utilities	9%
Electronics, appliances	29%	Aerospace	7%
Food processing	27%	Petrochemicals	5%
Industrial and farm equipment	24%	Crude oil	3%
Retailing	23%	Commercial banks	2%
Oil and refining	19%	Railroads	−8%
Diversified financial	17%	Paper and wood	−14%

Source: Joint Committee on Taxation, Taxation of Banks and Thrift Institutions (March 9, 1983), table 2. There are a number of ways to compute effective tax rates, and some computations generate results slightly different from these; but regardless of methodology, great disparities exist.

TABLE 2. Percentage of Research and Development Funded by the Federal Goverment, by Industry

Aircraft and parts	70%	Motor vehicles	8%
Transportation equipment (excludes autos)	55%	Nonelectrical machinery	7%
Fabricated metals	53%	Petrochemicals	2%
Communications equipment, electronic components	49%	Primary metals	2%
Electrical equipment (excludes communications)	26%	Drugs and medicines	<1%
Scientific instruments	22%	Textiles and apparel	<1%

Source: National Science Board, *Science Indicators, 1978* (Washington D.C.: U.S. Government Printing Office, 1979).

although the results were not exactly intended by the legislators who wrote the tax laws.

In some cases, tax breaks (most notably in the matter of depletion allowances favoring a minority of the largest, most integrated oil companies) have been quite intentionally of a piece with foreign policy under every president since Eisenhower and endorsed by every postwar presidential candidate but Hubert Humphrey. Thus the so-called Seven Sisters have played major roles, as de facto accredited plenipotentiaries, in acting to assure oil supplies to America's friends and allies and to assure "stable governments" in oil-exporting countries, and in guaranteeing the dominance of American firms in world oil trade. These companies have been invited, *at every critical turn of events in the Middle East since World War II,* to function as broadly empowered representatives of the State Department in adjusting the international supply to international demand for oil in ways that have consequently tempered kings, shahs, sheiks, emirs, presidents, and leaders of sundry other stripes. The companies did their patriotic work with powers essentially delegated to them, quietly but explicitly, without much fear and with very considerable favor, by leaders in the White House and in Congress and in both of our major political parties.[14] Whatever agreements or disagreements my readers may have with the wisdom of private controls exercised by a few citizens in oil companies—often affecting in significant ways the welfare of smaller independent oil companies and even whole nations, as well as the price of one of the world's most essential products, and so on and on—the facts of private controls are plain to see.

Anthony Samson reminds us that the chairman of ITT had no little influence over his private-sector company's holdings in Germany, *during* World War II, while serving as a general in the United States Army Signal Corps in Switzerland, presumably with the knowledge of highly placed civilian political leaders. After the war the United States government compensated ITT for the destruction of its Fokke-Wolf bomber plant by the Eighth Air Force.

The point I am urging, in short, is antecedent to questions about our personal dispositions regarding the best possible balance between public and private controls. The point is that it is a form of Orwell's Newspeak to conduct discourses about this balance of controls as if regulation refers exclusively to the exercise of power by public agents while pretending that deregulation refers, far less menacingly, to the exercise of mere initiatives by private agents. This main point, I may also suggest, could have been made almost as readily in reverse manner. I have chosen to deal with conservatives' tergiversations, in their rhetoric about public and private realms, because we are currently wrestling with views about American life of which their leaders are the principal proponents. Conservatives have, for example, been heard to argue that the traditionally agreeable dispositions of liberals toward regulatory measures are not one whit less destructive of the liberties of some individuals or groups for being labeled, self-servingly, in the appealingly benign language of social and economic reformers.

MANAGERS, WORKERS, AND CONTROLS

I have made several allusions in the preceding sections to the abundant literature on organizations in which proposals for reforms have focused on the tensions between the preferences and even the needs of psychologically healthy citizens in a democracy and managers who design the structures of organizations around rationalistic criteria.

The first social science studies formally addressing these tensions, conducted and interpreted by Elton Mayo and his colleagues from the Harvard Business School in the 1930s and elevated into management principles in *The Functions of the Executive,* a classic by Chester Barnard of AT&T, began with studies of industrial hygiene, that is, of the effects on workers of sundry aspects of their physical environments. After the Hawthorne studies, in the late 1930s, the Harvard group launched full-scale attacks on the then influential scientific-management movement on the grounds that it disregarded workers' social and psychological needs for group membership under the anomic conditions of modern society, and that it anthropomorphized the theory of the firm in what they termed economists' "rabble hypothesis."

Mayo and his students were much taken by evident worker interests in returns from their work that often subtracted from their interests in economic returns per se. These investigators were also convinced that managers could be taught to develop social scientific sensibilities and that, by applying the results of social-scientific studies of work groups, they could head off unions whose membership drives illegitimately stressed the extent to which these workers' organizations could usefully balance the unilateral power of corporate leaders. The majority of these human relationists believed firmly in broadening what they specifically called workers' "zones of acceptance" of management control through counselling workers about their "nonrational" ways.

Some human relationists moved somewhat to Mayo's ideological left, urging that unions, for example, could indeed make an important contribution to industrial democracy. They accordingly sought to wed some of the results of social psychological studies to the constructive results they claimed to have observed in studies of collective bargaining. This subgroup became a scholarly subdiscipline, linked to the work of the members of the so-called Wisconsin School, which still does business under the title of Industrial Relations. But the impact of these human relations revisionists was never terribly great, and it has lately become negligible.

The post–World War II era was one of economic growth and of only occasionally serious labor-management conflicts. In retrospect it seems quite clear that our favorable postwar circumstances—especially the worldwide demand for American products, our monopoly of the supply of both producers' and consumer goods, and the high profits reaped from selling American goods—served to temper the traditional impatience of management with employees' ways as well as management's longstanding resentment of third-party representatives of workers' putative interests. After all, the costs of what Gouldner called an "indulgency pattern" in the exercise of employers' authority could, for a number of years, be passed on to customers. Even public intervention—on behalf of consumers, workers, and their natural and work environments—was initially resisted, in the early seventies, in ways, we must now reckon, that were more ritualistic than determined. Thus *unions* are now blamed for expensive cost-of-living allowances—COLAs—but they were originally offered in the early 1950s (when inflation rates were well under 2 percent) by Charles Wilson of General Motors to negotiators of the United Auto Workers, in return for longer-term contracts and in lieu of larger wage settlements. It is doubtful that the top-level leaders of GM today are not aware of their predecessors' initiatives even as they complain of the inflationary implications of wage escalation.

A few managers were, however, responsive to work reformers in the social sciences and acted, at least, as if they were truly concerned about the allegedly growing discontents of American workers in the 1970s, about the brakes this discontent put on productivity increases and the dents it made on product quality, and about the benefits that would accrue if work-reform schemes were introduced and the human relations tradition revivified. It is my judgment, though, after a survey of the subject, that managers who professed have been attracted to the new calls for humanized workplaces, worker participation, quality circles, and the rest, during the 1970s have, in the main, been not entirely candid.[15]

Unions are reeling under the impact of plant shutdowns, collectively bargained "give backs," or, as they might as well be called, "get backs," membership losses and failed organizing drives. Managers, meanwhile, have embarked on drives of their own to make their organizations lean and mean, to meet the claims of foreign competitors to American and other foreign markets and to dismantle public controls and collective bargaining frameworks, and even to disassemble whole communities in the industrial Northeast. No faithful reader of newspapers can have much doubt that the velvet gloves of human relations, "we gotcha now" style, are coming off mailed fists in industry after industry.

Symptomatic of the drive to rewrite the social contract, or Pax Americana, of the fifties and sixties are the arrangements at the truck-making Japanese subsidiary of Nissan in Smyrna, Tennessee. The resident American managers there are waist deep in work participation and quality circles and are proud of their happy circumstances and sky-high worker morale as they prepare to quintuple the plant's initial annual output. The fact is, however, that they interviewed and otherwise screened twenty thousand applicants to find the two thousand workers they needed. Whether or not they scored better than Columbia University, Berkeley, or Harvard did in selecting organizationally complaisant persons back in the mid-1960s remains to be seen. It is a perfectly reasonable bet, though, that they were not especially looking to hire large numbers of unemployed members of the United Auto Workers Union or underutilized UAW organizers. Nissan's careful screening program, meanwhile, is entirely consistent with a view of social control, itself inconstant as it removes from macro- to microcosmic matters. The conservative ideological convention, as I have been at pains to delineate, holds that one can simultaneously seek significant reductions of macrocosmic controls and meaningful if subtle increases in control in the economy's plants and shops, where realists' aims, as they put it, are to get the iron out the back door.

That well-intended "change agents" who help managers reform workers join with more candidly opportunistic "union avoidance specialists" in serving employers' needs for better motivated workers, meanwhile, reflects their belief that the needs of their business clients can be made to seem essentially consistent with the complex of needs attributed to workers. If such beliefs are far-fetched, as the checkered history of the human relations tradition in its various guises and several incarnations suggests, the faithful idealists can say to themselves that they have at least helped put velvet gloves on their employer-clients' fists. 'Tis better, perhaps, to have gloved a boss than never to have gloved at all.

In the narrow bands of the economy where employers and their charges still relate to each other as parties to collectively bargained agreements we can observe a very substantial shift, from the exchanges of quids for quos between the parties in a given worksite, to highly legalistic encounters between visiting lawyers from distant corporate headquarters and local unionists. Local managers in many, many settings are simply discouraged from settling grievances in a process that once served both local parties well.[16] Instead these local managers are urged to provoke arbitration cases in which they have themselves increasingly become mere observers of the skills of visiting attorneys who define the relationship in accord with the canons of contract law rather than the tenets of what William O. Douglas, in a 1959 case, called "the industrial common law."[17] Control processes themselves, once the most important grist for the bargaining mill, day in and day out in accord with an agreement, have become the subjects of an essentially legal-adversarial relationship involving a contract. Modern-day industrial cases are, in the narrowest possible sense, settled, but the problems of which they are symptomatic are left essentially unattended.[18]

Beyond the masses of organized and unorganized Americans are the relatively few who, having tried but failed to persuade employers to change a course of conduct—the installation of a faulty device in an Eastern Airlines aircraft that subsequently crashed, for example—have brought their charges to the attention of regulators or the public. The mounting evidence that these whistleblowers are made to suffer for their actions suggests, very persuasively indeed, that employers' proclamations about worker participation need to be edited to allow for the limitations they so often wish to impose on the actual character of workers' roles in these events.[19] When the initiatives of corporate persons are fettered by natural persons, the scene becomes like the one once described by Andrew Hacker, in an analysis at larger and smaller corporations, in which "elephants are dancing among the chickens."

CODA

Norman Podhoretz, the distinguished editor of *Commentary,* recently wrote that it would not have surprised him if Orwell, had he lived, would have become a so-called neoconservative. I have forgotten Mr. Podhoretz's reasons, but a rereading of *Nineteen Eighty-Four* and attentive consideration to a recent National Public Radio series on Orwell lead me to believe that Mr.

Podhoretz's estimate is reasonable. Orwell, as we all know, was totally opposed to Soviet-style communism. It is perhaps less well known that his misgivings about fascism in Germany were considerably more temperate.

I am less certain how Orwell, who was obviously a major contributor to the vast literature on social control, would view Gouldner's distinction between natural and rational systems approaches to the subject. Nor am I very sure how he would view my observation that people who write on social control alternate between natural and rational system views depending on whether they are liberals or conservatives and on whether they are looking at microcosmic or macrocosmic social arrangements. The controls Orwell maligned are portrayed, after all, as operating at both of these analytical levels in his most celebrated novel. Thus, unlike the majority of writers, he appears to be critical of many controls regardless of the social level at which they are applied.

In his writings, otherwise, he was more than a little patronizing of the workers his socialism was intended to redeem. And, on his romantic side, he admired Hitler's parades and his spectacular pageants without *quite* saying openly that they were very visibly important ways of mobilizing the German public's emotions. Orwell, on studying a photo of Hitler, for example, thought he saw a remarkable likeness between the German dictator and Jesus Christ.

Judging from these hints and after observing the intellectual "career trajectories" of many writers and intellectuals from the old political left, those in Orwell's generation, one should perhaps not be any more shocked than Podhoretz to see Orwell as a potential member in good standing of the neoconservative congregation.

Orwell, in his own way, did, however, seek to serve that version or segment of the socialist cause in which concerns about industrial democracy have been very prominent, indeed. The term, in common usage in the thirties and forties, consistently denoted a distinction between political democracy—involving "government by the people"—and the extension of democratic arrangements into the organizational settings and contexts in which citizens live and, especially, work. The term reflected the interest of many, after the tempestuous period of organizing strikes that preceded (and abetted) the passage of the National Labor Relations Act, in adjusting our system of governance to the fact of industrialization and the emergence of America into what A. A. Berle defined as an "economic republic." The term *industrial democracy* allows for no inconstancy, no tergiversation between macro- and microworlds of human affairs, because it specifically denies the legitimacy of such a discontinuity. Proponents of industrial democracy were at great pains to deny the possibilities that political democracy could be coupled with significant politicoeconomic inequalities.

To the extent that we relocate significant margins for the exercise of macro social controls from public to private powerholders, on one side, rather than redesign and thus improve the work of public officials (like the work of regulators in "captured" regulatory agencies), we limit industrial democracy in its macromanifestations. To the extent, on the other side, that we paint employers' controls in shops, offices, and laboratories *en coleur de rose,* using the brushes and palettes of human relationists, we obscure microcosmic manifestations of what are not infrequently highly undemocratic limits on individual rights.

The time may well come—as Samuel Huntington implies it will, in the study I mentioned earlier—during which we will see hysterical reactions to the present eclipse of industrial democracy. It could thus be that the leaders of a movement to reregulate, for example, will be as effective in the future as the outraged critics of public regulation have been who have reversed the nearly fifty years of macrointerventions since the National Labor Relations Act. Readers will, of course, make up their own minds whether such a development is desirable.

It may be useful though, *whichever way one's preferences lead one,* to recognize, at least, that the flip-flopping in our views, left and right, in our conceptualization of social controls will continue. Contending partisans seem to need their individual conceits and thus to honor, at least implicitly, each other's hypocrisies. For my own part, I am about equally offended by what Robert Burns called a Holy Willy, "a saint abroad and a devil at home," whether he is Democrat or a Republican. I fondly wish, in short, that it were far less often the case, as Sam Goldwyn put it, that "where you stand depends on where you sit."

It is, of course, one of the hallmarks of true partisans that they are humorless in direct proportion to their dedications to their causes. And it is unfortunately the case that humorless people are especially well protected against any appreciation for the comedy of their own posturings. What is remarkable is that, like Laurel and Hardy, each side is obliged to play by the same script and, thereby, to give each other credibility. By doing so, the rest of us may end up as witnesses to a consensus that is sufficient to avoid a revolution in our thinking about social control. But among the problematical results are our failures to come fully to philosophical grips with questions concerning the legitimacy and effects of various social controls and thus with a host of sociological, political, and moral questions pertaining to the rights of persons, corporate not less than natural, especially pertaining to the rights of those two types of legal persons when they are in juxtaposition or conflict with each other.

For those who may feel that these juxtapositions and conflicts have essentially been addressed in our democratic society I urge a close perusal of James Coleman's recent book *The Asymmetric Society,* an impressive, closely reasoned volume in which one of our most distinguished social scientists offers us better reasons, by far, than Orwell's *Nineteen Eighty-Four* for being concerned about the matter of social controls—especially in connection with childrearing and the fates of our children. Our children, as he points out at the end of his striking analysis, live at the bottom of an archaic system in an industrial society—the family—in which they and their parents, natural persons, are on the light side of a teeter-totter. On the other, well-weighted, end of the board sit corporate persons, a sizeable number of whose leader-agents currently operate many of the most critical levers of social control at both macro- and microcosmic levels.

NOTES

1. Many Americans, we may recall, were upset about the treatment of youthful offenders as criminals and succeeded in reforming the law so that they would be treated as "juvenile offenders." As we discovered later, the legal machinery wrought by the reformers essentially stripped accused youths of some of the civil liberties guaranteed in the Bill of Rights.
2. Another invaluable effort, by my Vanderbilt colleague Jack P. Gibbs, is currently gaining the attention of specialized students of social control, especially criminologists. The model he describes is based on a relatively large number of very suggestive but subtle distinctions that I have simply not yet mastered. See his *Norms, Deviance and Social Control: Conceptual Matters* (New York: Elsevier, 1981).
3. The article "Organizational Analysis" appeared in Robert Merton, Leonard Broom, and Leonard S. Cottrell, eds., *Sociology Today* (New York: Basic Books, 1959).
4. For examples, in the labor-management field, see James W. Kuhn, *Bargaining in Work Rules Disputes* (New York: Columbia University Press, 1960). For a classic "mesocosmic" case, see Philip Selznik, *TVA and the Grass Roots* (Berkeley and Los Angeles: University of California Press, 1949).
5. Because the conservatives are now in power, this essay will concentrate on their position. For examples of the liberal position, see Barry Bluestone and Bennett Harrison, *The Deindustrialization of America: Plant Closings, Community Abandonment, and the Dismantling of Basic Industry* (New York: Basic Books, 1982), in which the authors move from a "rationalistic critique" of macroeconomic developments, stressing the need for more centralized direction and regulatory re-

form (not deregulation), to the need for "naturalistic" work reforms and the legitimacy of inventive community efforts to salvage abandoned enterprises.

6. Samuel Huntington, *American Politics: The Promise of Disharmony* (New York: Basic Books, 1981).

7. There are, of course, some notable exceptions. The leaders of NOW, for example, are equally concerned with the favored legal status of men and with the widely held norms, unconnected to formal sanctions and operative at the household level, that make second-class citizens of women. And one need only reread Sinclair Lewis's *Main Street* and *Babbitt* to rediscover the ransoms that studiously hypocritical communities exact of their hostages to virtue.

8. For an early effort to conduct an analysis along the lines of the present essay, see Eli Ginzberg, *The House of Adam Smith* (New York: Columbia University Press, 1934). The author was singularly concerned with saving Smith from those malevolent ideologues who have read into him precisely what they wished. For a lucid discussion of Adam Smith's ambivalence toward corporations and capitalism, see the comparison of Smith's differing treatment of the subjects in *The Wealth of Nations* and *Theory of Moral Sentiments* in Albert O. Hirschman, *Shifting Involvements: Private Interest and Public Action* (Princeton, N.J.: Princeton University Press, 1982), pp. 47–50.

10. For a detailed study of a noble and generously motivated effort to help one of the nation's leading newspapers serve itself and its employees better (an effort that was eventually rejected by top management) see Chris Argyris, *Behind the Front Page: Organizational Self-Renewal in a Metropolitan Newspaper* (San Francisco: Jossey-Bass, 1974). For a report of the ultimate rejection by employers in the 1980s of one of the two or three most highly touted work-reform programs of the 1970s (at the Gainesburger pet-food plant in Topeka, Kansas) see David A. Whitsett and Lyle Yorks, "Looking Back at Topeka: General Foods and the Quality of Life Experiment," *California Management Review* 25, no. 4 (Summer 1983). The failure of the second of these two limited managerial engagements with intraorganizational reform was forecast in my *Managers and Work Reform* (New York: Free Press, 1978), because the reformers' preconditions for success were precisely that almost none of the problems to be solved should be present in the first place; see especially pp. 157–70 and 246–61.

10. For a disarmingly evenhanded discussion of the pajama case, the collapse of the consumer movement, and the aborted efforts to form a federal consumer-protection agency, see Michael Pertschuk, *Revolt Against Regulation: The Rise and Fall of the Consumer Movement* (Berkeley and Los Angeles: University of California Press, 1982). Pertschuk is a member (and former director) of the Federal Trade Commission.

11. A few efforts have not been altogether modest, of course. Thus the Temporary National Economic Committee hearings in the period before World War II come to mind, as does the classic book by Thurman Arnold, FDR's antitruster, *The Folklore of Capitalism* (New Haven, Conn.: Yale University Press, 1938).

12. See my "Social Control in the Economy: In Quest of Common Denominators," in

Social Control: Views from the Social Sciences, ed. Jack P. Gibbs (Beverly Hills, Calif.: Sage, 1982), pp. 165–82.

13. Ibid., p. 168.
14. See Jack Anderson, *Fiasco* (New York: New York Times Books, 1983) for a brilliantly executed review of the energy crisis of the 1970s.
15. See Ivar Berg, Marcia Freedman, and Michael Freeman, *Managers and Work Reforms: A Limited Engagement* (New York: Free Press, 1978).
16. See Kuhn, *Bargaining in Work Rules Disputes.*
17. Actually there were three cases, collectively called the Trilogy Cases. For a brief outline see Berg et al., *Managers and Work Reforms,* pp. 145–46.
18. For a detailed analysis based on a seven-year-long study of labor relations and related employment matters in an industrial community in Michigan, see Ivar Berg and Janice Schack-Marquez, "Corporations, Human Resources and the Grass Roots: Community Profiles," in *The Impact of the Corporation,* ed. Betty Bok, Harvey J. Goldschmid, Ira M. Millstein, and F. H. Scherer (New York: Columbia University Law School, Center for Law and Economic Studies, 1984).
19. See Alan F. Westin, with the assistance of Henry I. Kurtz and Albert Robbins, *Whistleblowing: Loyalty and Dissent in the Corporation* (New York: McGraw-Hill, 1981).

Ruth Macklin

MODIFYING BEHAVIOR, THOUGHT, AND FEELING: CAN BIG BROTHER CONTROL FROM WITHIN?

t is not hard to identify the moral values most cherished in America and most threatened by George Orwell's vision in his book *Nineteen Eighty-Four*. Those values are freedom and privacy. Hallmarks of the philosophy of liberal individualism, the liberty and privacy of persons in our society have enjoyed constitutional protections and are embodied in numerous legal rights in statutes and in the common law. Threats to individual freedom or liberty and to personal privacy can be blatant or subtle, but they have rarely escaped the notice of observers ever watchful of Orwellian developments.

Consider, as an example of recently developed efforts to control behavior, technologies that intrude on privacy and freedom. In the field now referred to as psychotechnology, one technological device is a remote radio communications system using belt transceivers. This device is described as follows:

> Systems of this type can monitor geographical location in psychophysiological variables, as well as permit two-way coded communication with people in their natural social environment. Probable subjects include individuals susceptible to emergency medical conditions that occasionally preclude calling for help, (e.g., epilepsy, diabetes, myocardial infarctions), geriatric or psychiatric outpatients, and parolees. It is conceivable, for instance, that convicts might be given the option of incarceration or parole with mandatory electronic surveillance. In terms of cost . . . , treatment effectiveness, and invasion of privacy (few situations are *less* private than prison), an electronic parole system is potentially a feasible alternative. These systems can also be used for positive secondary reinforcement of pro-social behavior.[1]

The authors of this passage openly favor the development and use of these forms of psychotechnology and are correct in noting that one form of privacy or its invasion would be traded for another, if such devices were offered as alternatives to imprisonment. But not only is there an exchange of different types of privacy; the loss of privacy for the parolee is also offset by a corresponding gain in freedom to move about in society. Freedom and the right to privacy are two highly prized values that usually go hand in hand in our culture. The problem of having to choose between them is therefore especially acute, and not so easily resolved as these writers seem to think.

The book from which this passage is taken was published in 1973. Entitled *Psychotechnology: Electronic Control of Mind and Behavior,* it describes numerous other technologic advances that hold promise for controlling the behavior of mental patients and criminal offenders. That promise is now beginning to be delivered. The *New York Times* recently reported the use of an electronic transmitter strapped to the ankle of a man convicted of disobeying a police officer. The man was one of five criminal defendants in Albuquerque, New Mexico, whose sentences consisted of wearing an experimental "electronic monitoring anklet" instead of being jailed for a minor offense. Accepted in Albuquerque as an inexpensive alternative to incarceration, use of the device has nonetheless been questioned by civil libertarians. The electronic anklet is scheduled to be used in other states, and so far it has been offered to offenders as an alternative form of sentencing but has not been required. The fact that a choice was offered to convicted criminals is apparently what led a spokesman for the New Mexico chapter of the American Civil Liberties Union to remark, "At this stage we haven't seen anyone who wouldn't choose this over incarceration, so we see nothing constitutionally wrong." But the head of the district's public defender office expressed concern about what would happen if an offender resists. "Then I expect that we would challenge it as an invasion of privacy," he said.[2]

Less obvious than erosions of freedom and privacy, but as much a part of the warning Orwell issued in *Nineteen Eighty-Four,* are efforts to control behavior that raise concerns about autonomy. Consider another advance in electronic psychotechnology: the stimoceiver, a three-channel unit for radio stimulation and EEG telemetry. The unit is so named because it is both a cerebral stimulator and an encephalographic receiver. In describing the experimental design for research leading to the development of the stimoceiver, Dr. Jose Delgado, one of the leaders in brain manipulation, states that "the purpose of this study was to identify sites of abnormal intracerebral activity and to test brain excitability in order to guide contemplated therapeutic surgery."[3] As a proponent of psychosurgery as well as various modes of electrical intervention into the brain, Delgado is not troubled by the fact that some electrical methods of stimulating the brain are being developed for the purpose of helping make psychosurgery itself easier. In order not to mislead, however, it is important to note that electronic forms of brain intervention are often promoted or used because they serve as an alternative either to surgical intervention or to some other proposed method of therapy.

They also serve as an alternative of another sort—an alternative to imprisonment or institutionalization for some persons, such as the parolees described earlier. Physical or electrical manipulation of the brain is a form of control "from within," not only because it involves intrusion into the bodily space of an individual but, more important, because it is directed at the very core of what it is to be a human being: the locus of thoughts, ideas, and motivation. Physical, electrical, and chemical modes of altering brain function provoke a fearful response because of the technology itself. But their chief danger lies in potential threat to *autonomy,* in the sense of the ability to generate ideas.

A rich and ambiguous concept, autonomy is a psychological notion at once and value laden. Often identified simplistically with the idea of free action, autonomy is more correctly described as a mental capacity that different persons possess in greater or lesser degree. It is not surprising that the most feared threats to autonomy are those that stem from behavior-control technologies: mood-altering drugs, implantable electronic devices, highly refined techniques of psychosurgery, and methods of behavior modification using aversive stimuli or positive reinforcements. Whether the effects sought from these techniques are termed mood control, mind control, or thought control, the techniques themselves provoke fears of an Orwellian society because of their perceived power to alter the fundamental springs of human thought and action.

Yet it is worth questioning whether the capacity to implant intracranial electrodes is more to be feared than the ability to implant ideas. Behavior-control technologies have advanced to a point where emotions and moods can be induced or altered, certain patterns of behavior extinguished or stamped in by operant conditioning, and individual actions affected by mediating influences of a variety of sorts. Do newly developed methods of psychotechnology pose a greater threat to autonomy than nontechnical yet pervasive manipulations such as brainwashing (also called coercive persuasion)? Might there not be more to fear from a government's centralized, total control of information to its citizenry than from technological abilities to alter human behavior? Could it be that dangers to autonomy from without are as ominous as any efforts Big Brother may make to control from within? Understanding the multiple and varied meanings of the concept of autonomy is a necessary step in making judgments about the kind and degree of threats posed by technological advances in the ability to control human thought and behavior.

Lest we assume that causes for concern about behavior control in 1984 should be limited to present or future technological capabilities, recall the portrait of conformity Orwell paints in his novel. The book depicts several modes of inducing and enforcing conformity of ideas and behavior, but none is more effective or more threatening to autonomy than the language Newspeak. As one character notes, "the whole aim of Newspeak is to narrow the range of thought. In the end we shall make thoughtcrime literally impossible because there will be no words in which to express it." We can already find ample evidence that Newspeak has crept into our own society in the year 1984. The introduction of official terminology such as *correctional facility* to designate prisons and *corrections officer* to denote prison guards; *enhanced radiation,* a term used to mean "nuclear explosion," and *rapid oxidation* to mean "fire"; and *negative patient care outcome* in medical settings instead of "death." These and numerous other examples compel the conclusion that Newspeak is well on the way to becoming entrenched.

An especially insidious feature of Newspeak as Orwell described it is the technique called "doublethink." Involving no technology for mind control, yet probably a more powerful means of affecting people's ability to generate ideas, this mental technique consists of "the power of holding two contradictory beliefs in one's mind simultaneously, and accepting both of them. . . . The essential act of the Party is to use conscious deception while retaining the firmness of purpose that goes with complete honesty." Familiar for over three decades as a tool of language employed by Soviet governments in power, doublethink has become increasingly common in pronouncements by official spokesmen for our own federal government, and by authorities representing industry and other organizations in the private sector. *Peacekeeping forces* are military troops our government sends abroad; *peacekeeper* is a term invented to denote the MX missile; *negative economic growth* means "recession" when uttered by economists, to be *nonretained* is to be fired from one's job, and to engage in *terminal living* is to be in the process of dying. Such uses of language are effective in limiting the ability of society's members to think clearly about vital matters. Doublethink may be the ultimate means of squelching arguments mounted in opposition to governmental or other influential programs and policies.

PSYCHIATRY AND BEHAVIOR CONTROL

The scope of this essay precludes a look at the many other nontechnological factors contributing to conformity in our society. One symptom of the prevailing situation exists in the elaborate labeling system devised by psychiatry to characterize behavior that deviates from the norm. By inventing labels that designate deviant patterns as disorders, and by proposing interventions aimed at bringing such behavior into the normal range, psychiatrists are able to induce a desire for conformity in "patients" who come to accept their departure from the societal norm as pathological. Does the very practice of psychiatry, then, threaten the autonomy of those who become psychiatric patients? Perhaps. For the sake of clarity we need to distinguish, both conceptually and empirically, inroads into autonomy from erosions of privacy and freedom.

What does it mean to control "from within"? Can a sharp distinction be made between control from without and control from within? The distinction may initially seem plausible because of a linguistic debt to Cartesian dualism. Control from without implies that the source of behavior control lies spatially outside the human body. Such methods of control may take a variety of forms: ever-present television monitors eliminate privacy by scrutinizing one's every act, waking or sleeping; iron bars, steel shackles, concrete walls, locked gates, and strait jackets that restrict freedom of movement; beatings, burnings, administering electric shocks with cattle prods, and other modes of torture designed to produce confessions or overt adherence to an official ideology.

Television monitors are a product of modern technology and appear, therefore, to depart from age-old methods of invading privacy. Yet their use is, in principle, no different from such traditional methods as the use of informers, private detectives, and ever-present spies. External physical restraints on freedom can take many forms and probably constitute the oldest and most prevalent form of behavior control aimed at restricting personal liberty. But do those methods differ in kind, rather than in degree, from contemporary methods used to alter motivation, mood, or behavior? It is worth recalling that powerful drugs such as the phenothiazines and other antipsychotic medications have been dubbed chemical strait jackets, a term that underscores their continuity with physical restraints. Although they are ingested, thus becoming activated from within, Thorazine, Mellaril, Prolixin, and their chemical cousins represent one point on a continuum from more traditional physical restraints on freedom to methods of behavior control that directly invade autonomy. A conception of the Orwellian nature of such chemical means of control is reflected in the title of an article by a civil libertarian lawyer: "Prolixin Decanoate: Big Brother by Injection?"[4]

Although psychiatrists offer a therapeutic justification for the use of drugs to treat mental patients, it is well documented that antipsychotic medications are widely used for the purpose of social control. Mental patients, adult offenders, juvenile delinquents, and other institutionalized persons have been regularly "treated" with a variety of mood-altering drugs. The line between therapy and social control is easily blurred: prisons renamed correctional facilities, following the introduction of the concept of rehabilitation to replace the traditional notion of punishment. Such shifts in terminology demonstrate the practical effects of Newspeak once the new terms replace the old. It becomes possible to offer a different justification for methods of altering mood, motivation, and behavior when the desired alterations are termed therapeutic and when behavior is conceptualized as disordered rather than as bad or criminal. This conceptual shift may be defended as humane, since the offender is treated as a sufferer deserving rehabilitative treatment. But the use of behavior-control technologies under the medical model may at the same time bypass constitutional provisions that protect criminals from being subjected to cruel and unusual punishment by the state.

Disagreement is bound to arise concerning present and future capacities to alter or control human behavior by technological means. In a recent book about the powers of psychiatry, the author (himself a psychiatrist) assesses the situation as follows:

> Talking of even newer ways of controlling thoughts and feelings seems far fetched when the methods we now use already sound like the fulfillment of the most unlikely predictions of George Orwell, Aldous Huxley, and Anthony Burgess. In *1984, Brave New World,* and *A Clockwork Orange* we have a foretaste of a science-dominated world in which man will be controlled through the application of drugs, educational or brainwashing indoctrination techniques, and behavioral modification. The prediction of a population lulled into conformity by drugs has been at least partially fulfilled. . . . Some of the wilder aversive conditioning approaches to control of criminal behavior have only been curbed by the eternal vigilance of civil-libertarian lawyers. Certainly nothing in the futuristic predictions of novelists is any more bizarre or outlandish than the concept of forcing people, by the threat of imprisonment if they are on parole or probation, or by the threat of psychiatric commitment, to present themselves at biweekly intervals to be injected with a long-acting tranquilizer and so to have their thoughts, actions and sexual appetites quelled.[5]

Bleak as the foregoing description is, the current ability to use behavior control techniques is circumscribed in a number of ways that fall short of the society Orwell depicts. The chief difference lies in the present limitation of involuntary behavior-control techniques to some persons who have violated the laws of society and hence are subject to punishment under the name of rehabilitation, and to those who become mental patients either by virtue of their voluntary quest for help or as a result of involuntary commitment. The long-expressed concerns about proper criteria for involuntary commitment remain warranted, as are continuing worries about the involuntary use of methods of behavior control on mental patients or prisoners—methods ranging from behavior modification to drugs to electrical and surgical invasions of the brain.

Still, we do not (yet) live in a society in which the state may authorize the administration of such techniques to individuals who simply fail to conform to an official ideology or political viewpoint. Although some may fear that we are already sliding down that slippery slope, a great many more conditions would have to be met before our entire society could be characterized as approaching a use of behavior control reminiscent of Orwell's *Nineteen Eighty-Four*. While this may be a comforting thought, it is only part of the picture. An even greater danger to autonomy lies in the prospects for information control, whether it occurs through censorship, deceit, or limitations on members of the press or others to speak and write. While such control appears at first to limit the liberty only of those who speak or write, its widening use contributes to the more worrisome consequence of intruding on the autonomy of all.

CONCEPTS OF BEHAVIOR CONTROL

Several familiar concepts denote the ways in which people can be influenced to do what others want them to do. Each of these concepts embodies elements important for understanding autonomy, but a separate conceptual analysis of that notion will be required before we can assess the threats posed by recent technological advances enabling more powerful means of behavior control.

The concept most widely invoked to refer to ethically unacceptable means of controlling behavior is *coercion*. In its extreme form—in accordance with the so-called gunman model—coercion involves a threat of force or bodily harm by one person against another or another's relative—a child, for example.

The purpose of the coercer is to get the person coerced to do what the coercer wishes him or her to do—something that person would not do voluntarily and intentionally. On this account, a threat of force is always an element in coercive situations; for this reason they can be kept conceptually distinct from other forms of influence that have the effect of controlling behavior.

There is much debate, however, over whether merely offering people things they cannot (psychologically) refuse should properly be considered a form of coercion, when no threat of force or bodily harm is involved. Is an offer of five million dollars to commit a petty crime coercive? Is an offer of job promotion to a rising young executive, a grade of A to a premedical student, or a presidential cabinet appointment to an ambitious politician coercive, if the offer is made to secure some favor or as a promised reward for cooperating? Such acts are often termed coercive, although they lack the element of force. To keep the language clear, it would be best to restrict the term *coercion* to those acts directly involving threats of force and to use the term *manipulation* for situations that do not involve force. When someone makes generous offers of material goods or higher status in return for a favor, it might appropriately be called manipulation.

But making generous offers is not the only way of manipulating people into doing what you want them to do; there is another, even better known, method of behavior control in ordinary life. That form of manipulation takes place when one person deceives another in order to gain something for himself. Some kinds of deception are intended to help the person deceived: lying for benevolent motives (the white lie) or deceiving children to protect them from information they can't handle. But selfish or egoistic lies are motivated by the deceiver's perception of his own interests.

To manipulate people is to "handle" them, a figurative image calling to mind the way a puppeteer pulls the strings of his marionettes. That people are not mere marionettes is clear, in spite of the apparent implications of psychic determinism. Marionettes are simple creations and therefore are not comparable to humans with their biological and psychological complexity. That humans are not organic computers is a much more difficult hypothesis to refute. But the puppet image is a useful one, particularly in two situations: when the subjects of manipulation are especially weak or dependent and when they are in a situation in which they are more vulnerable than they would normally be—as in a prison, hospital, school, or other institutional setting. While manipulative acts might appropriately be termed coercion, it is best to keep distinctly separate those cases in which people may have some reasonable alternative course of action and those like the gunman model, in which they may suffer physical harm or even death if they fail to comply.

Weaker still than manipulation is seduction or temptation—offering people pleasures or goods they would like to have, but not so much that they can do nothing but accept. People who readily give in to seductions or temptations are often described as suffering from weakness of the will. The language may be quaint, but it suggests an important link between moral and psychological concepts. A person whose will is weak—who readily gives in to temptations—is generally held morally responsible and open to blame for backsliding from acceptable social behavior. Contrast this with the two preceding categories of action: doing what someone else wishes because of a threat of force (coercion) and doing what someone else wishes because of offers of great sums of money or positions of power and prestige (manipulation). Experience makes it clear why so many people give in to temptations or seductions in some form, at one time or other, and so perform acts they otherwise would not freely choose to do. But such acts are not made ethically acceptable by the mere fact that we understand why people perform them. Further justification is needed to excuse a person who acts wrongly as a result of being sorely tempted.

We come next to the concept of persuasion. Acts of persuasion often begin with the presumption that the persons to be persuaded stand roughly on an equal footing in both reason and power with those using the persuasive techniques. The techniques may include reason, argument, and entreaty. Propaganda, too, is a mode of persuasion. But insofar as propaganda or advertising uses deceit or fraud, it is more like manipulation than like persuasion. These categories are not perfectly clear and distinct, since acts of persuasion that proceed by reasoning are surely different in method and effect from persuasive techniques that appeal to the hearers' emotions. A fuller account is needed to distinguish between behavior-control techniques that bypass rational processes and those that employ them.

Distinguishing between the rational and the nonrational is also important in another pair of concepts. There is probably no sharp line between indoctrination and the notion of education. The process of educating usually involves activities (for example, role modeling) that go beyond the mere giving of information. More important, however, is the development of critical skills, which requires an ability to reason soundly. This difference between the methods of education and those of indoctrination may lie in the form of instruction, in the intentions of teachers versus indoctrinators, or in the setting—for example, a retreat run by members of a cult as opposed to a public school, where cultural and religious differences are supposed to be respected and tolerated. But indoctrination usually has other elements as well—elements of persuasion, especially those that appeal to emotions or attitudes. A special mode of indoctrination is the form of behavior control known as thought reform or brainwashing. These terms lack a clear, objective meaning, and mental health professionals are puzzled over whether the terms actually refer to some special psychological phenomenon, and if so, what it is. Different settings in which brainwashing is said to have occurred have a number of features in common: the victims are prisoners or captives, such as prisoners of war in Korea or Vietnam; or they were manipulated or enticed into joining a single-purpose group, such as the Moonies, in which leaders use extreme emotional arousal of subjects and cut them off almost totally, psychologically and socially, from their previous supports—family, friends, religion, or other ideological commitments. Similarities between the methods of behavior control used by religious cults and those employed by political or ideological groups have been described as follows:

> The persuader and his group represent a comprehensive and pervasive world view, which incorporates supremely powerful suprapersonal forces. That communism identifies these forces with the Party, while religious regard them as supernatural is relatively unimportant for the purpose of this discussion. The world view is infallible and cannot be shaken by the sufferer's failure to change or improve. The suprapersonal powers are contingently benevolent; the sufferer may succeed in obtaining their favor if he shows the right attitude. . . .
>
> The means by which changes in the sufferer are brought about include a particular type of relationship and some sort of systematic activity or ritual. . . . The systematic activity characteristically involves means of emotional arousal, often to the point of exhaustion, leading to an altered state of consciousness that increases susceptibility to outside influences.[6]

Whether these methods of behavior control are called brainwashing, thought reform, or coercive persuasion, they differ fundamentally from education in the role that reason plays in education but not in indoctrination. Yet education has another quality that makes it a powerful mode of behavior control: its lasting effect on the way people think and act. As Plato pointed out in *The Republic,* the process of education is among the most effective means of shaping later behavior, particularly when the learners are still at an impressionable age.

AUTONOMY

It is more or less evident when the freedom and privacy of individuals are restricted. It is much less clear when autonomy is being violated. Not all of the concepts of behavior control just described involve threats to autonomy. In explicating this concept, I will draw on two philosophical accounts. The first is the analysis offered by Gerald Dworkin in his article "Autonomy and Behavior Control"; the second is a paper by Bruce Miller, "Autonomy and the Refusal of Life Saving Treatment."[7] Dworkin proposes the formula autonomy equals authenticity plus independence as shorthand for a theory he fleshes out in detail. Both authenticity and independence are features that characterize a person's motivation, so Dworkin's account presupposes a psychological theory of persons in which motives are a necessary component of actions. Furthermore, since persons are able to reflect on their decisions, motives, desires, and habits, they may have positive or negative attitudes toward them. Dworkin develops his account of authenticity as a second-order trait: a person "may not simply be motivated by jealously or anger. He can also desire that his motivations be different (or the same)."[8]

This characterization of what it is to be authentic in one's motivational structure acknowledges the existence of causal determinants of behavior. What is crucial, however, is the attitude a person takes toward the influences motivating him. If one identifies with those influences, assimilates them, and wishes to be motivated in these particular ways, then they are to be considered *his* and are thus authentic. "If, on the contrary, a man resents his being motivated in certain ways, is alienated from those influences, resents acting in accordance with them, would prefer to be the kind of person who is motivated in different ways, then those influences, even though they may be causally effective, are not viewed as 'his.' "[9]

The human capacity for this sort of second-order reflection makes it possible to distinguish between authenticity and its absence. Unlike the traditional existentialist account of authenticity, Dworkin's theory does not presuppose a freedom to choose or decide what kind of person to be. It only requires that people be capable of reflecting on their motives and desires, and that they be able to develop some attitudes concerning them. Any form of psychotechnology that rendered people incapable of developing such reflective attitudes would destroy the very possibility of authenticity, and hence autonomy.

Authenticity is a necessary condition for autonomy, but taken alone it is not sufficient. Also required is that a person's motivational structure be his *own.* Dworkin offers a twofold account of what it is for a person's motivational structure to be not only *his,* but also his *own.* To this end he provides an account of two sorts of independence: procedural independence and substantive independence. Focusing on the former notion, Dworkin holds that there is a lack of procedural independence when a person's identification with his motives or the choice of the type of person he wants to be comes about as a result of manipulation, deception, and the withholding of relevant information. It is difficult, Dworkin acknowledges, to distinguish ways of influencing a person's higher order judgments (that is, judgments about what sort of person he desires to be) from those that do not result in a lack of procedural independence. "With respect to autonomy, conceived of as authenticity under conditions of procedural independence, the paradigms of interference are manipulation and deception."[10]

Which specific methods of behavior control interfere with the ability of the individual to reflect on his first-order motivations? Dworkin cites several general categories into which such specific methods fall. First are those that keep the person ignorant of the true determinants of his behavior, such as methods that rely on causal influences of which the person is unaware, for example, subliminal messages; and methods of changing attitudes and behavior that rely on the theory of cognitive dissonance, for example, getting people to shift their preferences by creating a situation of conflict in which they cannot assess or act on their true preferences. Second are methods of influence that destroy the ability of a person to reflect critically and intelligently on his motivations. These would include physical intrusion into the brain, such as psychosurgery or electrode implantation; and "processes which make the psychic costs of such examinations so painful that something analogous to coercion takes place."[11] Dworkin does not give specific examples of such processes but presumably has in mind methods such as brainwashing or coercive persuasion. He claims, however, that autonomy is in greater danger from manipulative methods of influence than from outright assaults on the individual.

Bruce Miller claims that four senses of autonomy can be distinguished: (1) autonomy as free action; (2) autonomy as authenticity; (3) autonomy as effective deliberation; and (4) autonomy as moral reflection. The first of these senses is equivalent to liberty or self-determination. According to Miller, "autonomy as free action means an action that is voluntary and intentional. An action is voluntary if it is not the result of coercion, duress or undue influence. An action is intentional if it is the conscious object of the actor."[12]

Miller's second concept of autonomy captures half of the sense of Dworkin's. Miller explicates this second sense as follows: "Autonomy as authenticity means that an action is consistent with the person's attitudes, values, dispositions, and life plans. Roughly, the person is acting in character. . . . For an action to be labeled 'inauthentic' it has to be unusual or unexpected, relatively important in itself or its consequences, and have no apparent or proffered explanation."[13] At least two features of this sense of autonomy are worth noting in the present context. First, in order to judge whether a person is acting autonomously, it is necessary to know more about that person than simply the facts surrounding the action or decision in question. To determine whether someone is acting in character, it is necessary also to have some background knowledge of that person's enduring character traits. In order to know whether or not an action or decision is consistent with a person's attitudes, values, and life plans, we must have some acquaintance with them. It is evident that a necessary element for judging the authenticity of persons will often be lacking.

The second feature to note about autonomy as authenticity is that since a person's action or decision is not to be judged in isolation, all manner of seemingly irrational decisions may turn out to be genuinely autonomous if they are found consistent with the person's character, values, or life plans. In this meaning of the concept, a person with a lifelong history of mental illness may nonetheless turn out to possess autonomy so long as his attitudes and values have remained consistent or "in character."

Miller's third sense of autonomy is autonomy as effective deliberation. This means "action taken where a person believed that he or she was in a situation calling for a decision, was aware of the alternatives and the consequences of the alternatives, evaluated both, and chose an action based on that evaluation." Miller argues that effective deliberation is distinct from authenticity and free action by virtue of the following considerations: "A person's action can be voluntary and intentional and not result from effective deliberation, as when one acts impulsively. Further, a person who has a rigid pattern of life acts authentically when he or she does the things we have all come to expect, but without effective deliberation."[14]

The fourth and final sense of autonomy Miller identifies is autonomy as moral reflection. Just as the second sense captures one of the elements of Dworkin's formula, autonomy equals authenticity plus independence," Miller's fourth sense embodies the other half of Dworkin's concept. According to Miller: "Autonomy as moral reflection means acceptance of the moral values one acts on. . . . One has reflected on these values and now accepts them as one's own. This sense of autonomy is deepest and most demanding when it is conceived as reflection on one's complete set of values, attitudes, and life plans. It requires rigorous self-analysis, awareness of alternative sets of values, commitment to a method for assessing them, and an ability to put them in place."[15] Given this characterization, it is questionable whether most people possess autonomy even some of the time. While the concept makes perfectly good sense analytically, it is probably more of an ideal notion of autonomy than one typically achieved in reality.

In addition, this sense poses an epistemological problem. It may be difficult if not impossible for anyone to assess whether another person possesses autonomy in this meaning of the term. It is hard enough to be objective about one's self when reflecting on one's own values, attitudes, and life plans. But to determine whether another person has succeeded in doing that presents an almost insuperable epistemic barrier. Miller is careful to distinguish this last sense of autonomy from that of effective deliberation: "One can do the latter without questioning the values on which one bases the choice in a deliberation."[16]

It is important for our analysis to distinguish behavior-control methods that government authorities may employ on the general population, from those developed for use on mental patients. It is entirely possible that mental patients lack what the rest of us have, that is, the basic fundamentals of autonomy. Many unfortunate individuals may suffer diminished autonomy during a bout of mental illness, or throughout their lives. Truly autonomous agents, who may sometimes act in ways that other people believe to be against their own interest, nevertheless have the moral and legal right to be let alone. Those who are mentally incompetent lack full autonomy, and so that very quality cannot be violated by imposing a method of behavior control designed to restore or produce autonomy. If there is a reasonable likelihood that medication or some form of electrical stimulation of the brain can restore or preserve a patient's autonomy, then a paternalistic intrusion can be justified by the same ethical precepts that render autonomy valuable to us in the first place.

To be autonomous in any but the most minimal sense is to have what Kant referred to as "self-legislating will." To be autonomous is to be the author of one's own beliefs, desires, and actions. The autonomous agent is one who is self-directed rather than one who blindly obeys the commands or dictates of others. These descriptions of autonomy assume the existence of an authentic self, a self that can be distinguished from the reigning influences both of other persons and of alien motives. Intuitively plausible as this concept of autonomy is in theory, it may nevertheless fail to provide practical, workable criteria for distinguishing those who have autonomy from those who lack it. But the concept remains useful for pinpointing the most devastating threats that lurk in the tools and techniques of behavior control.

MENTAL AUTONOMY AND THE LAW

In a totalitarian state, where the government is monolithic and its power absolute, citizens have little or no recourse when their rights are violated. One of the strongest defenders of human rights in the United States has been the judicial system, established by the Constitution as a branch of government separate from the legislature and the executive. It is largely the courts, at both federal and state levels, that have articulated and protected an array of individual rights in a wide variety of settings and circumstances. Among these is the right to freedom of thought, interpreted as including the protection of mental autonomy under the first amendment.

Two courts in recent years have invoked the first amendment as the basis for protecting the rights of individuals against medical treatment designed to alter their mental functioning. The first case was in 1973: the celebrated "Detroit Psychosurgery Case"—*Kaimowitz* v. *Department of Mental Health*.[17] In its decision the Michigan court prohibited physicians from performing experimental psychosurgery on an involuntarily confined mental patient. The patient had been committed under a state statute as a "criminal sexual psychopath." Although other considerations contributed to the court's decision, notably the difficulty of obtaining truly informed, voluntary consent from an incarcerated mental patient, the court's appeal to the first amendment right to freedom of thought marked the first judicial acceptance of this legal theory. In its opinion, the court made the following observations:

A person's mental processes, the communication of ideas, and the generation of ideas, come within the ambit of the First Amendment. To the extent that the First Amendment protects the dissemination of ideas and the expression of thoughts, it equally must protect the individual's right to generate ideas. . . .

Experimental psychosurgery, which is irreversible and intrusive, often leads to the blunting of emotions, the deadening of memory, the reduction of affect, and limits the ability to generate new ideas. Its potential for injury to the creativity of the individual is great, and can impinge upon the right of the individual to be free from interference with his mental processes. . . .

To allow an involuntarily detained mental patient to consent to the type of psychosurgery proposed in this case, and to permit the State to perform it, would be to condone State action in violation of basic First Amendment rights of such patients, because impairing the power to generate ideas inhibits the full dissemination of ideas.[18]

Although *Kaimowitz* v. *Department of Mental Health* was the first case in which a court applied the first amendment to a situation involving the use of psychiatric techniques of behavior control, it was not the first general statement of the legal theory that the first amendment is designed to permit individuals to think freely and to develop their unique personalities.[19] The specific application of this theory to behavior-control technologies was put forward in 1972 by M. H. Shapiro, in an article entitled "The Use of Behavior Control Technologies: A Response."[20] In a subsequent elaboration of his view, a law-review article that appeared the year after the Detroit psychosurgery case was decided, Shapiro referred explicitly to the concept of mental autonomy. He set out six criteria for distinguishing those influences that are so "assaultive of our mental autonomy, individuality or personhood" that the state must show a compelling reason to employ them against our will.[21]

A second, more recent court case that invoked the first amendment as a basis for prohibiting the forcible use of mind-altering medical treatments is *Rogers* v. *Okin*,[22] a federal district court case in Massachusetts, which held that mental patients, including those who have been involuntarily committed, have a right to refuse standard psychiatric treatment in the form of psychotropic (mind-altering) drugs. In a suit initially filed in 1975, a group of patients at Boston State Hospital claimed that their constitutional rights were being violated. Judge Joseph L. Tauro issued a temporary restraining order that prohibited seclusion of patients and forcibly medicating them in nonemergency situations without gaining properly informed consent. The temporary restraining order was made permanent in October 1979, following an extended trial.

A major criticism of this judicial decision focused on the question of the competency of mental patients to grant or refuse consent for medically recommended treatment. Yet Judge Tauro had invoked a Massachusetts law holding that mental patients are presumed competent to manage their affairs. The judge claimed that because psychotropic drugs carry risks as well as benefits, the presumption of competency should apply to a mental patient's refusal of such drugs. The court cited two grounds in defense of mental patients' right to refuse psychoactive drugs. One constitutional provision cited was the right to privacy, a right also noted in the *Kaimowitz* psychosurgery case. The second provision cited in the *Rogers* case was the first amendment's protection of communication, held to include protection of thought. "The court reasoned that the freedom to produce ideas is a necessary precondition of the freedom to communicate ideas. Because they affect a person's mood, attitude and thinking processes, Judge Tauro held that the involuntary administration of psychotropic drugs violates the first amendment right to freedom of thought." This case, along with similar developments in other jurisdictions, has led to a growing clash between civil libertarians and the psychiatric establishment.[23] Civil libertarians hail these judicial decisions as marking an important gain in the rights of mental patients against forcible treatment. On the other side, prominent psychiatrists are dismayed by these decisions because of their presumed consequences for the welfare of patients and their overall best interests.

It is only recently, as illustrated by the two cases just described, that psychiatric patients have been granted legal protections against the forcible administration of treatments deemed medically beneficial by their caregivers. In other cases, state courts have held that a patient's consent is required before "intrusive" forms of treatment such as electroshock can be given. These latter cases, however, did not rest on first amendment grounds protecting freedom of thought or mental autonomy but rather on the now widely accepted doctrine of informed consent for biomedical treatment and research. There remains a problem, however, with the rationale used in the *Rogers* case to grant mental patients the right to refuse psychotropic drugs.

The problem with the rationale was noted at the end of the preceding section: laws and precedents designed to protect the autonomy of persons only make sense when those persons can legitimately be judged as having autonomy in the first place. Although it is very likely that some mental patients have disorders that do not compromise their preexisting autonomy, it is equally likely that other patients lack autonomy because of their mental illness. The relationship between autonomy, as characterized in this essay, and the legal-psychological concept of competency is vague and uncertain. The conceptual links stand in need of clarification, and empirical data about such patients would help in understanding their ability to function in a variety of settings. The most telling criticism of Judge Tauro's decision is that he failed to acknowledge the likelihood that a good many psychiatric patients are mentally incompetent and therefore lack a reasonable basis for refusing drugs that may be beneficial. This point can be expressed better using the notion of autonomy: mental autonomy cannot be violated when it is lacking in the first place. For those mental patients in whom genuine autonomy is lacking, it may well be that psychoactive medication can instill or promote the ability to generate ideas, rather than the other way around. The resolution of this problem must rest ultimately on empirical findings, on theoretical progress in psychiatry, and on a conceptual decision regarding the nature of mental autonomy and the conditions for ascribing it to persons.

THREATS TO AUTONOMY IN 1984

It is tempting to view the society Orwell depicts in *Nineteen Eighty-Four* as more threatening to autonomy by virtue of its methods of information control than by its direct modes of manipulating behavior, which invade individual privacy and severely limit liberty. The parolee in whose skull an electronic device is implanted would thus suffer less loss of autonomy than one whose thoughts and actions are manipulated by what those in power allow him to see and hear, and by the vocabulary available for forming concepts and reflecting critically. The parolee's privacy is invaded by a device that records his brain waves and monitors his geographic location with remote monitoring able to keep track of these features of his brain and bodily behavior. The present state of scientific knowledge pertaining to brain processes and mental functioning is nowhere near unlocking the mysteries that would make possible inferences about the meaning and purpose of thoughts from a graphic or auditory record of electroencephalographic activity. The parolee's brain waves may be monitored, but it is impossible to interpret the nature of his thoughts—their meaning and content—solely from those brain waves. So long as the parolee knows of the existence of the device implanted in his head, the threat to his autonomy is only indirect. The parolee's ability to move about freely will surely be affected by an implanted device that reports his physical location to a central station, especially if that station can transmit messages back to him. In the case of the parolee, then, the knowledge that his brain and bodily behavior are being monitored and recorded surely restricts his freedom and privacy. The direct inroads into his autonomy are far fewer.

Consider, in contrast, the situation regarding individuals who are regularly or systematically deceived, from whom information is withheld or distorted, and who have no independent means of discovering, verifying, or falsifying information they are allowed access to. The deliberate and total control of information by a central source, be it the state, the church, the military, teachers, parents, or jailors, poses a direct threat to autonomy in the terms described by Dworkin and Miller. People can experience little in the way of procedural independence, not to mention substantive independence, when all information that reaches them is censored or when the terms in which information is parceled out are couched in Newspeak.

Recall again the aims of the state in Orwell's *Nineteen Eighty-Four,* and the means used to achieve those ends. "In a Party member, . . . not even the smallest deviation of opinion on the most unimportant subject can be tolerated. . . . A Party member is required to have not only the right opinions, but the right instincts." These ends are achieved by a variety of methods, all working together to produce conformity in behavior and orthodoxy in thought and feeling. "An elaborate mental training, undergone in childhood and grouping itself round the Newspeak words *crimestop, blackwhite,* and *doublethink,* makes a Party member unwilling and unable to think too deeply on any subject whatever." Applying Dworkin's analysis to Orwell's fictional society, we see how both procedural and substantive independence are precluded by the distortion of facts and manipulation of the thinking processes resulting from the use of Newspeak.

The proper exercise of a *doublethink* by individuals marks the successful completion of the Party's ultimate goal of thought control. It also demonstrates one way in which autonomy can be eradicated. "To tell deliberate lies while genuinely believing in them, to forget any fact that has become inconvenient, and then, when it becomes necessary again, to draw it back from oblivion for just so long as it is needed, to deny the existence of objective reality and all the while to take account of the reality which one denies—all this is indispensably necessary."

As for the other ingredient in autonomy—authenticity—whether that is present or absent requires that a further story be told. Authenticity involves the ability to engage in second-order reflection on one's motivations and desires. If we possess authenticity, "we always retain the possibility of stepping back and judging where we are and where we want to be."[24] In order to determine whether total and deliberate centralized control of information affects an individual's authenticity, we would have to supply numerous specific details. Such determinations would have to be made on a case-by-case basis. Furthermore, to specify just what is involved in the ability to engage in second-order reflection on one's motives or desires requires a well-developed personality theory accepted as providing an overall explanation of human behavior. It thus becomes a complex exercise in theory, as well as in practice, to ascertain the circumstances in which the "authenticity" component of autonomy is present and when it is not.

Here again, George Orwell presents a striking account of how authenticity can be eliminated entirely from the ingredients of an individual's personality. The means of achieving this end need not include invasive methods or advanced technology, but can be limited to age-old techniques of behavior control, combined with the power of Newspeak to affect the way ideas are generated.

> The first and simplest stage in the discipline, which can be taught even to young children, is called, in Newspeak, *crimestop. Crimestop* means the faculty of stopping short, as though by instinct, at the threshold of any dangerous thought. It includes the power of not grasping analogies, of failing to perceive logical errors, of misunderstanding the simplest arguments if they are inimical to Ingsoc, and of being bored or repelled by any train of thought which is capable of leading in a heretical direction.

Control of the ability to generate ideas, in ways that require few technological advances and not much sophistication in the latest developments in neuropsychiatry, is the most chilling aspect of Orwell's tale. It reminds us that we have as much to fear from the implantation of ideas in the mind as from the insertion of electrodes in the skull. Insofar as modern psychotechnology poses a threat to autonomy, it carries the danger to our Western democratic values often attributed to it. Ultimately, however, the danger lies not so much in the type of technological intrusion, nor even in the degree of invasiveness of such methods. Instead, as Orwell portrays with such insight, it is the power of those with authority to affect people's ability to authentically and independently generate ideas that we need most to guard against.

NOTES

1. Robert L. Schwitzgebel, "Emotions and Machines: A Commentary on the Context and Strategy of Psychotechnology," in *Psychotechnology: Electronic Control of Mind and Behavior,* ed. Robert L. Schwitzgebel and Ralph K. Schwitzgebel (New York: Holt, Rinehart and Winston, 1973), p. 15.
2. *New York Times,* February 12, 1984.
3. Jose M. R. Delgado, "Intracerebral Radio Stimulation and Recording in Completely Free Patients," in *Psychotechnology,* Schwitzgebel and Schwitzgebel, p. 188.
4. Thomas Zander, "Prolixin Decanoate: Big Brother by Injection?" *Journal of Psychiatry and Law* 5, no. 1 (1977): 55–75.
5. Jonas Robitscher, *The Powers of Psychiatry* (Boston: Houghton Mifflin, 1980), pp. 457–58.

6. Jerome D. Frank, *Persuasion and Healing* (New York: Schocken Books, 1974), pp. 103–4.
7. Gerald Dworkin, "Autonomy and Behavior Control," *Hastings Center Report* 6 (1976): 23–28; Bruce Miller, "Autonomy and the Refusal of Lifesaving Treatment," *Hastings Center Report* 11 (1981): 22–28.
8. Dworkin, "Autonomy and Behavior Control," p. 24.
9. Ibid., p. 25.
10. Ibid., p. 26.
11. Ibid.
12. Miller, "Autonomy and Refusal," p. 24.
13. Ibid.
14. Ibid.
15. Ibid., p. 25.
16. Ibid.
17. *Kaimowitz* v. *Department of Mental Health*, Civ. No. 73-19434-AW (Cir. Ct. Wayne County, Mich., July 10, 1973).
18. Court's opinion in *Kaimowitz*, reprinted in Willard M. Gaylin, Joel S. Meister, and Robert C. Neville, eds., *Operating on the Mind* (New York: Basic Books, 1975), pp. 200–203.
19. See Nancy Rhoden, "The Right to Refuse Psychotropic Drugs," *Harvard Civil Rights Civil Liberties Law Review* 15 (Fall 1980), especially pp. 388–96.
20. Michael H. Shapiro, "The Use of Behavior Control Technologies: A Response," *Issues in Criminology* 7 (1972).
21. Michael H. Shapiro, "Legislating the Control of Behavior Control: Autonomy and the Coercive Use of Organic Therapies," *Southern California Law Review* 47 (1974): 261.
22. *Rogers* v. *Okin*, 478 F. Supp. 1342 (D. Mass. 1979), rev. in part, 634 F. 2d 650 (1st Cir. 1980).
23. Rhoden, "Right to Refuse"; quotation from p. 373.
24. Dworkin, "Autonomy and Behavior Control," p. 25.

Mark Crispin Miller

BIG BROTHER IS YOU, WATCHING

The only comprehension left to thought is horror at the incomprehensible. Just as the reflective onlooker, meeting the laughing placard of a toothpaste beauty, discerns in her flashlight grin the grimace of torture, so from every joke, even from every pictorial representation, he is assailed by the death sentence on the subject, which is implicit in the universal triumph of subjective reason.

—T. W. Adorno, *Minima Moralia*

he opening sentence of *Nineteen Eighty-Four* recalls some of the oldest of English poetical traditions, but only to imply that they mean nothing in the novel's world: "It was a bright, cold day in April, and the clocks were striking thirteen." With its two trimeter clauses and marked caesura, the sentence initially suggests the opening couplet of a folk ballad; but then this familiar rhythmic evocation is abruptly canceled out. The line's quasi-nostalgic appeal is undercut, first of all, by the futuristic revelation that Oceanic clocks strike more than twelve. And the effect of this surprising news is reinforced by the ending's metrical dislocation, as that spondee "thirteen" falls jarringly in place of the expected monosyllable. Moreover, as with the sentence's balladic rhythm, so with its peculiar April day, another reference that at first seems half-familiar, then wholly alien. Despite its vaguely comforting reverberations, this April day does not exemplify that balmy, revivifying April sung by the English poets since Chaucer, but is strangely "bright" and "cold," suggesting that, within the world we are about to enter, such antique associations have been eliminated.

The sentence seems at first to beckon us back home but ends by leaving us bewildered, as on a sunny morning when you think you are awake until you sense that you are dreaming it. And yet the dreamlike eeriness of this new world is merely the final consequence of the most clear-sighted practicality. In the world liberated by the Inner Party, all vestiges of literary culture—both popular and learned—have long since been discarded as fantastic nonsense. Those obsolete texts by Chaucer, Shakespeare, Eliot, and others, with their impressionistic references to April, have now been modernized for good, made equally accessible and clear in Newspeak versions; and the rustic traditions that once sustained the ballad have also been wiped out, even from among the unenlightened proles. Moreover, in its drive to junk all preexistent myth, the Party has excised not only poetry, but even those arbitrary terms and structures once used to mark the passage of time. Whereas before the Revolution the clocks had been attuned to go from one to twelve twice every day, that purely customary sequence need not persist in the Party's readjusted world, where the military scheme of hours makes better sense. Indeed, that bright, cold afternoon that starts the novel may not, in fact, represent an unseasonable "day in April," but a day in what we still call March or January, since the months need not refer any longer to the quaint divisions of the Roman calendar; nor, for that matter, does the Oceanic 1984 necessarily denote a point along our temporal continuum, which still refers to the legendary birth of a deity outmoded by the Party.

"It was a bright, cold day in April, and the clocks were striking thirteen." This disorienting line of antipoetry does not just alienate us, then, but implicitly refers us to the intellectual origins of all contemporary alienation. Although, in effect, the sentence is surrealistic, with its sudden vision of a world that seems to have gone mad, this new world actually represents the final triumph of rationality itself, the distant source of the Oceanic madness that has so disastrously betrayed it. Thus the object of Orwell's horrific satire is not any one totalitarian regime, but the necessary modern urge that has indirectly brought about all modern tyrannies, whether of the left or right, whether centralized or pluralistic. What Orwell understood with such intolerable clarity was the appalling likelihood that the most destructive modern systems have emerged, paradoxically, out of the very impulse to transcend destruction: the impulse of Enlightenment.

Orwell had begun to intuit this paradox in the late thirties, when he wrote the controversial second part of *The Road to Wigan Pier;* and as war broke out and then persisted, his intuition seemed to be continually reconfirmed by the massive barbarism that had somehow emerged out of civilization at its latest moment: "As I write," begins "The Lion and the Unicorn," composed in 1940, "highly civilized human beings are flying overhead, trying to kill me."[1] It was the war, a conflict at once atavistic and sophisticated, that led Orwell and certain others to contemplate the long self-contradiction of Western progress. In 1943, as Orwell was making notes toward his last novel, two other observers, although working out of intellectual traditions wholly different from Orwell's, were collaborating on a brilliant, dismal essay that illuminates precisely the same ruinous process that is the implicit subject of *Nineteen Eighty-Four.* Exiled in Los Angeles, Max Horkheimer and T. W. Adorno wrote the *Dialectic of Enlightenment* to elaborate their argument that mechanistic "Progress," as Orwell had once put it, "is just as much of a swindle as reaction."[2]

For Horkheimer and Adorno, "Enlightenment" refers not simply to the optimistic moment of the *philosophes,* but to the drive, as old as civilization, toward the rational mastery of nature; or, to put it more accurately, that drive toward mastery which is itself the source and purpose of civilization. The authors subvert complacent faith in progress by disproving the absolute distinction between primitive societies and the modern world that seems to have transcended them; for the aim of men, both then and now, has been to turn the natural world into the instrument of their own power. Just as archaic groups attempted to manage the inchoate forces of their universe through priestly ritual and human sacrifice, so too have modern men, from the time of Bacon's first intellectual prospectus, worked to make the material world both useful and predictable, through the application of technology and scientific method. What distinguishes the historical era which we call the Enlightenment, then, is not its objectifying tendency per se, but its total rationalization of that tendency, proclaimed "under the banner of radicalism."[3] Now nature will serve those who study it most coolly and relentlessly, having freed it from the obfuscations of folk wisdom, church doctrine and Aristotelian dogma: "The program of the Enlightenment was the disenchantment of the world; the dissolution of myths and the substitution of knowledge for fancy."[4]

This program was conceived by its earliest proponents as a means of universal renewal, "the Effecting of all Things possible," as Bacon put it.[5] And yet the unrestrained demythifying impulse has led us not to rejuvenation but toward apocalypse. In its efforts to appropriate the natural world by wiping out the myths that had made it legible, the Enlightenment began a process of erasure that soon moved beyond the defunct beliefs of tribe and church, to subvert *all* metaphysical conceptions, particularly those which had justified the process in the first place: God, then Nature went the way of the countless spirits that had animated the global wilderness; and now such later abstractions as History, Man, the people, social justice, and the like, also impossible to defend as strictly rational, have also therefore come to seem mere sentimental fabrications: "For the Enlightenment, whatever does not conform to the rule of computation and utility is suspect. So long as it can develop undisturbed by any outward repression, there is no holding it. In the process, it treats its own ideas of human rights exactly as it does the older universals."[6]

Enlightenment, then, is finally bent on leaving nothing extant but its own implicit violence. As it proceeds to blast away each of its own prior pretexts, this explosive rationality comes ever closer, not to "truth"—which category it has long since shattered—but to the open realization of its own coercive animus, purified of *all* delusions—including, finally, rationality itself.[7] Into the ideological vacuum which it has created so efficiently there rushes its own impulse to destroy and keep destroying: Orwell perceived the same suicidal process at work in Western thought and explicitly described it several years before elaborating that perception in his last novel.

In a piece written for *Time and Tide* in 1940, Orwell considers that modern moment when Christianity had finally proven indefensible. At that moment, "it was absolutely essential that the soul should be cut away," for religious belief had "become in essence a lie, a semi-conscious device for keeping the rich rich and the poor poor." And so the major writers of the last two centuries, the heroic standard-bearers of Enlightenment—"Gibbon, Voltaire, Rousseau, Shelley, Byron, Dickens, Stendhal, Samuel Butler, Ibsen, Zola, Flaubert, Shaw, Joyce"—proceeded to demolish what was left of that old falsehood; but the outcome of that just campaign seemed to be a total, irreversible injustice: "For two hundred years we had sawed and sawed and sawed at the branch we were sitting on. And in the end, much more suddenly than anyone had foreseen, our efforts were rewarded, and down we came. But unfortunately there had been a little mistake. The thing at the bottom was not a bed of roses after all. It was a cesspool filled with barbed wire."[8]

Like Horkheimer and Adorno, Orwell saw the unprecedented horrors of mid-century not as the aberrant results of any single system of beliefs, but as the inevitable consequence of the dumb, persistent onward urge that had devastated one belief after another. It was the relentless impulse of Enlightenment that had enabled the conceptions of the death camp, the atomic bomb, the machinery of total propaganda—each one a highly rational construction, devoted to a terminal irrationality. And that autonomous rationality, Orwell believed, would quickly supersede even those new myths devised to justify it in the present. Soon such notions as "the master race" and "socialism in one country" would seem as quaint as "Harry, England, and St. George," as Enlightenment approached that perfect disillusionment whereby the Inner Party keeps itself in power: "We are different," says O'Brien, "from all the oligarchies of the past in that we know what we are doing." For Orwell and his German counterparts, the expert atrocities of the late Enlightenment foretold the emergence of a world wholly dominated by the self-promoting urge to dominate, an urge whose only manifesto might be expressed in these infamous tautologies: "The object of persecution is persecution. The object of torture is torture. The object of power is power."

And yet Enlightenment is necessary. "We are wholly convinced," write Horkheimer and Adorno, "that social freedom is inseparable from enlightened thought,"[9] a conviction to which Orwell too always held firmly. Neither he nor the two Germans ever called crudely for the repeal of the

Enlightenment; for if progress "is as much of a swindle as reaction," the reflexive movement backward can only end up in that same abyss toward which the automatic movement forward always speeds. Rather, these critical advocates of Enlightenment recognized that progressive thought, while indispensable, at the same time "contains the seed of the reversal universally apparent today"; and so it was their project to salvage the best original intentions of Enlightenment, by encouraging "reflection on [its] recidivist element." "The point is . . . that Enlightenment *must consider itself,* if men are not to be wholly betrayed."[10] We must therefore read and reread *Nineteen Eighty-Four,* not as a piece of cold war propaganda, but as a work that might enlighten us as to the fatal consequences of Enlightenment, including the current glare of publicity that has all but blacked out the text itself.

"It was a bright cold day in April, and the clocks were striking thirteen." Having thus adroitly engineered its total severance from the past, the Party represents the demythifying mechanism of Enlightenment at its most successful; but such success amounts to failure, since the Party's efforts to annihilate the past have only reimposed it. The Party's system, founded upon the total extirpation of cruel nature, has itself reverted to cruel nature. Life in the state of Oceania is nasty, brutish, and short, a furtive passage through an urban sprawl that is as primitive and dangerous as any jungle: London swarms with "gorilla-faced guards" and "small, beetle-like" men, and even its machines suggest the wilderness which they oppose: "In the far distance a helicopter skimmed down between the roofs, hovered for an instant like a bluebottle, and darted away again with a curving flight." And, as nature has been recreated at its most inimical, so has the patriarchal God, an overseer more wrathful and alert than ever: "The little sandy-haired woman had flung herself forward over the back of the chair in front of her. With a tremulous murmur that sounded like 'My Savior!' she extended her arms toward the screen. Then she buried her face in her hands. It was apparent that she was uttering a prayer." And even the defunct conventions of poetry reemerge uncannily from the mechanism that was built to obliterate them. Although "composed without any human intervention whatever on an instrument known as a versificator," the lines sung continually by the washerwoman outside Charrington's shop repeat that strangely inexpungible allusion: "It was only an 'opeless fancy, / It passed like an Ipril dye."

Thus Enlightenment hurries forward toward the very state from which it flees, a grand pattern that recurs in small and subtle ways throughout the novel, just as it defines the general structure of the narrative itself. As Winston Smith helplessly observes, "the end was contained in the beginning." Therefore the fateful number 101 does not only designate the room wherein the hero relapses forever into primal incoherence but also symbolizes all such reversion, the terminal arrival at the point of origin. Nor is this process only temporal, but spatial and psychological as well, informing every movement, every thought, with an absoluteness that conveys more poignantly than any dissertation the full horror of whatever is "totalitarian." In Oceania there is no possible escape from Oceania, but only continual rediscoveries of Oceania where one least expects it. "It was a bright, cold day in April . . ." Although it seems at first to proffer a venerable pastoral solace, this "April" is merely one more of the Party's inventions, a term irrelevant to that April known before the Revolution; and so this "day in April" is as "bright" and "cold" as "the place where there is no darkness," another promised refuge that turns out to have been devised by the very forces from which it seemed at first to offer sanctuary. And so it is with the Brotherhood, with Charrington's retreat, with Charrington himself.

And, as there is no refuge for the novel's hero, neither is the hero himself a solid refuge for the novel's readers; for even Winston Smith embodies that cruel force which he ostensibly opposes. Like the April day that chills.him, he too appears at first to represent an exception that turns out to be the rule: "It was a bright, cold day in April, and the clocks were striking thirteen. Winston Smith, his chin nuzzled into his breast in an effort to escape the vile wind, slipped quickly through the glass doors of Victory Mansions, though not quickly enough to prevent a swirl of gritty dust from entering along with him."

Although, until his "reintegration," Winston Smith is clearly different from the rest of Oceania, it would be a sentimental overstatement to insist that, once the Party has hollowed him out, it has extinguished the world's last sturdy subject. Even at first, "the last man in Europe" is already losing his fragile selfhood, which is entirely contingent on his furtive, doomed refusal to accept the status quo. The figure who "slipped quickly through the glass doors of Victory Mansions" already seems as insubstantial as a breeze; whereas, conversely, that "swirl of gritty dust," by "entering along with him," seems to walk in on human legs. But this first image of the hero implies not just that he is losing his tenuous uniqueness and coherence, but that he loses them precisely in attempting to retain them, since it is in making "an effort to escape the vile wind" that Winston Smith seems to turn into mere wind himself.

Until his final degradation, Winston Smith is repeatedly undone by this same paradox, as his very efforts to escape or to combat the Party become themselves the proof of this inviolable membership. In starting a diary, he deliberately commits what is probably a capital offense against the Party; and yet the first result of this dissident gesture is an effusion of perfect orthodoxy, enthusiastic praise for an atrocious war film seen the night before. Similarly, after his first sexual encounter with Julia, he realizes that the same belligerent coldness had entered into even this forbidden pleasure, thereby undoing it: "Their embrace had been a battle, the climax a victory. It was a blow struck against the Party. It was a political act." And his most explicit act of defiance—his promise to O'Brien that he will commit whatever subversive crimes "the Brotherhood" requires of him—only demonstrates the futility of his ardent opposition, which makes him sound less like the Party's clearsighted enemy than like one of its deluded founders:

> "You are prepared to give your lives?"
> "Yes."
> "You are prepared to commit murder?"
> "Yes."
> "To commit acts of sabotage which may cause the death of hundreds of innocent people?"
> "Yes."

And so on, the hero recalling those steeliest revolutionaries of the past, whose self-discipline prepared the way, not for some hoped-for earthly paradise, but for the enlightened Party that would vaporize them.

In opposing the Party, Winston Smith approximates it, because the Party has arisen from the same impulse that motivates his opposition: the impulse of Enlightenment. Having long since disabused itself of every metaphysical distraction, the Party not only sees all, but—more frighteningly—sees through all. What makes the Party's gaze so devastating, then, is not just its sweep, enabled by the telescreens, but its penetration. The Party sees through anyone who would see through the Party, because the Party has seen through itself already, demythifying itself, not to defeat itself, of course, but to make itself eternal. In struggling to see through the Party, therefore, Winston Smith inadequately emulates it. Each of his rebellious actions puts him in the ludicrous position of clumsily anticipating the system that he wants to terminate. Whether surreptitiously writing, defiantly rutting, or conspiring to subvert an odious regime, he merely reenacts old battles long since fought and won by the Enlightenment on its way to Ingsoc.

Nor does the Party thus superannuate only its opponents. In its relentless onward thrust, sooner or later it simultaneously bypasses and exterminates everyone above ground level, whether they hate the Party, or zealously applaud it, or vacuously go about their business: Syme is vaporized, despite his exemplary commitment to Enlightenment linguistics, because, Winston thinks, "he sees too clearly and speaks too plainly"; but then Parsons too is vaporized—for "thoughtcrime," although he seems to have no thoughts.

However, to describe the Party as a force that indiscriminately kills is to mistake its sway for simple tyranny, like the reign of Caligula or of Henry VIII; whereas the Party's sway is total, at once more subtle and extensive than the rule of any mere dictator, however bloodthirsty. For it is not the Oceanic bloodshed per se that proves the Party's destructiveness, but the object of that bloodshed, the extinction of all resistant subjectivity. As Orwell put it in "Lear, Tolstoy and the Fool," it makes no difference whether one's would-be oppressors work cruelly or seductively, since, in either case, their intention toward the subject is to erase him in the name of their own power, to "get inside his brain and dictate his thoughts for him in the minutest particulars." In Oceania, the victim is extinguished long before his heart is stopped by force, or even if it never is, since, even while still breathing, that victim has already become a mere Oceanic repetition of the state that may or may not have him shot, redundantly, one day. Thus Syme, "a tiny creature," is nothing more than the linguistic diminution that consumes him, and Parsons too, wet and energetic, in only a particle of the general flood. Once vaporized, therefore, these nonentities are still no less extant than those model citizens who have survived them—Winston's wife, for instance, without "a thought in her head that was not a slogan," or the functionary whom Winston hears "quack-quack-quacking" at lunch, each official phrase "jerked out very rapidly, and, as it seemed, all in one piece, like a line of type cast solid."

If all of these blank members of the Outer Party have succumbed to the state's hollowing process, then perhaps the members of the Inner Party, the supervisors of that process, have not themselves been emptied by it: O'Brien, a representative of that invisible elite, does seem somehow to stand above the universal nullity, or so the hero thinks, yearning desperately for some communion with this ostensible exception, who "had the appearance of being a person that you could talk to, if somehow you could cheat the telescreens and get him alone." It is O'Brien's curiously aristocratic mien that excites this vague hope: his "peculiar grave courtesy," and "urbane manner" that contradicts his "prizefighter's physique." Winston Smith is heartened by O'Brien's strange detachment, his air of irony and secret knowledge, which suggests a sympathetic rebel hidden deep within the oligarch.

And yet O'Brien too is wholly a microcosm of the system that has both empowered and undone him. "So ugly yet so civilized," he embodies Oceania itself, or rather, that process of Enlightenment whereby Oceania has been forced forward to its origins. The hero has misread him absolutely. The discrepancy between O'Brien's coarse bulk and smooth deportment is not the sign of some dialectical potential, as Winston Smith had assumed, but, on the contrary, just another instance of the same final contradiction that has arrested the whole world, its managers included. And, more important, O'Brien's air of ironic detachment, in which the hero had discerned a promise of transcendence, is in fact the deadliest of all the Inner Party's secret weapons. "More even than of strength, [O'Brien] gave an impression of confidence and of an understanding tinged with irony." Even more than through relentless terror, it is through relentless irony that the Party subverts anyone who, explicitly or even inwardly, tries to resist its gaze.

Long before they have seized Winston Smith, the Party leaders have already neutralized his dissidence through derisive imitation, thereby transforming his struggle into an empty joke for their own unhappy entertainment. O'Brien himself helped write the book attributed to Goldstein, and so that "heavy black volume," Winston's Bible, turns out to be a satire; and even O'Brien's first encounter with the hero, in "the long corridor at the Ministry," is an implicit parody of the hero's first encounter with Julia in the same place. And the gentle "Mr. Charrington" is also an ironic spectacle, meant to draw the hero out, not to entrap him—an unnecessary step in lawless Oceania—but to make his desire laughable. But even if it never bothered thus actively to set the hero up for ridicule, the Inner Party would still have played him for a laugh, simply by looking on, unseen and delighted, at the torment which he thought was private.

More fundamentally than by its instruments of torture, then, the Party is made mighty by its own mimetic subtlety and keen spectatorship—the weapons of pure irony, which is, necessarily, the attitudinal vehicle and expression of Enlightenment. Both like Enlightenment and fostered by it, pure irony denudes the world of every value, devastating, just with a little smile and deft repetition, whatever person, concept, feeling, belief, or tradition it encounters, until there is nothing left but the urge to ironize. And so the ironist, at last contemptuous even of the values that had previously bolstered his contempt, is forced to keep on being ironic, because that attitude is all that can distinguish him from the nullity that underlies and enables it. Such an attitude depends, however, on the persistence of objects worthy of derision, even if all such objects have already been wiped out by enlightened thought and ridicule. The ironist must therefore revive anachronistic postures, reinvent the enemies long since put to rest, or else he becomes depleted. Thus the ironist is forced to follow the ruinous trajectory of Enlightenment, succumbing to his own process of erasure, and in that process merely reevoking the objects which he had intended to destroy.

Posing as a conspirator, O'Brien "filled the glasses and raised his own glass by the stem. 'What shall it be this time?' he said, still with the same faint suggestion of irony. 'To the confusion of the Thought Police? To the death of

Big Brother? To humanity? To the future?' " Only later do we realize that these apparent exhortations are nothing more than sardonic little jokes: O'Brien is sadistically equivocating, since, as he knows already, "the death of Big Brother" is impossible, "the confusion of the Thought Police" redundant, and "humanity" an essence that he means not to vindicate, but to extinguish in "the future," which, we learn eventually, O'Brien sees as "a boot stamping on a human face—forever." Thus the hero's cherished, vague ideals are played for laughs by the resolute O'Brien; and yet, for all his resoluteness, O'Brien is, without the selfhood which he mimics, nothing. Similarly, once Winston's guardian agent doffs his excellent disguise as "Mr. Charrington," he at once regresses from the individuality which he performs into "a member of the Thought Police," alert, hostile, and anonymous, like the Party that deploys him.

The obsessive thoroughness with which the Party re-creates what it purports to have transcended attests to a distorted longing for it. Although intended as ironic, the spectacle that is Mr. Charrington and his shop is so fully and convincingly detailed, the agent's performance so finely nuanced, that the actor and directors must unknowingly desire the past which they have parodied so expertly. And when O'Brien finally reveals his true identity (or nonidentity) to Winston Smith in the actual "place where there is no darkness," the ambiguity of his reply also suggests that his very irony is itself an expression of the desire which it keeps cruelly mimicking:

> "They've got you too!" [Winston] cried.
> "They got me a long time ago," said O'Brien with a mild, almost regretful irony.

What the Party leaders laugh at in their victim, then, is not, in fact, a desire which they themselves have transcended, but, on the contrary, a desire which they themselves still feel, and which they express pervertedly through their permanent campaign against it. And even in this perversion Winston Smith resembles and anticipates them. At the beginning of the novel, we recognize the hero's longing in his posture: "Winston Smith, his chin nuzzled into his breast in an effort to escape the vile wind," is a figure trying to evade Oceania by mothering himself, trying to escape the coldness of Enlightenment by re-enacting that primal situation which Enlightenment attacks and yet restores in a perverted form. Although still capable of acting on this desire, however, he is, like any other proper Oceanic citizen, both unconscious of it, and, while driven by it, quick to side with every other Oceanic citizen against it—an indirect self-censure which he too carries out through ironic spectatorship.

Just after he has slipped into Victory Mansions in that revealing attitude, he writes, "only imperfectly aware of what he was setting down," an orthodox denunciation of the desire which he has just expressed out on the street, and which now continues to impel his jeering at it: "April 4th, 1984. Last night to the flicks. One very good one of a ship full of refugees being bombed somewhere in the Mediterranean." Both in the midst of this spectatorship and in recounting it, Winston Smith shares with the other members of the audience a cruel, sheltered pleasure in the methodical explosion of every figure on the screen: "a great huge fat man trying to swim away with a helicopter after him," then disappearing, torn by bullets, the "audience shouting with laughter as he sank." And yet this sadistic joy in the destruction of those fictitious "refugees" is also masochistic, as the hero unwittingly reveals in describing, still with evident approval of their fate, the next few victims, whose image expresses vividly his own desire as he has just betrayed it to us: "there was a middle-aged woman might have been a jewess sitting up in the bow with a little boy about three years old in her arms. little boy screaming with fright and hiding his head between her breasts as if he was trying to burrow right into her."

When, at the end, Winston Smith is rapt for good in credulous spectatorship, he is himself just like those refugees, a visible example of floundering and defeated opposition, shunned by all and waiting to be shot. The Inner Party is surely gratified by this atrocious spectacle—we can imagine them, sitting and jeering his submersion into Oceanic nonconsciousness, just like that earlier "audience shouting with laughter as he sank." But there is no ultimate distinction between such viewers and the disintegration that amuses them. In cheering the destruction of their own prototype, they cheer their own destruction. And so, in the end, all collapses into hateful liquid. Weeping "gin-soaked tears," his memory ebbing, the ex-hero, an old joke in the eyes of those who have been drenched along with him, clings to the image of Big Brother's nonexistent face, as Enlightenment fulfills itself, and humanity breaks down into a flood as vast and absolute as the flood in which all life originated.

As we leave the world of Orwell's novel dissolving into its own flux, we must turn back to our more tangible society, wherein the novel now receives so much perfunctory attention, and ask how Orwell's vision reflects on American life in 1984. We can best begin to answer this unpleasant question by pointing out that most of those who have raised it have done so only to dismiss it, proclaiming in a flood of essays, editorials, and advertisements that *Nineteen Eighty-Four* cannot relate to our free society, whereas the novel does, of course, apply directly—and exclusively—to the Soviet Union. This conception of the novel is nearly as old as the novel itself, which, once published, was immediately hailed by some American conservatives as a vivid anti-Communist manifesto. Although Orwell himself publicly deplored this propagandistic reduction of his work,[11] in the work itself he had already satirized just such warlike interpretation. In Oceania there can be no lasting animus against the status quo, since every individual reaction to the Party's rule is deflected by the Party into collective hatred of the Party's latest enemy. Thus the reader who appropriates the novel as a weapon succeeds only in resembling its most benighted characters, who also bolster their own system through the very discontent in which it keeps them. (As we might expect, the chauvinistic misreading of *Nineteen Eighty-Four* suits the purposes of those Soviet ideologues who jeer America, just as it has helped express the American condemnation of the Soviet Union.[12])

Such jingoistic interpretation exemplifies the paralysis of Enlightenment, wherein the means of liberation becomes an object that prolongs captivity: the warlike reader keeps himself forever moving forward in aggressive readiness, justifying his repressive posture with the very text that calls it into question.[13] However, it is not only such reactionary misreadings that inadvertently demonstrate the truth of *Nineteen Eighty-Four*. Because the novel's power derives primarily from Orwell's apprehension that the most progressive attitudes demand their own eventual reversal, the ruthless left-liberal reader vindicates that apprehension even more directly than his right-wing counterpart. That enlightened reader who, in the name of justice or equality, treats the novel as a guide to some vast campaign of mechanistic social engineering therefore only advocates the same process that motivates the Inner Party. What we may call the vulgar feminist position, for instance, which argues that we must get rid of "traditional sexual love" in order to preempt Big Brother,[14] repeats O'Brien's way of thinking and even anticipates one feature of his program: "We shall abolish the orgasm. Our neurologists are at work upon it now."

In short, those who, whether on the left or the right, use the novel as a social or political instrument thereby betray their inability to step outside of it, much less read it, illuminating nothing but their own inclusion in the iron process which the novel criticizes. But *Nineteen Eighty-Four* enables us to read with clarity not just itself but the whole current moment in which it is so widely celebrated and distorted. Orwell was, of course, not thinking of this moment in America when he conceived and wrote his novel; nor would it make sense to demonstrate a crude equation of America with Oceania. Orwell wrote not as a prophet but as an artist. Rather than simply itemize the world of *Nineteen Eighty-Four* into those details that have "come true" and those that haven't, then, we must discover within this satire of Enlightenment its oblique reflections on our own enlightened culture, whose continuities with Orwell's time and place demand our critical consideration. We can best begin this project of discovery by analyzing one explicit similarity between the novel's world and ours. In Oceania, as in America, the telescreens are always on, and everyone is always watching them.

The Oceanic telescreens are not actually televisual. Writing in the late forties, Orwell could not come to know TV's peculiar quality but conceived the telescreen, understandably, as a simple combination of radio and cinema.[15] Its sounds and images therefore suggest these parent media, which, beginning at mid-century, turned out to be alike in their capacity to drum up violent feeling. The telescreens' voices are abrasive and hysterical, like the mob whose regulated violence they catalyze; and the telescreens' images are also explicitly suasive, arousing primitive reactions, paradoxically, through sophisticated cinematic techniques. Ingenious tricks of Eisensteinian montage enable the telescreens to inspire extreme reactions, whether foaming hatred of this year's foe or cringing reverence for Big Brother (reactions that are fundamentally the same).

Television, on the other hand, inspires no such wildness, but is as cool and dry as the Oceanic telescreens are hot and bothered. Its flat, neutralizing vision automatically strains out those ineffable qualities wherein we recognize each other's power; nor can it, like film, reinvest its figures with such density, but must reduce all of its objects to the same mundane level. In order to overcome the muting effect of TV's essential grayness, the managers of all televisual spectacle try automatically to intensify each broadcast moment through the few sensational techniques available: extreme close-ups, marvellously heightened colors, dizzying graphics, high-pitched voices trilling choral harmonies, insistent bursts of domesticated rock'n'roll, and the incessant, meaningless montage that includes all things, events, and persons. And yet these compensations for the medium's basic coolness merely reinforce its distancing effect. Repeatedly subjected to TV's small jolts, we become incapable of outright shock or intense arousal, lapsing into a constant dull anxiety wherein we can hardly sense the difference between a famine and a case of body odor. And the televisual montage bolsters our inability to differentiate, its spectacle of endless metamorphosis merely making all those images seem as insignificant as any single image seen for hours.

Because of these formal properties, TV is casually inimical to all charisma and therefore seems an inappropriate device for any program like the Inner Party's. Televised, the "enormous face" of Big Brother would immediately lose its aura of "mysterious calm," and so those omnipresent features would appear about as menacing as Ricky Schroder's. On TV, furthermore, the maniacal intensities of actual Party members would also lose their sinister allure, not by being cancelled out but by coming off as overheated, alien, and silly. At those moments when his face takes on a "mad gleam of enthusiasm," even

O'Brien would seem to have been bypassed, and therefore exterminated, by TV.

Thus TV would seem to be an essentially iconoclastic medium; and yet it is this inherent subversiveness toward any visible authority that has enabled TV to establish its own total rule—for it is *all* individuality that TV annihilates, either by not conveying it, or by making it look ludicrous. TV would therefore suit the Party's ultimate objective perfectly, if Orwell had lived to watch and understand it. As TV would neutralize Big Brother's face and O'Brien's transports, so would it undercut the earnest idealism of Winston Smith, dismissing his indignant arguments about "the spirit of Man" by concentrating coolly on his "jailbird's face," just as O'Brien does. With its clinical or inquisitorial vision, TV appears to penetrate all masks, to expose all alibis, thereby seeming to turn the whole world into a comic spectacle of unsuccessful lying, pompous posturing, and neurotic defensiveness, behaviors that appear to be seen through the moment they are represented. It is from this apparent penetration that TV's documentary programs derive the ostensible incisiveness that makes them so engrossing: "Sixty Minutes," "The People's Court," "Real People," and so on. And it is the need to withstand TV's derisive penetration that has dictated the peculiar self-protective mien of all seasoned televisual performers, whether they play love scenes, read the news, or seem to run the country. The muted affability and thoroughgoing smoothness that make these entertainers seem acceptable on TV also serve as a defense against its searching eye; and yet by thus attempting to avoid subversion, these figures—finally interchangeable as well as evanescent—merely subvert themselves, giving up that individuality which TV would otherwise discredit.

Thus, within the borders of its spectacle, TV continues automatically that process of Enlightenment which the Party hastens consciously—the erasure of all lingering subjectivity. Whereas the Oceanic telescreens are the mere means used by the ironists in power, our telescreens are themselves ironic, and therefore make those powerful few unnecessary. For it is not only *on* TV that TV thus proceeds to cancel selves; it also wields its nullifying influence out in the wide world of its impressionable viewers. Television's formal erasure of distinctness complements—or perhaps has actually fostered—a derisive personal style that inhibits all personality, a knowingness that now pervades all TV genres, and the culture which those genres have homogenized. That corrosive irony which emanates from the Oceanic elite has been universalized by television, whose characters—both real and fictional—relentlessly inflict it on each other and themselves, defining a negative ideal of hip inertia which no living human being is able to approach too closely. On the sitcom, for example, TV's definitive creation, the "comedy" almost always consists in a weak, compulsive jeering that immediately wipes out any divergence from the indefinite collective standard. The characters vie at self-containment, reacting to every simulation of intensity, every bright idea, every mechanical enthusiasm with the same deflating look of jaded incredulity. In such an atmosphere, those already closest to the ground run the least risk of being felled by the general ridicule. And so those characters most adept at enforcing the proper emptiness are also the puniest and most passive: blasé menials, blasé wives and girlfriends, and—especially—blasé children, who, like Parsons's daughter, prove their own orthodoxy by subverting their subverted parents.[16]

Nearly all of TV's characters—on sitcoms and in "dramas," on talk shows and children's programs—participate in this reflexive sneering, because such contemptuous passivity reflects directly on the viewer who watches it with precisely the same attitude. TV seems to flatter the inert skepticism of its own audience, assuring them that they can do no better than to stay right where they are, rolling their eyes in feeble disbelief. And yet such apparent flattery of our viewpoint is in fact a recurrent warning not to rise above this slack, derisive gaping. At first, it seems that it is only those eccentric others whom TV belittles. Each time, on a sitcom, some deadpan tot responds to his frantic mom with a disgusted sigh, or whenever the polished anchorman punctuates his footage of "extremists" with a look that speaks his well-groomed disapproval, or each time Johnny Carson comments on some "unusual" behavior with a wry sidelong glance into our living rooms, we are being flattered with a gesture of inclusion, the wink that tells us, "*We* are in the know." And yet we are the ones belittled by each subtle televisual gaze, which offers not a welcome but an ultimatum—that we had better see the joke or else turn into it.

If we see the joke, however, we are nothing, like those Oceanic viewers "shouting with laughter" at the sight of their own devastation. All televisual smirking is based on, and reinforces, the assumption that we who smirk together are enlightened past the point of nullity, having evolved far beyond whatever datedness we might be jeering, whether the fanatic's ardor, the prude's inhibitions, the hick's unfashionable pants, the snob's obsession with prestige. Thus TV's relentless comedy at first seems utterly progressive, if largely idiotic, since its butts are always the most reactionary of its characters—militarists, bigots, sexists, martinets. However, it is not to champion our freedom that TV makes fun of these ostensible oppressors. On the contrary: through its derision, TV promotes only *itself*, disvaluing, not Injustice or Intolerance, but the impulse to resist TV.

Despite his broad illiberality, what makes the butt appear ridiculous in TV's eyes is not his antidemocratic bias but his vestigial individuality, his persistence as a self sturdy and autonomous enough to sense that there is something missing from the televisual world, and to hunger for it, although ostracized for this desire by the sarcastic mob that watches and surrounds him.

Like Winston Smith, the butt yearns for and exemplifies the past that brought about the present, and which the present now discredits through obsessive mockery. Whether arrogantly giving orders, compulsively tidying up, or longing for the good old days when men were men, the butt reenacts the type of personality—marked by rigidity and self-denial—that at first facilitated the extension of high capitalism but that soon threatened to impede its further growth. And it is just such endless growth that is the real point and object of TV's comedy, which puts down those hard selves in order to exalt the nothingness that laughs at them. Whereas the butt, enabled by his discrete selfhood, pursues desires that TV cannot gratify, we are induced, by the sight of his continual humiliation, to become as porous, cool, and acquiescent as he is solid, tense, and dissident, so that we might want nothing other than what TV sells us. This is what it means to see the joke. The viewer's enlightened laughter at those uptight others is finally the expression of his own oceanic dissolution, as, within his distracted consciousness, there reverberates TV's sole imperative, which, once obeyed, makes the self seem a mere comical encumbrance—the imperative of total consumption.

Guided by its images even while he thinks that he sees through them, the TV viewer learns only to consume. That inert, ironic watchfulness which TV reinforces in its audience is itself conducive to consumption. As we watch, struggling inwardly to avoid resembling anyone who might stand out as pre- or non- or antitelevisual, we are already trying to live up, or down, to the same standard of acceptability that TV's ads and shows define collectively, the standard that requires the desperate use of all those goods and services that TV proffers, including breath mints, mouthwash, dandruff shampoos, hair conditioners, blow-driers, hair removers, eye drops, deodorant soaps and sticks and sprays, hair dyes, skin creams, lip balms, diet colas, diet plans, lo-cal frozen dinners, bathroom bowl cleaners, floor wax, car wax, furniture polish, fabric softeners, room deodorizers, and more, and more. Out of this flood of commodities, it is promised, we will each arise as sleek, quick, compact, and efficient as a brand-new Toyota; and in our effort at such self-renewal, moreover, we are enjoined not just to sweeten every orifice and burnish every surface, but to evacuate our psyches. While selling its explicit products, TV also advertises incidentally an ideal of emotional self-management, which dictates that we purge ourselves of all "bad feelings" through continual confession, and by affecting the same stilted geniality evinced by most of TV's characters, the butts excluded. The unconscious must never be allowed to interfere with productivity, and so the viewer is warned repeatedly to atone for his every psychic eruption, like Parsons after his arrest for talking treason in his sleep: " 'Thoughtcrime is a dreadful thing, old man,' he said sententiously. 'It's insidious. . . . There I was, working away, trying to do my bit—never knew I had any bad stuff in my mind at all.' "

Thus, even as its programs push the jargon of "honesty" and "tolerance," forever counseling you to "be yourself," TV shames you ruthlessly for every symptom of residual mortality, urging you to turn yourself into a standard object wholly inoffensive, useful, and adulterated, a product of and for all other products. However, this transformation is impossible. There is no such purity available to human beings, whose bodies will sweat, whose instincts will rage, however expertly we work to shut them off. Even Winston Smith, as broken as he is at the conclusion, is still impelled by his desires, which the Party could not extinguish after all, since it depends on their distorted energy. For all its chilling finality, in other words, the novel's closing sentence is merely another of the Party's lies. And what O'Brien cannot achieve through torture, we cannot attain through our campaigns of self-maintenance, no matter how many miles we jog or how devotedly, if skeptically, we watch TV.

Like the Party, then, whose unstated rules no person can follow rigidly enough, TV demands that its extruded viewers struggle to embody an ideal too cool and imprecise for human emulation. Like Winston Smith, we are the victims of Enlightenment in its late phase, although it is the logic of consumption, not the deliberate machinations of some cabal, that has impoverished our world in the name of its enrichment. And as the creatures of this logic, we have become our own overseers. While Winston Smith is forced to watch himself in literal self-defense, trying to keep his individuality a hard-won secret, we have been forced to watch ourselves lest we develop selves too hard and secretive for the open market. In America, there is no need for an objective apparatus of surveillance (which is not to say that none exists), because, guided by TV, we watch ourselves as if already televised, checking ourselves both inwardly and outwardly for any sign of untidiness or gloom, moment by moment as guarded and self-conscious as Winston Smith under the scrutiny of the Thought Police: "The smallest thing could give you away. A nervous tic, an unconscious look of anxiety, a habit of muttering to yourself—anything that carried with it the suggestion of abnormality, of having something to hide." Although this description refers to the objective peril of life in Oceania, it also captures the anxiety of life under the scrutiny of television. Of course, all televisual performers must abide by this same grim advice or end up canceled; but TV's nervous viewers also feel themselves thus watched, fearing the same absolute exclusion if they should ever show some sign of resisting the tremendous pressure.[17]

And TV further intensifies our apprehension that we are being watched by continually assuring us that it already understands our innermost fears, our private problems, and that it even knows enough about our most intimate moments to reproduce them for us. The joy of birth is brought to us by Citicorp, the tender concern of one friend for another is presented by AT&T, the pleasures of the hearth are depicted for us by McDonald's. And on any talk show or newscast, there might suddenly appear the competent psychologist, who will deftly translate any widespread discontent into his own antiseptic terms, thereby representing it as something well known to him, and therefore harmless. As we watch TV, we come to imagine what Winston Smith eventually discovers: "There was no physical act, no word spoken aloud, that they had not noticed, no train of thought that they had not been able to infer."

TV, however, is not the cause of our habitual self-scrutiny, but has only set the standard for it, a relationship with a complicated history. It is through our efforts to maintain ourselves as the objects of our anxious self-spectatorship that we consummate the process of American Enlightenment, whose project throughout this century has been the complete and permanent reduction of our populace into the collective instrument of absolute production. This project has arisen not through corporate conspiracy but as the logical fulfillment, openly and even optimistically pursued, of the imperative of unlimited economic growth. Thus compelled, the enlightened captains of production have employed the principles, and often the exponents, of modern social science, in order to create a perfect work force whose members, whether laboring on products or consuming them, would function inexhaustibly and on command, like well-tuned robots. As the material for this ideal, Americans have been closely watched for decades: in the factory, then in the office, by efficiency experts and industrial psychologists; in the supermarkets, then throughout the shopping malls by motivational researchers no less cunningly than by the store detectives; and in the schools, and then at home, and then in bed, by an immense, diverse, yet ultimately unified bureaucracy of social workers, education specialists, and "mental health professionals" of every kind.[18] The psychic and social mutations necessarily induced by this multiform intrusion have accomplished what its first engineers had hoped for, but in a form, and at a cost, which they could never have foreseen: Americans—restless, disconnected, and insatiable—are mere consumers, having by now internalized the diffuse apparatus of surveillance built all around them, while still depending heavily on its external forms—TV, psychologistic "counseling," "self-help" manuals, the "human potential" regimens, and other self-perpetuating therapies administered to keep us on the job.

And so the project of industrial Enlightenment has only forced us back toward that same helpless natural state that Enlightenment had once meant to abolish. Both in America and in Oceania, the telescreens infantilize their captive audience. In *Nineteen Eighty-Four* and in 1984, the world has been made too bright and cold by the same system that forever promises the protective warmth of mother love, and so each viewer yearns to have his growing needs fulfilled by the very force that aggravates them. So it is, first of all, with Orwell's famished hero. The figure who had slipped quickly into Victory Mansions, "his chin nuzzled into his breast," had tried unknowingly to transcend the Oceanic violence by mothering himself, but then ends up so broken by that violence that he adopts its symbol as his mother: "O cruel, needless misunderstanding!" he exults inwardly before the image of Big Brother's face. "O stubborn, self-willed exile from the loving breast!" And, as it is with Winston Smith in his perverted ardor, so it is with every vaguely hungry TV viewer, who longs to be included by the medium that has excluded everyone, and who expects its products to fulfill him in a way that they have made impossible.

What is most disconcerting, then, about the ending of *Nineteen Eighty-Four* is not that Winston Smith has now been made entirely unlike us. In too many ways, the ex-hero of this brilliant, dismal book anticipates those TV viewers who are incapable of reading it: "In these days he could never fix his mind on any one subject for more than a few moments at a time." At this moment, Winston Smith is, for the first time in his life, not under surveillance. The motto, "Big Brother Is Watching You," is now untrue as a threat, as it has always been untrue as an assurance. And the reason why he is no longer watched is that the Oceanic gaze need no longer see through Winston Smith, because he is no longer "Winston Smith," but "a swirl of gritty dust," as primitive and transparent as the Party.

As this Smith slumps in the empty Chestnut Tree, credulously gaping, his ruined mind expertly jolted by the telescreen's managers, he signifies the terminal fulfillment of O'Brien's master-plan, which expresses the intentions not only of Orwell's fictitious Party, but of the corporate entity that, through TV, contains our consciousness today: "We shall squeeze you empty, and then we shall fill you with ourselves."[19] The Party has now done for Winston Smith what all our advertisers want to do for us, and with our general approval—answer all material needs, in exchange for the self that might try to gratify them independently, and that might have other, subtler needs as well. As a consumer, in other words, Orwell's ex-hero really has it made. "There was no need to give orders" to the waiters in the Chestnut Tree. "They knew his habits." Furthermore, he "always had plenty of money nowadays." In short, the Party has paid him for his erasure with the assurance, "We do it *all* for you." And so this grotesque before-and-after narrative ends satirically as all ads end in earnest, with the object's blithe endorsement of the very product that has helped to keep him miserable: "But it was all right, everything was all right, the struggle was finished. He had won the victory over himself. He loved Big Brother."

It is a horrifying moment; but if we do no more than wince at it, and then forget about it, we ignore our own involvement in the horror, and thus complacently betray the hope that once inspired this vision. Surely Orwell would have us face the facts. Like Winston Smith, and like O'Brien and the others, we have been estranged from our desire by Enlightenment, which finally reduces all of its proponents into the blind spectators of their own annihilation. Unlike that Oceanic audience, however, the TV viewer does not gaze up at the screen with angry scorn or piety, but—perfectly enlightened—looks down on its images with a nervous sneer that cannot threaten them, but that only keeps the viewer himself from standing up. As you watch, there is no Big Brother out there watching you, not because there isn't a Big Brother, but because Big Brother is you, watching.

NOTES

1. George Orwell, "The Lion and the Unicorn: Socialism and the English Genius," in *The Collected Essays, Journalism and Letters of George Orwell*, ed. Sonia Orwell and Ian Angus, 4 vols. (New York: Harcourt, Brace and World, 1968), 2:56 (hereafter cited as *CEJL*.)
2. "The Rediscovery of Europe," *CEJL*, 2:205. Orwell makes this point in the course of comparing the optimistic works of the Edwardian writers with the darker mood of their postwar successors. The entire passage will reproduce the specific context of the observation: "Compare almost any of H. G. Wells' Utopia books, for instance *A Modern Utopia*, or *The Dream*, or *Men like Gods*, with Aldous Huxley's *Brave New World*. Again it's rather the same contrast, the contrast between the over-confident and the deflated, between the man who believes innocently in Progress and the man who happens to have been born later and has therefore lived to see that Progress, as it was conceived in the early days of the aeroplane, is just as much of a swindle as reaction."
3. Max Horkheimer and T. W. Adorno, *Dialectic of Enlightenment*, trans. John Cumming (New York: Continuum, 1982), p. 92.
4. Ibid., p. 3.
5. Francis Bacon, *New Atlantis*, ed. Alfred B. Gough (Oxford: Clarendon Press, 1924), p. 35.
6. Horkheimer and Adorno, *Dialectic of Enlightenment*, p. 6.
7. "The only kind of thinking that is sufficiently hard to shatter myths is ultimately self-destructive" (ibid., p. 4).
8. "Notes on the Way," *CEJL*, 2:15.
9. Horkheimer and Adorno, *Dialectic of Enlightenment*, p. xiii.
10. Ibid., p. xv.

11. Orwell repudiated the anti-Communist misreading in a letter, now lost, to Francis A. Henson of the UAW. A crucial excerpt from this letter was preserved, however, and appeared both in *Life* and the *New York Times Book Review*, these two published versions differing slightly. For an amalgam of both versions, see *CEJL*, 4:502.

12. "Soviet Says Orwell's Vision Is Alive in the U.S.," *New York Times*, Sunday, January 8, 1984, p. 8.

13. For a full elaboration of this Enlightenment posture, see the discussions of Odysseus in Horkheimer and Adorno, *Dialectic of Enlightenment*, pp. 32–36, 43ff.

14. Elaine Hoffman Baruch advances this position in " 'The Golden Country': Sex and Love in *1984*," in *1984 Revisited*, ed. Irving Howe (New York: Harper and Row, 1983), pp. 47–56, esp. pp. 55–56.

15. Horkheimer and Adorno also assumed that television would be such an amalgam, although their remarks on the emergent medium's potential suasiveness have proven more accurate than Orwell's conception, since they expected the televisual hegemony to arise out of the medium's tendency toward total homogenization and not out of that inflammatory capacity envisioned in *Nineteen Eighty-Four*. See *Dialectic of Enlightenment*, p. 124. For a wholly celebratory discussion of the same televisual tendency uneasily foretold by Horkheimer and Adorno, see Marshall McLuhan's remarks on TV and synesthesia in *Understanding Media* (New York: New American Library, 1964), pp. 274–75.

16. The absolute interchangeability forever represented on, and valorized by, TV is not, of course, only a formal illusion, but also an expression of the triumph of exchange value, which is at once the ultimate reason for TV's hectic display of goods, and a major ideological message arising out of that display. Within the televisual atmosphere, determined, as it is, by the equalizing power of money, a blasé manner is downright obligatory. "The blasé person," Simmel writes, "has completely lost the feeling of value differences. He experiences all things as being of an equally dull and grey hue, as not worth getting excited about, particularly where the will is concerned. . . . Whoever has become possessed by the fact that the same amount of money can procure all the possibilities that life has to offer must also become blasé" (*The Philosophy of Money*, trans. Tom Bottomore and David Frisby [Boston: Routledge and Kegan Paul, 1978], p. 256). Although Simmel refers here to the jaded rich of his own era, his full analysis of the blasé attitude (pp. 256–57) also applies to TV's creatures—that is, viewers and characters alike—whose jadedness is not so much an expression of material satiation as it is a response to the flood of mere *images* of "all the possibilities that life has to offer."

17. "Cameras and recording machines not only transcribe experience but alter its quality, giving to much of modern life the character of an enormous echo chamber, a hall of mirrors. Life presents itself as a succession of images or electronic signals, of impressions recorded and reproduced by means of photography, motion pictures, television, and sophisticated recording devices. Modern life is so thoroughly mediated by electronic images that we cannot help responding to oth-

ers as if their actions—and our own—were being recorded and simultaneously transmitted to an unseen audience or stored up for close scrutiny at some later time" (Christopher Lasch, *The Culture of Narcissism* [New York: Norton, 1978], p. 47).

18. This development has, of course, been as complex as influential, and has therefore been analyzed widely and variously. Only a comparatively few references are appropriate here. For a history of the surveillance carried out by social scientists in the American workplace, see Loren Baritz, *The Servants of Power: A History of the Use of Social Science in American Industry* (Middletown, Conn.: Wesleyan University Press, 1960). For discussions of the intrusions planned and/or committed by the advertising industry, see Stuart Ewen, *Captains of Consciousness: Advertising and the Social Roots of the Consumer Culture* (New York: McGraw-Hill, 1976), and Vance Packard, *The Hidden Persuaders* (New York: David McKay, 1957), which, despite its occasional inaccuracies, is still an illuminating account. And for the history of the gradual displacement of familial functions by the state, see Christopher Lasch, *Haven in a Heartless World: The Family Besieged* (New York: Norton, 1975) and *The Culture of Narcissism*. Also, see the writings collected in *The Culture of Consumption: Critical Essays in American History, 1880–1980,* ed. Richard Wrightman Fox and T. J. Jackson Lears (New York: Pantheon Books, 1983).

19. Although Horkheimer and Adorno, both in the *Dialectic of Enlightenment* and (separately) elsewhere, draw comparisons between totalitarian domination and the implicit coerciveness of advertising, Orwell tended, in his journalistic writings, to regard advertising not as comparable to totalitarianism but as the excrescence of a different, much preferable system. He often condemned advertising for its corruptiveness rather than for its animus against the subject. For instance, he deplored its incitements to snobbery (*CEJL*, 3:183–84, 194) and condemned its emphasis on trivialities in the midst of war (2:343–45 et passim).

However, such moralistic complaints do not express Orwell's deepest reservations about advertising, whose most pernicious effect, he argued, was its "indirect censorship over news" (2:68). He regarded advertising as the force that ensured the total fatuity of what we now call "the media," that invisible yet inescapable environment which imperceptibly blunts and diminishes every mind within it: "Between the wars England tolerated newspapers, films and radio programmes of unheard-of silliness, and these produced further stupefaction in the public, blinding their eyes to vitally important problems. This silliness of the English press is partly artificial, since it arises from the fact that newspapers live off advertisements for consumption goods" (3:35).

Although such "stupefaction" results from universal trivialization rather than from terror, it evidenced, for Orwell, the drastic reduction of the subject. "This silliness of the English press" has its clear Oceanic equivalent in the calculated inanities devised by the Ministry of Truth, whose job it is to keep the proles as dim and vacant as Winston Smith ends up, even if the proles are reduced by films, novels and newspapers, not through torture. There is, then, a distant relationship between advertising and the moronized masses in *Nineteen Eighty-Four*, despite the fact that the Party has long since smashed the apparatus of consumerism. And there is further evidence for this relationship in Orwell's earlier novel *Keep the Aspidistra Flying* (1936), which contains this very telling description of the ideological atmosphere inside an advertising agency:

> The interesting thing about the New Albion was that it was so completely modern in spirit. There was hardly a soul in the firm who was not perfectly well aware that publicity—advertising—is the dirtiest ramp that capitalism has yet produced. In the red lead firm [where the hero had worked previously] there had still lingered certain notions of commercial honor and usefulness. But such things would have been laughed at in the New Albion. Most of the employees were the hard-boiled, Americanised, go-getting type—the type to whom nothing in the world is sacred, except money. They had their cynical code worked out. The public are swine; advertising is the rattling of a stick inside a swill-bucket. And yet beneath their cynicism there was the final naïveté, the blind worship of the money-god. (London: Secker and Warburg, 1954, pp. 65–66)

Having blown apart the myth of "commercial honor and usefulness," the devotees of advertising, "completely modern in spirit," are now entrapped by "the final naïveté," serving wholeheartedly the very mechanism which they see through. Thus the enlightened employees of the New Albion are the prototypes of the doublethinking members of the Inner Party.

James Billington

THREE VIEWS OF REVOLUTION

New forms of dehumanizing authoritarianism have come into being in the modern world, forms that are widely designated as "Orwellian" and are, alas, widely in force in the calendar year 1984. Many of the intellectual origins of this totalitarian tendency lie in the dominant political faith of the modern world: the belief in revolution. And I believe that close study of the body of experience in which the ideas of the modern revolutionary tradition originated—Europe in the late eighteenth and nineteenth centuries—shows that the new authoritarianism of our times owes a great deal to the two new types of revolutionary belief based on nationalism and socialism that grew out of the French Revolution and have dominated world revolutionary movements of the twentieth century. These two European traditions differ far more than is generally realized from the liberal, constitutional tradition of the earlier American Revolution.

Three secular ideas basically define the three different branches of the revolutionary faith in the modern world: *liberty, fraternity, equality*—the component parts of the main slogan of the French Revolution.

The tradition of revolution for liberty predated the French Revolution and grew out of the political experience of the North Atlantic entrepreneurial, primarily Protestant world. A wave of political upheavals moved from Holland in the sixteenth century to England in the seventeenth century, culminating in the American Revolution. The American tradition (which was echoed in the Belgian and Swiss revolutions of the nineteenth century) mobilized already-established social forces for a limited political struggle to overthrow tyranny and define a constitutional order, usually in the form of a republic. The aim was to restore concrete liberties by limiting and dividing central political power.

The French Revolution also began as a revolution of this type—for constitutional liberties—and seemed to confirm this identity when the most powerful king in Christendom was replaced by the First French Republic in 1792. Almost immediately, however, the ideal of a political revolution for liberty was overtaken—indeed overwhelmed—by the prototypical example of the second form of the revolutionary faith—the revolution for *fraternity*. This was an unlimited, emotional military struggle on the part of hitherto inarticulate masses seeking not to limit tyranny and divide power, but to defend and extend the authority of the sovereign territorial nation and to galvanize its citizenry into a neotribal brotherhood.

Salut et fraternité was the greeting of the new blood brotherhood. Its favorite political slogan—what Nodier called *le mot talismanique*—was no longer *république*, but *nation* (a word rarely used in America before the 1790s), and soon *la grande nation*. Revolutionary nationalism subsequently spread primarily through Catholic, largely southern Europe, reaching on to Latin America and Poland, becoming the dominant faith of the revolutionary movement as a whole until the last French revolution was defeated in 1871 and French leadership discredited.

By then, the center of revolutionary gravity had moved east, producing in Germany and Russia its third variant: revolution for *equality*. Egalitarian social revolution called for the establishment of a universal *communauté* or *commune* of socioeconomic equality that would render both liberal constitutions and national identities irrelevant. Babeuf's Conspiracy of Equals of 1797 was the precursor; the Paris Commune of 1871 provided the model and martyrology. But the new ideal of social revolution and its characteristic slogans—social democracy, socialism, communism—were most warmly adopted in the authoritarian hierarchical societies of Lutheran Prussia and Russia (whose Orthodox church had been structurally Lutheranized in the eighteenth century). In the wake of World War I, revolutionaries came out of the wilderness and into power in Russia—and nearly did so in Germany.

The original tradition of revolution for liberty differs radically from both later traditions of national and social revolution in three important ways. First, the earlier constitutional revolutionaries had always used the word *revolution* in its Copernican sense of a re-volution back from a temporary tyranny to a more just and natural norm that was presumed to have existed previously. Both national and social revolutionaries used the word revolution in the new sense of something totally new and totally redemptive that first appeared only in the French Revolution. The American founding fathers did not call themselves revolutionaries.

Second, the earlier revolutionaries for liberty generally continued to affirm the preromantic belief in a divine creator and in an objective moral order—never accepting the belief that anything approaching salvation could be found on the secular political plane through a nation or a community.

Finally and most important, these revolutionaries of the American type believed the immediate postrevolutionary task was the creation of complexity to preserve liberty rather than radical simplification to enshrine fraternity or equality. The prototypical liberal revolutionary document was the American constitution, which moved from the simplicity of declaring independence to the complexity of separating central powers and layering federal authority.

The French Revolution, in contrast, moved from the immense complexity of reform struggles throughout the 1780s to the "terrible simplifications" of the mid-1790s: from many estates to one state; from many titles to the one of *Citoyen;* from many formal ways to address to the one familiar *tu;* from many points of power to one—from a national assembly to a twelve-man committee, to a five-man directorate, to one emperor; from the complexity of discussion to the simplicity of slogans.

The French revolutionaries sought to begin time over again with a new calendar; to reshape space with pyramids and spheres, and society with triangles and circles; to link life itself with prime numbers, primal incantations, primeval nature. The classical no less than the Christian heritage was swept aside for the occult druidism of a pyramidal earth mound in place of the high altar in Notre Dame Cathedral, which was itself said to camouflage an earlier shrine to Isis, whose name in turn was said to derive from the sound that came when fire first met water and produced *is-is.*

Out of the French Revolution came the noun *revolutionary* and the novel idea that being dedicated to making a revolution could be the very essence of one's human identity. The professional revolutionary was basically a thirsting politician lifted up by ideas, not a hungry worker or peasant bent down by toil. There are two little-appreciated general features of the authentically innovative revolutionaries who appeared in the French Revolutionary era, which I have traced elsewhere and can only briefly itemize here.

First, the new revolutionary faith grew out of not just the critical rationalism of the Enlightenment but also the occultist revival of the late eighteenth century evidenced in higher-order Masonry and intermingled with a protoromanticism filtering in from Germany. This romanticism tinged politics with a new sense of magical, promethean possibility. Romanticism in my view was a partial cause as well as an effect of the French Revolution. The kind of emotional assault on traditional authority that precludes rational remedy began with the fascination of the *Sturm und Drang* artist-intellectuals in Prussia with the political antitraditionalism of Frederick the Great, prefiguring the love-hate fascination of romantic Europe with Napoleon. The word *ideology* no less than the megalomania of seminal ideologists of revolution like Hegel and Saint-Simon was born during the reign and under the spell of Napoleon.

A second element in the new revolutionary faith was the new sense that total secular happiness really was possible on earth. This belief, releasing thinkers from traditional inhibitions and limitations, was incubated in the immediate prerevolutionary period in the sensual café subculture of the Palais-Royal of Choderlos Laclos and the marquis de Sade. There, nowhere (the literal meaning of utopia) suddenly seemed to exist somewhere; and in the dialectic formation of a new revolutionary vocation, the ascetic pursuit of public virtue tended to follow the erotic indulgence of private vice.

This dialectic was exemplified in the transition from Danton to Robespierre, but also in the inner spiritual life of many of the most authentically creative ideological innovators of the revolutionary era. Mirabeau, the first to use the word *revolutionary* in its new sense of "totally new, secular, and salvific"; Restif de la Bretonne, the first to invent the word *communist;* Sylvain Maréchal, the author of the *Manifesto of Equals* and the first to propagate the idea of a second social revolution to come; as well as the famous Saint-Just—all four of these were literary pornographers before becoming revolutionary visionaries. The mob storming the Bastille formed in front of the cafés in the Palais-Royal; and the subsequent choreography of revolutionary processions in Paris tended to move literally as well as figuratively from the Café de Venus to the Champs de Mars, where the first of the great revolutionary festivals was held on the first anniversary of the fall of the Bastille.

The two new mythic ideals presented by the French Revolution—a nation of brothers or a commune of equals—emerged in two successive, very different waves of incendiary simplification: the nationalistic mobilization heralded by the *Marseillaise* and the rationalistic conspiracy announced by the *Manifesto of Equals.* The words used ever since to describe these new authoritarian ideals—*nationalism* and *communism*—were both first coined in the late 1790s.

I believe it is possible to extract from the subsequent historical record in Europe characteristics of a prototype if not an archetype for both the national and the social revolutionary movements. Each of course may have some qualities of the other type and almost always used rhetoric from the older liberal tradition. But there are at least four areas where these two more authoritarian traditions tend to differ from each other as well as from the older North Atlantic tradition of revolution for political liberty. Let me contrast, then, the typical national revolutionary from the Catholic Franco-Italo-Polish context up to the 1860s with the typical social revolutionary that arose in the Lutheran-Orthodox Prusso-Russian context thereafter.

First, in basic aims, national revolutionaries seeking fraternity sought to create a nation through the emotional unification of a people. Social revolutionaries seeking equality sought rather to create a commune or community through the rational manifestation of truth. The basic mobilizing device of the one was the transrational call to the national emotions in the *Marseillaise;* of the other, the transnational revelation of a universal rationality in the

Manifesto of Equals. Contrast the exultation, simplification, and absolutism of either one with the relative specificity of grievances itemized in the Declaration of Independence or the complexity, practicality, and relative dullness of the Constitution of 1787, the prototypical documents of the earlier American revolution for liberty.

The two traditions also had contrasting basic mechanisms for broadening their appeal: lyrical for national revolutionaries and cerebral for social revolutionaries. Both the emotive *Marseillaise* and the rationalistic *Manifesto* pointed toward a closed and absolute social objective in contrast to the open, argumentative mode of a federal dialogue and representative legislatures to perpetuate open-ended debate in America.

The lyrical mechanisms of national revolutionaries included mythic history, evocative folklore, and above all the romantic vernacular poetry that spilled into politics through Lamartine, Mickiewicz, and Petöfi—and escalated into musical heroism in the new vernacular operas of national liberation. Live operatic performances literally started two major revolutions (in Piedmont in 1820 and Belgium in 1830).

In sharp contrast, the social revolutionary tradition relied on cerebral methods of mobilization, which required not an inspiring example but an ideological high commander. The socialist's weapons were polemic prose for an atomized reading public, not lyric poetry for an assembled audience. The realistic, social novel aroused the social revolutionary consciousness in some of the same ways that romantic national opera aroused that of the national revolutionaries. Unity among social revolutionaries was provided by the occult truth distilled from dross within the secret inner circle of a revolutionary elite and then made manifest to the masses, whose most active and ambitious leaders could then seek initiation into the intellectually aware leadership group. The leadership image was not the heroic conductor arousing a chorus but the intellectual alchemist enlisting apprentices. His secret task was to transform the macrocosm through the microcosm of a vanguard. The word *manifesto*—from Maréchal to Marx and on to its vulgarization in Germany, Russia, and points east—never loses altogether its connections with the occult.

The prototypical social revolutionary subculture emerged, of course, in Russia, where a suddenly swollen student population in the 1860s cut loose traditional religious moorings and floated out into a sea of polemic prose where islands of egalitarian community suddenly seemed to provide the most solid ground for an intellectual vanguard. The Russian word coined in this period to describe this new elite, *intelligentsiia,* can be traced back through its earlier Polish form to the long use of the Latin *intellegentia* in the occult tradition.

In addition to contrasting aims and means of mobilization, national and social revolutionaries differed in their models of organization. Each tradition seems to have unconsciously derived the model for its soft organizational technology from the particular form of hard material technology that dominated its particular time and place. The era of romantic nationalism was under the spell of an architectural structure; the era of socialism, of an industrial machine. The microcosmic model for national revolutionaries of the Franco-Italo-Polish era was almost always that of the Masonic lodge: a structure that suggested the world itself being transformed into a rebuilt Temple of Solomon. Whether transferred into tents in Germany, shops in France, or Carbonari grottoes in Italy, the national revolutionary movements saw themselves as the personalized agents of some static but unique structure that was itself the model of the new nation. For social revolutionaries of the subsequent Germano-Russian era, organization was modeled on a machine, which is by its nature dynamic but impersonally uniform. The social revolutionary was the interchangeable part in a machine rather than a differentiated dweller in a structure.

Illustrative of this difference are the contrasting places where the young were characteristically mobilized for national or social revolution. These places played the same role in their traditions that the Palais-Royal had played in the original French revolution: as a privileged sanctuary under imperial patronage in which junior members of the old order could indulge in pleasures denied ordinary people—including the ultimate one of undermining the inherited order itself. This role of a kind of "liberated zone" unwittingly nurturing revolution was played for national revolutionaries by the Italian opera houses of the Hapsburgs in which explicitly anti-Hapsburg works like *William Tell* or *Don Carlos* inspired young audiences to dream of national uprisings. A similar role was played by the Imperial Technological Institute in St. Petersburg, where the first modern dynamo in Russia stood like a totem at the center of a complex directly created and patronized by the Romanovs—yet where both the first Leninist circle and first Soviet of Workers were born—and became the leading elements in the social revolution that overthrew those same Romanovs.

A fourth area of difference between national and social revolutionaries lay in their preferred forms of violence, which were generalized and emotional for the former, targeted and scientific for the latter. National revolutionary violence was linked with music from the very time in April 1792 when revolutionary France first went to war with monarchical Europe. Within a few hours of each other in the same city of Strasbourg were created the first modern national anthem, the *Marseillaise,* and the first guillotine—the anthem of arousal being first played on a piano built by the same firm which designed the instrument of execution.

The romantic appeal of generalized violence in the cause of revolution be-gan not with Wordsworth's readers smelling flowers but with Schiller's au-diences smelling power. The insurrectionary impulse idealized in his pre-revolutionary *Robbers* and *Don Carlos* was translated into French by Nicholas Bonneville; fortified by music in the works of Charles Nodier, the inventor of melodrama and founder of the first anti-Napoleonic revolutionary group, the Philadelphians; intensified by the antitraditional beat of the plays written by Nordier's protégé, Victor Hugo; and transposed into Verdi's cascading operas of national liberation, which more than anything else accounted for the suc-cessful Italian revolution against the Hapsburgs, the great success story of the age of national revolutions.

The violent tactics of the national revolutionary movements in the early nineteenth century evolved largely out of the experience of anti-Napoleonic military-resistance movements, which invented the words *guerrilla* and *partisan* to describe their mass-based, irregular forms of total war against traditional armies. Violence throughout the romantic era was expressive and heroic—seeking to overcome apathy and inspire a nation by providing exam-ples and arousing emotions.

But Napoleon himself, who was the target of much generalized violence from national revolutionaries, recognized that there was another, more ra-tional approach to violence, represented by the sole survivor and later histo-rian of the Conspiracy of Equals, Filippo Buonarroti. Writing from St. Hele-na, the mathematician in Napoleon found much to admire in the original Italian social revolutionary, whom he described as "a man of good faith, pure, a terrorist."

Thus, half a century before the word *terrorist* was first adopted as a badge of pride by Russian social revolutionaries, Napoleon seemed to have sensed the basically different approach of social revolutionaries, for whom violence was to be more calculated and impersonal: a controlled use of applied tech-nology, designed systematically to soften a political structure for revolutionary change.

The expressive, histrionic form of struggle designed to awaken a sleeping nation by heroic example died with the brutal repression of the Polish revolu-tion of 1863, and of the Paris commune in 1871. Thereafter, Petersburg re-placed Paris as the Mecca of revolution. Social revolution became the rallying cry in a rigidly hierarchical Russian society and replaced national revolution as the dominant revolutionary ideal in Europe generally.

Rather than using the assassin's dagger or pistol in a theater or the randomly destructive "infernal machine" on the streets outside, the new Russian revolu-tionaries developed a calculated campaign of escalating violence using ap-plied science—particularly chemistry, for which a Russian had discovered the periodic table, and experiments in Russia had proven the new power of nitro-glycerine in the 1860s. Russian revolutionaries discussed using acid both to disguise their own personal identities and to brand slogans with scar tissue on their skin—so that they would literally become bearers of an idea rather than recognizable and distinct human beings. Assembling bombs became a ritual act; and the main revolutionary organization of the late 1870s—in which the word *terrorist* was first used as a badge of pride—did not publicly announce even its existence (let alone its name, The People's Will) until after they had exploded the first lethal bomb in the series that led up to the assassination of Alexander II in 1881.

Proclamation by explosion represented the ultimate simplification of the revolutionary tradition—announcing one's very existence not with a man-ifesto, a slogan, or even a shout, but with a destructive detonation. Yet it was an act not of emotional gratification but of rational strategy. The People's Will sought systematically to remove enough key authorities to force those that remained either to end the Tsarist system or to relinquish power. No less important than isolating and targeting the oppositional hard core were the functions of recruiting and testing one's own revolutionary leaders and ter-rorizing the populace as a whole into frightened neutrality.

Since terrorism seems to be an increasingly prevalent feature of revolution-ary activity in this age of nuclear stalemate, it might be well to note some key characteristics of these very first revolutionary terrorists: the Russian social revolutionaries during the decade from their first adoption of the label in 1877 to the liquidation of their last important cell (and the execution of Lenin's older brother, who was one of its recruits) in 1887.

Terrorism was, first of all, a product of positive conviction, not of random criminality. It was a product of the aroused expectation of a rapidly enlarged educated class that had been rooted in, but was suddenly torn away from, traditional religious values as they moved from a seminary, village education to a secular, urban university. Both Leo Tolstoy, who was deeply antiterrorist, and Serge Kravchinsky, who was proterrorist, independently described Dmi-try Lizogub, the first to call himself a terrorist, as "a saint."

Terrorism was a tactic designed for cities (in contrast to the guerrilla ideal of a rural-based revolution advanced by the national revolutionaries of an earlier era). The turn to terrorism first in Kiev then in Petersburg occurred at the end of a period of liberalization, when the aroused expectations of newly urbanized students outran the opportunities for political reform and vocational reward. As Frederick the Great and Napoleon had done for earlier romantic revolutionaries, Alexander II widely raised hopes, then attracted the hatred of unrealized dreams rather than credit for partial reforms.

Terrorists used the new potentiality of the modern mass media against established domestic authority. In the late 1870s they turned almost every trial of terrorists into a countertrial of the government, contrasting their own selfless idealism to the flabby self-indulgence of Russian society, appealing to foreign readers through newly installed wire-service reporting, using their rights to public defense in the newly installed system of trial by jury for irrelevant but hypnotic ideological oratory. Liberal judges confronted by revolutionary youth tended to overlook the violence of their acts out of fascination with the sincerity of their motives. Finally, and perhaps most important, was the key role of women in the moral validation of terrorism (and indeed in the social revolutionary tradition as a whole, where women—from Flora Tristan to Rosa Luxembourg—played a far more important role than in the earlier national revolutionary tradition). The energizing passion of women, their willingness to undertake the most difficult assignments within the terrorist cause, created heightened emotional interest in, and human sympathy for, what might otherwise have been seen as an ascetic, impersonal organization. The spectacle of placing a pregnant woman on trial for the assassination of Tsar Alexander II brought letters of protest to his son and successor not against the murder of the tsar but against the proposed execution of one of the assassins.

All of this suggests too many contemporary parallels for comfort—as does the last and most important fact about these original terrorists: their fateful legacy of generating counterterrorism within and even beyond the government itself. The interaction, interborrowing, and at times interpenetration of the terrorist left with the counterterrorist right undermined all hope for moderate reform and constitutional liberalism in late imperial Russia. The pogroms of the 1880s, extralegal organizations like the Black Hundreds, and the florid growth of the Tsarist secret police gave way dialectically in the Soviet era to the "Extraordinary Commission" or Chekha, and the other successor instruments of the unprecedented state terrorism of the Stalin era.

Terrorism has, of course, not been the preferred weapon of the triumphant Marxist-Leninist version of the social revolutionary tradition. Leninism arose in Russia as a rival to the terrorist tradition and continuously has rejected strategic reliance on terrorism in its formal doctrine. But Lenin was initiated into social revolution by his terrorist older brother; Soviet Leninism never repudiated terrorism as a subsidiary tactic; and the victory of a more terrorist-based strategy in Vietnam along with the increasing Soviet acceptance of the Cuban line in Central America indicate a growing accommodation to a view of Leninist revolution in which terrorist techniques are more central than in the traditional Soviet view based on Marxist doctrine and Russian example.

Terrorism may be likely to increase not just because of added Soviet and Communist bloc support, but because it has rooted itself in national revolutionary movements often with a religious base (Palestinians, Armenians, and

Shiite Moslems) as well as in traditional social revolutionary movements (such as the Italian Red Guards). Terrorism makes use of the new medium of television to compensate for the lack of ritual life in the atomized modern world, and it feasts on the growing often extralegal terrorism of right-wing groups in Latin America, the Middle East, and elsewhere.

The consequences of losing a moderate liberal alternative in such a violently polarized situation was noted eloquently by Yeats in 1919 as he watched the extralegal Black and Tans rise on the right to ravage Ireland in reaction to the failed left rebellion of 1916.

> Turning and turning in the widening gyre
> The falcon cannot hear the falconer;
> Things fall apart; the centre cannot hold;
> Mere anarchy is loosed upon the world,
> The blood-dimmed tide is loosed, and everywhere
> The ceremony of innocence is drowned;
> The best lack all conviction, while the worst
> Are full of passionate intensity.

Yeats went on to suggest that "surely some revelation is at hand," but he ended his poem with the suggestion of dread rather than hope:

> And what rough beast, its hour come round at last,
> Slouches towards Bethlehem to be born?

The rough beast was the totalitarian state which harnessed modern technology to the combined authoritarian ideals of both national and social revolutionary traditions. Hitler's cause was "national socialism," Stalin's socialism in one nation. Both depended on a kind of state-sponsored terrorism that moved beyond traditional categories of right and left in the 1930s. Similarly in the 1970s a fusion of the guerrilla tactics of national revolutionaries and the terrorism of social revolutionaries created the most authoritarian forms of revolutionary mobilization in the weak political cultures of the Third World.

Faced with the armed might of revolutionary socialists in the Second World and the aroused expectations of revolutionary nationalism in the Third World, the partisans of constitutional democracy in the First World confronted the difficult task of effectively resisting (without repressively overreacting to) both missiles beyond and guns within their borders.

Of course, Orwell's nightmare was supposed to apply to the liberal democracies; and in America, the homeland of the original revolution for liberty, there were indeed by 1984 authoritarian tendencies evident in the passion for both nationalistic fraternity on the right and egalitarian community on the left.

But the two causes were never joined in America, whose deepest failings were probably not so much the new ones envisaged by Orwell as the classical decadence described by Gibbon.

The new revolutionary ideals of fraternity and equality that arose from the French Revolution each contained a structural flaw that assumed mammoth proportions with the gaining of power. Fraternity—in the phrase of one perceptive critic of the French revolutionary era—invariably meant the fraternity of Cain with Abel. Blood brotherhood within a nation required bloody opposition to those outside. And equality—openly ending old hierarchies everywhere—required secretly beginning a new hierarchy somewhere. And in the Babeuf-Lenin lineage, the new hierarchy seemed compelled to extend its authority everywhere.

There may, of course, also be an inherent flaw in the older ideal of liberty. Liberty for some often seems to imply bondage for others. But this is surely not a necessary consequence of freedom so much as the severing of liberty from its Siamese twin of responsibility. Even in an age of increasing physical limitations, one man's freedom in the pursuit of the good, the true, and the beautiful is not a threat but an invitation to others. In the intellectual and spiritual domain the horizons of freedom remain unlimited and uncompetitive; and in the material domain, freedom can still be shared if it is linked to responsibility.

Ordinary people even in 1984 are inclined to answer the question, Responsibility to what? by affirming a responsibility to God—thus fortifying themselves in their personal life against the modern intellectuals' tendency to accept those God-substitutes called ideologies in their political thinking. Perhaps the hidden weapon of the original revolutions for liberty was that they came from people who believed in covenants before they crafted constitutions. Perhaps that dimension is not altogether absent from the lands that have adopted liberal democratic ideals since World War II: not just in Germany and Italy, but in other traditional authoritarian regions in southern Europe, South America, and indeed south Asia.

The revival of the ideal of liberty at the heart of the Communist empire through the astonishing growth of the Polish Solidarity movement clearly illustrates how the independent moral authority of a vital church can help revalidate freedom within a closed society. The most remarkable (and frequently most overlooked) features of the Solidarity movement were that it was overwhelmingly nonviolent in means and evolutionary in objectives. Unlike the more authoritarian revolutionary ideals, that of liberty is not necessarily linked to violence or even to revolution in the militantly innovative and secular sense that the word has been understood since the French Revolution. The original revolutions for liberty of the American type were limited re-volutions for practical redress of specific grievances rather than unlimited revolutions for some general form of secular salvation. Liberty is most at home in a world of peaceful evolution in which people are not only free, but responsible—to an independent moral authority higher than, and independent from, politics. Liberty was won—and will only be preserved—by those who resist the claims of absolute state authority that reached their apogee in Orwell's time and have continued to be validated for modern man by the revolutionary mystique of fraternity and equality, nationalism and socialism. At the base of the American experience during the century and a half before revolution, and perhaps of the Judaeo-Christian world generally, lies the memory and example of a corporate calling that came from the God of ancient scripture, not the leader of a modern movement: the call to be special people by building justice in time rather than just extending power in space.

CONTRIBUTORS

IVAR BERG is dean of the College of Arts and Sciences at the University of Pennsylvania, where he was formerly chairman of the Department of Sociology. He is the author of many articles and several books, including *Industrial Sociology* and *Managers and Work Reform*.

JAMES H. BILLINGTON is the director of the Woodrow Wilson International Center for Scholars. He has written extensively on Russian history and culture. His most recent book is *Fire in the Minds of Men: Origins of the Revolutionary Faith*.

ROBERT COLES is professor of psychiatry and medical humanities at the Harvard Medical School. He is the author of over twenty-five books and numerous articles and has received many awards, including an Everett N. McDonnell Foundation grant. For volumes two and three of his five-volume study *Children in Crisis,* he received the Pulitzer Prize.

BERNARD CRICK is emeritus professor of politics at Birkbeck College, the University of London. He has written many articles and several books, including *George Orwell: A Life*.

HUGH KENNER is Andrew W. Mellon Professor of Humanities at the Johns Hopkins University. He has written numerous essays for popular and scholarly journals. Among his many books are *Ulysses* and *The Pound Era*.

RUTH MACKLIN is associate clinical professor of community health at the Albert Einstein College of Medicine in New York and philosopher-in-residence at the Bronx Municipal Hospital. She has written many articles on bioethics, applied value theory, and moral philosophy.

MARK CRISPIN MILLER is head of the Film Study Program and teaches in the Writing Seminars at the Johns Hopkins University. He is a contributing editor for the *New Republic* and has written many articles for popular and scholarly journals.

MURRAY N. ROTHBARD is professor of economics at the Polytechnic Institute of New York. He is the associate editor of *Inquiry*. He has written several books, including *Man, Economy, and State,* and many articles for scholarly journals.

ROBERT C. SOLOMON is associate professor of philosophy at the University of Texas, Austin. Among his many books are several on nineteenth- and twentieth-century philosophy. In addition, he has written two books on the philosophy of the emotions, *The Myth of the Passions* and *Love*.

JOSEPH WEIZENBAUM is professor of computer science and a member of the Laboratory for Computer Science at the Massachusetts Institute of Technology. He wrote the natural-language computer program ELIZA and is the author of *Computer Power and Human Reason.*

SHELDON S. WOLIN is professor of politics at Princeton University. He has written many articles and several books, including *Politics and Vision: Continuity and Innovation in Western Political Thought.* He is the editor of the journal *Democracy.*

INDEX

Index

Index